FALLING LEAVES

FALLING LEAVES

THE TRUE STORY OF AN UNWANTED CHINESE DAUGHTER

ADELINE YEN MAH

John Wiley & Sons, Inc.

New York • Chichester • Weinheim • Brisbane • Singapore • Toronto

This publication is designed to provide accurate and authoritative information in regard to
the subject matter covered. It is sold with the understanding that the publisher is not
engaged in rendering professional services. If professional advice or other expert
assistance is required, the services of a competent professional person should be sought.

Library of Congress Cataloging-in-Publication Data:

Mah, Adeline Yen
    [Falling leaves return to their roots]
    Falling leaves : the true story of an unwanted Chinese daughter /
Adeline Yen Mah.
       p.   cm.
  - Originally published: Falling leaves return to their roots. London
: M. Joseph, c1997.
    Includes index.
    ISBN 0-471-24742-1 (cloth : alk. paper)
    1. Mah, Adeline Yen, 1937–   . 2. Chinese Americans—California—
Biography. 3. Women physicians—California—Biography.
4. California—Biography. 5. China—Social life and customs.
I. Title.
CT275.M45115A3 1998
305.48'8951073'092—dc21
[B]   97-40144

Printed in the United States of America

10 9 8 7 6 5 4 3 2 1

Dedicated to my Aunt Baba, whose unwavering belief
in my worth sustained me throughout my tormented childhood.
And to my husband, Bob, without whose love this book
could not have been written.

Contents

vii

Author's Note

This is a true story. Much of it was painful and difficult to write but I felt compelled to do so. I continue to have deep feelings towards many members of my family and harbour no wish to hurt anyone unnecessarily. I have therefore disguised the Christian names of all my living siblings, their spouses and their children. However, my parents' names are real, so are all the events described.

FALLING LEAVES

Hong Kong, 19 May 1988

It would not be quite truthful to say that we were all together for the first time in nearly forty years. Each of us, severally and separately and sometimes stealthily, had gathered before but there had always been a common denominator of absence. Today it was Father.

Susan, our youngest sister, well-known socialite and wife of billionaire banker Tony Liang, was also absent. She had not been invited to Father's funeral or to the subsequent will reading. Her name was left out in the obituary published in the *South China Morning Post*. 'Joseph Tsi-rung Yen,' it read, 'dearly beloved husband of Jeanne Prosperi Yen, father of Lydia, Gregory, Edgar, James and Adeline, died on 13 May 1988 peacefully at the Hong Kong Sanatorium.'

That very morning, Father had been buried at the Catholic cemetery in North Point, on the east side of Hong Kong Island. Now, at four thirty in the afternoon, we were assembled at the impressive law offices of Johnson, Stokes & Masters on the seventeenth floor of Prince's Building in Hong Kong, for the reading of his will.

We waited nervously in the conference room around a large, oval table with a polished granite top. It gleamed, like the matching granite floor, in the afternoon sunlight that flooded through huge windows from the harbour. Lydia, my oldest sister, moved close to me and placed her right arm protectively around my shoulder. My three older brothers, Gregory, Edgar and James, sat sombrely next to each other. Louise, James's pretty wife, gazed solicitously at our French–Chinese stepmother whom we called 娘 Niang, a Chinese term for mother. She sat with her solicitor at the head of the table; a cloud of cigarette smoke floated from her gold cigarette holder, tightly clutched between meticulously manicured fingers. The room seemed enormous and I felt sick with grief.

He had been a very wealthy man, my father, something of a risk-taker but certainly one of Hong Kong's more successful businessmen. Escaping from Shanghai in 1949, he had started an import and export company, then diversified into manufacturing, construction, trading and property, and had even listed a company on the highly competitive Hong Kong stock exchange. James and Niang had managed his financial affairs when he became too ill to deal with them himself.

Niang was immaculately dressed in an expensive Parisian black silk suit. On her lapel was a large diamond brooch which matched the glittering diamond on her finger. Her dyed jet black hair was carefully coiffed above her broad forehead. From a black alligator handbag she extracted a pair of glasses in designer frames which she put on her nose. She nodded towards her solicitor, who now handed us each a copy of Father's will.

He cleared his throat and said, 'Your mother, my client Mrs Jeanne Yen, has requested that you don't turn the page for the time being. I shall explain the reason later.' He began to read the first page with each of us hanging on his every word. I felt as if I was seven years old and living back in Shanghai.

'This is the last will and testament of me, Joseph Yen, of No. 18 Magazine Gap Road, No. 10a Magnolia Mansions, Victoria, in the colony of Hong Kong,' he began. There followed the usual phrases about revoking all wills and codicils made previously. Father then appointed his wife Jeanne Yen to be the sole executrix of his will. 'And give devise and bequeath to her my entire estate whatsoever and wheresoever.' Should Niang not survive him, the solicitor continued, then James would be the sole executor and trustee of Father's will.

The solicitor had already reached the bottom of the page. He now coughed nervously and said, 'It is my duty to inform you that I have been instructed by your mother, Mrs Jeanne Yen, to tell you that there is no money in your father's estate.'

We stared at him in astonishment. No money? All eyes turned to Niang, our stepmother. She gazed at us one by one. 'Since there is no money in the estate,' she said, 'there is no need for you to go on reading the will. There is nothing there for any of you. Your father died penniless.' She held out her hand and slowly, reluctantly but obediently, each of us handed over his or her copy of Father's will without reading the next page, exactly as we had been instructed.

No one said anything. The prolonged silence carried an uneasiness as we looked expectantly at Niang for an explanation.

'None of you seem to understand,' Niang said. 'Your father's will is meaningless because he had no money in his estate.'

She stood up and handed all the copies of Father's unread will back to the solicitor. The will reading was at an end.

No one questioned the legitimacy of Niang's actions, or turned the first page to peruse the next. Baffled and bewildered as we all were, we accepted Niang's command. We had no idea in what manner Father had wished to dispose of his fortune or how he had foreseen the future of our family.

Father had been a man of great wealth and substance. Why did we each hand back Father's unread will as if we were mindless robots?

In order to explain our collective docility that afternoon, I have to go back to the very beginning. A Chinese proverb says that 落葉歸根 *luo ye gui gen* (falling leaves return to their roots). My roots were from a Shanghai family headed by my affluent father and his beautiful Eurasian wife, set against a

3

background of treaty ports carved into foreign concessions, and the collision of East and West played out within and without my very own home.

CHAPTER I

門當戶對

Men Dang Hu Dui

The Appropriate Door Fits the Frame of the Correct House

At the age of three my grand aunt proclaimed her independence by categorically refusing to have her feet bound, resolutely tearing off the bandages as fast as they were applied. She was born in 上海 Shanghai (city by the sea) in 1886 during the Qing dynasty when China was ruled by the child emperor Kuang Hsu, who lived far away up north in the Forbidden City. The pampered baby of the family, eight years younger than my grandfather, 爺爺 Ye Ye, Grand Aunt finally triumphed by rejecting all food and drink until her feet were, in her words, 'rescued and set free'.

Shanghai in the late nineteenth century was unlike any other city in China. It was one of five treaty ports opened up to Britain after the First Opium War in 1842. Gradually it burgeoned into a giant intermediary between China and the rest of the world. Strategically situated on the Huangpu River seventeen miles upstream from the mighty Yangtse, the city was linked by boat to the inner western provinces. At the other end to the east, the Pacific Ocean was only fifty miles away.

Britain, France and the United States of America staked out foreign settlements within the city. To this day, amidst the new high-rise buildings, Shanghai's architecture reflects the influence of the foreign traders. Some of the great mansions, formerly homes of diplomats and business magnates, possess the stately Edwardian grandeur of any fine house by the River Thames at Henley in England or the Gallic splendour of a villa in the Loire valley in France.

Extraterritoriality meant that within the foreign concessions, all subjects, be they foreign or Chinese, were governed by the laws of the foreigner and were exempt from the laws of China. Foreigners had their own municipal government, police force and troops. Each concession became an independent city within a city: little enclaves of foreign soil in treaty ports along China's coast line. China was governed not by written laws but by the rulings of magistrates appointed by the emperor and her citizens traditionally viewed these mandarins as demi-gods. For roughly one hundred years (between 1842 and 1941) westerners were perceived throughout China as superior beings whose wishes transcended even those of their own mandarins. The white conquerors were treated with reverence, fear and awe by the average Chinese.

Legal cases were tried before a Chinese magistrate but presided over by a foreign consular assessor whose power was absolute and whose word was final. The local populace was further humiliated by being barred from ownership of, or even free access to, many of the most desirable sections within their own city. Discrimination, segregation and abuse coloured most inter-racial dealings, with westerners viewing the Chinese as their vanquished inferiors. All this was bitterly resented.

Immediately south of the French Concession in Shanghai, my great-grandfather owned a tea-house in the old walled Chinese city of Nantao. These Chinese quarters, or the Old Town, were packed with low, dense buildings, small bustling markets and wandering alleyways overhung by colourful shop signs. Business was successful in spite of fierce competition from mobile stoves on bamboo poles, road-side stands and modest one-room cafés. When Grand Aunt was seven years old, her father relocated his tea-house to a more fashionable site in the International Settlement, formed by the merging of the former British and American Concessions. He then moved his entire family into a house a few streets away, in a quiet residential neighbourhood within the French Concession.

The French laid out gardens, apartment blocks, office buildings and tree-lined avenues which were given the names of French dignitaries. These boulevards became thick with café strollers and imported motor cars intermingling with wheelbarrows, rickshaws and pedicabs. Shanghai began to be known as the Paris of the Orient, though Grand Aunt always claimed that Paris should be called the Shanghai of Europe.

Grand Aunt's older siblings received little formal education, but they did learn to read and write at a private teacher's home. The youngest of five children, Grand Aunt was an afterthought. When she came of school age my great-grandfather had prospered. He enrolled her at the fashionable and expensive McTyeire Christian Girls' School, run by American Methodist missionaries. She was the first child in the Yen family to be given a foreign education.

By that time, Shanghai had become the centre of China's trade and industry. Opportunities were limitless. Grand Aunt's eldest brother had established a successful business manufacturing spare metal parts for rickshaws, pedicabs, bicycles and some of the more modern household appliances. He was to die young, probably from syphilis, for he succumbed to the three vices common to Chinese men at that time: opium, gambling and the brothels. Leisured women also gambled and took opium, but discreetly at home. Grand Aunt's second brother set up a thriving import–export tea business but he, too, became infected with venereal disease and was unable to sire children. Her sister had an arranged marriage and died from tuberculosis. Her third brother, my grandfather Ye Ye, was softspoken and gentle. A devout Buddhist, he was tall and slender, with poetic leanings and gentle ways. He disliked the required Manchu male hairstyle of shaving the brow and braiding long hair into a single queue. Even as a young man, he kept his head clean shaven (the only permitted alternative), wore a round skull cap, and sprouted a neatly trimmed moustache. Determined not to follow his brothers down the slippery path, he proved to be far more able than either of them.

While at McTyeire, Grand Aunt developed a lifelong passion for riding. She became fluent in English, was baptized as a Christian and made many western friends through her church. One of these, a fellow member of the Anti-foot-binding League, gave her a job as a clerk in the savings department of the Bank of Shanghai. During the twenty years that she worked there she learned every aspect of the banking business and was made manager of her division.

Grand Aunt never married. In those days, daughters could still be legally sold or bartered. A wife was often treated as an indentured servant in her husband's household, especially to her mother-in-law. If she failed to bear a son, one or more concubines would be brought in. Remarriage for widowers was routine but considered unchaste for widows. Most men of means routinely visited brothels but a woman who was unfaithful to her husband could be punished by death.

I remember Grand Aunt as a tall, imposing figure, treated with great esteem by every member of our family. Even Ye Ye and Father deferred to her every wish, which was remarkable in a society where women were disdained. Out of respect, we children were instructed to call her 公公 'Gong Gong', which meant Grand Uncle. It was common practice for high-achieving women within the clan to assume the male equivalent of their female titles.

At five feet seven inches she was only slightly shorter than Ye Ye. Erect, dignified, her feet unbound, she had a striking presence, in contrast to the obsequious demeanour befitting women of her time. Her black hair was cut short above her ears and combed backwards to reveal a smooth forehead above an oval face. Behind round, wire-rimmed, tinted glasses, her large eyes were penetrating. Always elegant, she favoured dark, monochrome, silk *qipaos* (Chinese dresses) with mandarin collars and butterfly buttons. Her complexion was fair with a tiny sprinkle of freckles across her nose. Habitually she wore face cream, a dab of rouge and a touch of lipstick, while her ears were adorned with exquisite stud earrings of pearls and jade. She moved with ease and athletic grace, riding and playing tennis into her sixties. I have a photograph of her smiling and confident astride a large black stallion, dressed in a white blouse, dark tie and well cut jodhpurs.

In 1924 Grand Aunt founded her own bank, the Shanghai Women's Bank. It is impossible to overestimate the scale of her achievement. In a feudal society where the very idea of a woman being capable of simple everyday decisions, let alone important business negotiations, was scoffed at, Grand Aunt's courage was extraordinary.

The reputation she had gained was such that Grand Aunt was able to raise the financing for her bank without difficulty. Shares were issued and fully subscribed to. Her bank was staffed entirely by women and designed to meet their specific needs. In they came: spinster daughters, with their inheritance and nest eggs; first wives (called big wives), with their dowries and winnings from mah-jong; concubines (called little wives), with cash presents from their men; and professional and educated women, who were tired of being patronized at male-dominated establishments. Shanghai Women's Bank was profitable from the very beginning and remained so until Grand Aunt's resignation in 1953.

With her profits she built a six-storey bank building at 480 Nanking Road which, in the 1920s and 30s, was considered *the* most prestigious business address in China. Her bank was situated at the nerve centre of the International Concession, adjacent to major office blocks and department stores, less than a mile from the Bund (nicknamed Wall Street of Shanghai), the famous park-like river-front promenade which, in those days, excluded Chinese ownership. Her staff lived in comfortable dormitories on the upper floors. The best building materials were used. Lifts were installed and modern plumbing put in with flush toilets, central heating, and hot and cold running water. Grand Aunt lived in a spacious penthouse on the sixth floor with her friend Miss Guang whom she had met through church. There were rumours about their relationship. They shared a room and slept in the same bed. In China, intimate friendship between single women was sneered at but tolerated. Miss Guang, born in 1903, had money of her own and was one of Grand Aunt's first investors. She became the bank's vice president. Later on, Grand Aunt adopted a daughter. (This was a common practice among childless women of means and required little formality.) They employed three maids, a chef and a chauffeur and entertained lavishly at home. Many a transaction was negotiated over a bowl of shark's fin soup during lunch at Grand Aunt's penthouse apartment.

At the age of twenty-six, Grand Aunt's third elder brother, my Ye Ye, entered into an arranged marriage through a *mei-po* (professional female marriage broker). My fifteen-year-old grandmother came from an eminently suitable Shanghai family. Theirs was a 門當戶對 *men dang hu dui* (as the appropriate door fits the frame of the correct house) marriage. Across the street from my great-grandfather's tea-house, her father owned a small herbal store filled with desiccated leaves, roots, powdered rhinoceros horns, deer antlers, dried snakes' gall bladders and other exotic potions. The bride and the groom saw each other for the first time on their wedding day in 1903.

On the eve of her wedding, Grandmother was summoned into her father's presence. 'Tomorrow you will belong to the Yen family,' she was told. 'From now on, this is no longer your home and you are not to contact us without permission from your husband. Your duty will be to please him and your in-laws. Bear them many sons. Sublimate your own desires. Become the willing piss-pot and spittoon of the Yens and we will be proud of you.'

Next day, the trembling bride, bedecked in a red silk gown and her face covered with a red silk cloth, was borne into the home of her parents-in-law in a red and gold sedan chair painted with a phoenix and dragon, rented from a store specializing in weddings and funerals. The wedding procession was a colourful, noisy affair accompanied by red lanterns, banners, trumpet blowing and the clanging of gongs. It was a point of honour for families to impoverish themselves for such occasions. However, in the case of my grandparents, friends and relatives gave many wedding presents including large cash gifts to defray the costs.

The young bride's fears were misplaced because Ye Ye proved to be loving and considerate. At her insistence, the young couple broke with tradition and moved out of the Yen family home into their own rented quarters in the French Concession. Grandmother taught herself mathematics and used it to great advantage in her daily mah-jong games. I remember her as a quick-witted and strong-willed chain-smoker with bound feet, short hair and a razor-sharp tongue.

At the age of three, Grandmother's feet had been wrapped tightly with a long, narrow cloth bandage, forcing the four lateral toes under the soles so that only the big toe protruded. This bandage was tightened daily for a number of years, squeezing the toes painfully inwards and permanently arresting the foot's growth in order to achieve the tiny feet so prized by Chinese men. Women were in effect crippled and their inability to walk with ease was a symbol both of their subservience and of their family's wealth. Grandmother's feet caused her pain throughout her life. Later, she braved social ridicule rather than inflict this suffering on her own daughter.

My grandparents grew to love each other and had seven children in quick succession. Of those, only the first two survived. Aunt Baba was born in 1905 and my father two years later.

On 10 October 1911, when Aunt Baba was six years old, the Manchu dynasty came to an end. Dr Sun Yat Sen, the leader of the Chinese revolutionaries, returned from exile to Shanghai in triumph on Christmas Day the same year. He was named President of the Republic of China. One of his first acts was to abolish the custom of foot-binding.

Ye Ye supported his family by buying and leasing out a small fleet of sampans (bum-boats) which plied the waters of Shanghai's busy Huangpu River. Goods were ferried in and out of China's interior and loaded on to giant ocean cargo steamers moored at the Bund. Ye Ye never gambled or wasted his money in brothels and opium dens. By the time he was forty, he had accumulated considerable wealth. He was approached by young K. C. Li, the dynamic proprietor of Hwa Chong Hong, a thriving import–export company, to manage their branch office in Tianjin, a port city one thousand miles north of Shanghai.

Ye Ye had a secret. He was prone to seasickness and hated to set foot on board one of his own sampans. So, though his business was profitable, he decided to sell and move up north, leaving his family behind as Aunt Baba and Father both attended local Catholic missionary schools which were considered the best in China and he did not wish to disrupt their education.

CHAPTER 2

點鐵成金

Dian Tie Cheng Jin
Converting Iron into Gold

In 1918, when Ye Ye moved to 天津 Tianjin, (Ford of Heaven), the last Qing emperor had been deposed and China had fragmented into fiefdoms governed by warlords. To the north, Japan already controlled Korea and now set her sights on China. At the Versailles Peace Conference held after the conclusion of the First World War, Japan was allowed by Britain and her allies to seize and keep Germany's colonial possessions in Shandong Province as a reward for having remained neutral. Emboldened, Japan began moving into Manchuria. Japanese soldiers then infiltrated south into Tianjin.

Situated in the level and fertile great plains to the north-east, Tianjin was the second largest of the treaty ports. It was opened up to trade after China's second defeat by Britain (and France) during the Second Opium War in 1858. The treaty of Tianjin added ten more ports between Manchuria and Taiwan. The city suffered from hot, dry summers and bitterly cold winters. It was prone to flooding because of its flat terrain crisscrossed by many branches of the Huai River. Between November and March, the rivers were icy and there were occasional dust storms. Whereas the architecture in Shanghai reflected mainly British and French influence, Tianjin adopted a bewildering kaleidoscope of building styles representing all the allied countries which had defeated Empress Tsu Hsi during the Boxer Rebellion in 1903. Besides Victorian office buildings and French churches, there were Russian dachas, a Prussian castle, Italian villas, Japanese tea-houses and German as well as Austro-Hungarian chalets, all situated in separate concessions adjoining each other along the river bank. Ye Ye again chose to live in a rented house in the French Concession, a tongue-shaped enclave sandwiched between the Japanese to the north, the British to the south and the Russians across the river. The area was neatly laid out with tree-lined avenues, tidy tramways, an imposing Catholic church, missionary schools and cheerful green parks.

Meanwhile, business had never been so good. Both Tianjin and Shanghai were booming. British, American, European and Japanese money poured back into China at the conclusion of the First World War. Concrete and steel buildings replaced the Victorian structures along the river. Factories sprang up at industrial sites manufacturing wool and cotton textiles, carpets, glass, concrete, tiles, paper, soap, matches, toothpaste, flour and other food stuffs. Under Ye Ye's management, Hwa Chong Hong prospered. To his delight, the traditional bonus paid to him at Chinese New Year greatly exceeded his annual salary. To celebrate his prosperity, fellow employees and friends urged him to take a young concubine to 'serve him'. Even Ye Ye's boss, the London-educated K. C. Li, jokingly volunteered to 'give' him a couple of girls with his bonus. Ye Ye reported all this in a matter-of-fact way in a letter to his wife, adding touchingly that he was a 'one-woman man'.

Soon after receiving this letter, Grandmother and fifteen-year-old Aunt Baba hurried to join Ye Ye in Tianjin, leaving my thirteen-year-old father in the care of Grand Aunt. Aunt Baba was told to drop out of school because advanced education was considered detrimental to the marriage prospects of young girls. Confucius had professed that 'only ignorant women were virtuous'.

Father remained in Shanghai and continued attending Chen Tien Catholic Boys' School. He excelled in English and Ye Ye advised him not to leave his excellent teacher, an Irish missionary. Father lived with Grand Aunt until graduation five years later. During this time, he converted to the Catholic faith and was given the name Joseph. He also developed a close relationship with my Grand Aunt, who became his mentor.

After completing middle school in 1924, Father chose not to go to university. He joined his family in Tianjin and was employed as an office boy under Ye Ye at Hwa Chong Hong. Although this was a menial post and the salary was minuscule, Father claimed in later life that it was the best possible education for a bright, inexperienced teenager. He learned all facets of the import–export business at first hand. Because of Father's fluency in English, K. C. Li soon relied on him to write and translate most of his firm's correspondence.

Father bought a second-hand typewriter and often typed important business letters after eating dinner at home, with his whole family clustered around the dining table in awed admiration. Once Ye Ye wondered aloud how the heads of these international companies would react if they found out that valuable documents worth hundreds of thousands of taels of silver were being banged out with one finger by an eighteen-year-old boy barely out of high school.

Hwa Chong Hong developed profitable relationships with various large pharmaceutical companies, including the German firm Bayer. Enormous quantities of the Chinese plant *ma huang* were purchased by Hwa Chong Hong and exported abroad. For many centuries, *ma huang* was used by Chinese herbal doctors to treat asthma and general malaise. Eventually, scientists working in the West identified and extracted the key component of the plant, ephedrine. This was then imported back into China in its purified form and sold to pharmacies prescribing western medicine.

Meanwhile, outside the foreign concessions, the Japanese military presence in Tianjin deepened. Well-armed and ruthless, they were a law unto themselves and treated the Chinese with contempt. Hwa Chong Hong's prosperity did not escape the notice of the Japanese. Company headquarters were situated outside the French Concession and unprotected by French law. K. C. Li was being increasingly harassed to 'collaborate'. There were no formal demands, just vague threats hinting at the need for 'protection against criminal elements'. During a routine 'visit' by Japanese inspectors, K. C.'s employees were randomly beaten for not showing sufficient respect to photos of the Japanese emperor in old newspapers, which were frugally being cut up and used as toilet paper. K. C. realized that at any time the situation might explode. Rather than give in to Japanese coercion, K. C. decided to move out of Tianjin altogether.

Father did not follow Hwa Chong Hong on its departure. Instead, at the age of nineteen, in 1926, he started his own firm, Joseph Yen & Company, within the French Concession in Tianjin.

Ye Ye had such faith in Father's business acumen that he invested his total life savings, about 200,000 taels of silver (equivalent to over one million US dollars in today's currency), in his son's company. Ye Ye resigned from Hwa Chong Hong and became the new firm's chief financial officer. No formal contracts were drawn up between father and son. It remained unclear whether the money was a gift or a loan. However, Ye Ye had authority to sign all company cheques and extracted an oral promise from Father that he would look after everyone in the family and pay all expenses, including Aunt Baba's dowry should she marry. At this time, my aunt had left Tianjin and was living in Shanghai. Grand Aunt's recently opened Women's Bank was flourishing. Reliable assistants were urgently needed and Aunt Baba had been dispatched to work at the bank.

Father's company prospered from the start, picking up much of the business left behind by the departure of Hwa Chong Hong. *Ma huang* continued to be exported, as did walnut kernels, straw hats, candle wax, pig bristles and dried fruits; imports included bicycles and pharmaceutical products. In the state of political unrest and increasingly ominous Japanese presence, many businesses came on the market very cheaply and Father expanded rapidly by buying up their assets. He soon acquired a lumber mill, a carpet-weaving concern and a bicycle spare parts assembly plant. Father retained the loyalty of key personnel by giving them incentive stock in his newly acquired companies. Grand Aunt and her bank played a crucial role in Father's early success and rapid growth. She had connections in Tianjin, including the manager of the local branch of the Bank of Shanghai. With her help Joseph Yen & Company was able to issue letters of credit for up to half a million US dollars guaranteed by Grand Aunt's Women's Bank. Their arrangement was for net profits after expenses to be split 70/30 in Father's favour. Hundreds of thousands of taels of silver changed hands with each transaction. Every deal was profitable. In three years, they never had a loss. Father began to be known in business circles as the 'miracle boy' who had the power of 點鐵成金 *dian tie cheng jin* (converting iron into gold).

Marriage brokers swarmed around the young business tycoon. But, with that same bit of swagger that gave him an edge in business, he declared that all Tianjin girls were dreary and provincial. He preferred the sparkle and sophistication of the young women in Shanghai.

CHAPTER 3

如影隨形

Ru Ying Sui Xing

Inseparable as Each Other's Shadows

Shanghai in the late 1920s was an exhilarating city for a young girl such as Aunt Baba. While the rest of China still travelled by push carts, sedan chairs and horse-drawn carriages, in Shanghai shining imported motor cars were speeding down well paved roads alongside trams and buses. Giant, colourful billboards advertising British cigarettes, Hollywood movies and French cosmetics gazed down at crowded pavements teeming with young men in suits and ties and girls clacking around in high-heeled shoes and stylish *qipaos*. The Bund, close to the Women's Bank on Nanking Road, had been transformed into a panorama of majestic buildings sweeping along the Huangpu River. Gun-boats, steamers, sampans and tug-boats festooned the muddy waters. Multi-storeyed department stores, such as Sincere, Wing-On, Dai-Sun and Sun-Sun, were crammed full of furs, jewellery, toys, household goods, ornaments and the latest Parisian fashions. Large enough to rival Selfridges of London or Macy's of New York, these emporiums promoted seasonal sales, gave away coupons and prizes, and even held concerts and theatrical performances on their roof gardens.

Aunt Baba had become friendly with a girl a year younger than herself, who worked in the new accounts department. Miss Ren Yong-ping could render complicated currency conversions in her head with astonishing speed and accuracy. Even when Grand Aunt checked her calculations with the abacus they were never wrong. Glowing with high spirits and vitality she had a ready smile and warm liveliness which made her attractive.

Miss Ren came from a middle-class Shanghai family which struggled somewhat after her father, a post office official, became addicted to opium and spent the last twenty years of his life in a drug-induced haze. An only daughter, she had three younger brothers, two of whom also worked in the post office, both rising later to become inspectors. She herself was soon promoted by Grand Aunt to head the new accounts department.

Working downstairs in the bank and spending their leisure hours upstairs in the dormitory, the two girls soon became best friends. Aunt Baba remembered one occasion when she and Miss Ren lunched by themselves in the restaurant at Sincere's, nicknamed 'Shanghai's Harrods' because of its physical resemblance to the famous London store. The two girls hired rickshaws which pulled them along the busy Nanking Road, where traffic lights were controlled manually by red-turbaned Sikh policemen stationed in cage-like boxes perched on poles twelve feet above ground. The restaurant was elegant, with white tablecloths, fresh flowers and crystal glasses. The menus listed only western food items with which they were unfamiliar. Chinese food was unavailable.

A little intimidated by the tuxedoed waiter, they hesitantly asked whether there was a 'daily lunch special'. Informed that it was *re gou* (dog meat, served hot), Aunt Baba was only slightly nonplussed. She had heard that in some provinces dog was considered a delicacy; but Miss Ren was much more dubious, remembering her family's pet Pekinese at home. She promptly remarked that 'today's special' usually meant 'yesterday's leftovers'.

The waiter became impatient. He was one of those Chinese who had adopted the haughtiness of the foreigners and preferred to serve the wealthy whites from the concessions. On this occasion the two girls were the only Chinese in the restaurant. They began to feel like gauche simpletons and, as much to be free of the arrogant waiter as anything else, they both ordered the dog dish. Aunt Baba was pleasantly surprised by the sausage that arrived wrapped in a bun and ate it with relish. Miss Ren, however, could not stop thinking about the little family pet and gave up after one bite. They laughed heartily when they eventually learned from Grand Aunt that 熱狗 *re gou* 'hot dog meat' was, in fact, the classic American hot dog.

On one of Father's frequent visits to Shanghai to discuss business at the Women's Bank, he was introduced to Miss Ren. 小巧玲瓏 *Xiao qiao ling long* (petite, vivacious and interesting) was Father's verdict. They began to correspond. Five months later, they were married. An enormous banquet was held at the Xin Ya (New Asia) restaurant in the International Concession just off Nanking Road. Besides immediate relatives, most of the guests were business associates of Grand Aunt's and Father's. It was 1930.

Father took his bride to Tianjin and bought a large house at 40 Shandong Road, conveniently located in the town centre of the French Concession and very near a public park. Across the street was St Louis Catholic Boys' School.

Their marriage was happy and they had four children in as many years. The young couple were 如影隨形 *ru ying sui xing* (inseparable as each other's shadows). First came a daughter. The baby was large and Dr Mary Mei-ing Ting, an obstetrician, applied forceps during the difficult delivery. Force had to be exerted and the baby (my eldest sister Jun-pei) was born with a partially paralysed left arm. Then came three sons (Zi-jie, Zi-lin and Zi-jun). There was a gap of three years before I (Jun-ling) came along.

The family house was spacious, with two storeys and a large attic where the servants slept. With its rounded bow windows, balconies, charming porch and pretty garden, the house was considered ultra-modern because of its flush toilets, running water and central heating. The latter constituted the height of luxury: most Chinese homes were still being heated by raised brick sleeping benches called *kangs*.

Father converted the ground floor of his house into offices for some of his staff. The rest of the family lived with Ye Ye and Grandmother on the second floor. There were seven servants to take care of the household. Father bought a large black Buick for himself and a black rickshaw for Grandmother to visit friends and play mah-jong.

Aunt Baba often took the train from Shanghai to Tianjin, a two-day journey in those days, and stayed for long visits. Father and Mother would meet her at the station in the Buick and the three would spend hours catching up on Shanghai gossip and Grand Aunt's latest business triumphs. There were outings to restaurants, films and the Chinese opera. According to Aunt Baba, it was an idyllic time for them all.

Mother's obstetrician, Dr Ting, was almost a member of the family by the time my three brothers were born. Like Grand Aunt, who was her classmate and childhood friend, she too had been educated at Shanghai's McTyeire School for Girls. She converted to Christianity and at the age of fifteen had spurned an arranged marriage. The intended bridegroom came from a wealthy family but was sickly, in pain and already addicted to opium. On her wedding day, the bride simply vanished. Her parents were sued and forced to pay the bridegroom's family a great many taels of silver in compensation for breach of promise, besides enduring considerable loss of face. With the help of her uncle, Mary escaped to Hong Kong where she continued her studies at another missionary school. Mary's uncle followed her to Hong Kong, cut off his queue (pigtail) and sent it to their family in Shanghai in a gesture of defiance. This was a serious crime and amounted to a public declaration of rebellion against the Qing emperor. (After the Manchus conquered China in 1644, they had imposed the partly shaven head and queue on every Chinese man to state their dominance.) Mary and her uncle were both disowned. He went to work in Hong Kong to pay for Mary's education. Later Mary won a scholarship to the University of Michigan Medical School and specialized in obstetrics and gynaecology. Returning to China, she settled in Tianjin rather than Shanghai where painful memories haunted her. She founded her Women's Hospital and became the best obstetrician in town. My sister and three older brothers were all delivered at Dr Ting's hospital.

When my mother became pregnant with me, the political situation in China had deteriorated drastically. In 1928 the Manchurian warlord, Chang Tso-lin, had been murdered by the Japanese while riding in his private railway coach. Over the next few years, Japanese soldiers invaded Manchuria. A puppet regime (Manchukuo or Nation of Manchu) was established under the former boy emperor Puyi in 1932. The United States refused to become directly involved. Britain looked the other way and recommended compromise. The League of Nations promised to investigate. Chiang Kai-shek, commander in chief of the army and head of the Nationalist party (Kuomintang), was fully occupied fighting the Communists, who had formed their own army and government in the rural strongholds of Yan'an in the north-west. Emboldened, Japan proceeded to launch a full scale attack on Tianjin and Beijing in July 1937. This was the beginning of the Sino–Japanese war which was to rage on for eight long years.

Japanese soldiers were everywhere, wearing surgical masks and carrying bayonets, demanding bows and obeisances, taking bribes and threatening violence. The foreign concessions remained neutral, small havens of uneasy independence amidst a vast sea of Japanese terror. The rest of Tianjin was now occupied territory under Japanese rule. In the evenings there were black-outs and curfews. Special permits were needed to cross key points at night, especially those conduit streets and bridges leading from the concessions into Japanese-patrolled areas.

My mother's labour pains started at four in the morning on

30 November 1937. Father did not possess the papers required to drive her past Japanese sentries on the way to the Women's Hospital. However, Dr Ting had been issued with a pass allowing her to travel freely at night. Her chauffeur-driven black Ford, flying a small US flag given to her by the American consulate, arrived at my parents' home an hour later. My birth was uneventful.

Dr Ting advised Father to transfer mother and baby to her hospital for a check-up and a few days' rest. Father demurred. The birth had been so smooth and rapid. He considered it unnecessary. He also rejected Dr Ting's advice to employ a nurse to care for my mother. He thought he could look after her himself, with the able assistance of Aunt Baba, who happened to be visiting at the time. Besides, trained nurses were expensive. A special bell was placed by mother's bedside so that she could call for Father as needed. Mother was weak, so instead of using the bathroom down the hall, it was easier to slip a bedpan under her. Afterwards Father would wipe her with a towel held in his bare, unwashed hands. Mother thought Father knew best. Father was convinced he knew best.

The headaches and fever started three days after I was born. Mother's temperature soared to 103 degrees and stayed there. Her lips were cracked and blistered. Her mind became cloudy and she was incoherent. Dr Ting diagnosed puerperal fever. In those days before penicillin this was virtually a death sentence.

Dr Ting immediately admitted my mother to the Women's Hospital. She was given fluids intravenously and various medications were administered in a desperate attempt to save her life. Her temperature rose to 106 degrees. She became delirious, refused all food and drink, and tried to pull out all her tubes, making wild accusations that Dr Ting was trying to imprison and poison her. Dr Ting realized that the prognosis was hopeless and finally gave permission for her to go home to die.

Her condition worsened. Doctor after doctor was consulted but to no avail. A dark cloud hung over the entire family.

Towards the end there was a short period of lucidity. With Father weeping at her side, she spoke to her parents-in-law and saw her children one by one, calling out each name with yearning. When Aunt Baba came in to say goodbye, Mother was weak but clear-headed. She smiled at my aunt and asked for a hot dog. Then she added sadly, 'I've run out of time. After I'm gone, please help look after our little friend here who will never know her mother.'

My mother died two weeks after my birth, with five doctors at her bedside. She was only thirty years old and I have no idea what she looked like. I have never seen her photograph.

CHAPTER 4

秀色可餐

Xiu Se Ke Can

Surpassing Loveliness Good Enough
to Feast Upon

After my mother's death, Grandmother and Father persuaded
Aunt Baba to resign her job at the Women's Bank and stay on
in Tianjin to take charge of the household. She was put on the
payroll of Joseph Yen & Company at the same salary that she
had been paid by Grand Aunt. She nagged and harried the
servants and ensured that the house ran along similar lines as
before. She became our surrogate mother, worrying about our
meals, clothing, schooling and health. An invisible silken
handcuff was thus slipped around her willing wrists, evaporat-
ing her chances of marriage and a family of her own. In those
days, women in China were expected to sublimate their own
desires to the common good of the family. In return, the men
felt honour-bound to protect and support them for the rest of
their lives.

Marriage brokers again clustered around, not for Aunt
Baba, but for her newly widowed brother. The double standard accorded men and women determined that single girls
not married off by the age of thirty often remained single
for life, whereas a man was expected to take at least one
wife, regardless of his age. Father had just turned thirty and
headed his own company, with properties, investments and
many thriving businesses. He had worked hard to achieve
all this, putting business affairs and family welfare before

personal gratification. Now he decided to please himself.

Cruising with his sons around the neighbourhood in his impressive Buick on a Sunday afternoon, he spotted his secretary, Miss Wong, standing by the door of a modest apartment complex conversing with a girlfriend. He immediately noticed that the friend was very young and possessed a 秀色可餐 *xiu se ke can* (surpassing loveliness good enough to feast upon).

Jeanne Virginie Prosperi was the seventeen-year-old daughter of a French father and a Chinese mother. Her features were an exquisite combination of Chinese delicacy and French sensuality. Her face was oval, with a white, porcelain-like complexion. She had lustrous, large, round, dark eyes, fringed by long lashes. Her head was crowned with thick, silky, jet-black hair. That day, her slender frame was dressed in a simple white blouse with a scooped-out square neckline and a royal-blue cotton skirt tied with a bow at the waist. Later on Father was to discover that Jeanne was a skilled seamstress and made all her own clothes.

Next day at work, Father made discreet enquiries and found out from Miss Wong that Jeanne was her classmate and had just started work as a typist at the French consulate. At lunchtime he drove over to the consulate on the pretext of applying for additional import–export licences from France, found her there and made her acquaintance.

Jeanne's father had been a soldier in the French army and was involved in the building of railways in China. He married a woman from Shandong Province. They had five children and times were hard. He left the army and found a job working as a security guard for a firm in the French Concession in Tianjin. He died suddenly in 1936, reputedly trying to break up a barroom brawl.

His widow coped as best she could. She had a small widow's pension. She and her spinster sister, Lao Lao, took in sewing to make ends meet. Being French citizens, all five children were given special scholarships by missionary schools within the

French Concession. Both Jeanne and her older sister, Reine, graduated from St Joseph's Catholic School for Girls, run by the Franciscan sisters.

Although Jeanne was not someone with an impressive social pedigree, she did graduate from the most exclusive convent school in Tianjin and, along the way, had acquired many of the social graces. Besides Mandarin, she spoke fluent French and English. Father was enchanted by her beauty and style. The fact that she was half European made her something of a trophy, to be prized, cherished and put on display.

During the 1930s, in the treaty ports such as Tianjin and Shanghai, everything western was considered superior to anything Chinese. A young, beautiful and educated European wife was the ultimate status symbol. Jeanne Prosperi, therefore, possessed considerable allure. She was always perfectly groomed and remained so all her life. Still in her teens, she displayed all the beguiling modesty instilled at the convent. In addition, there was a gleam in her eyes that suggested that she was a little more exciting than an ordinary girl barely out of school. Father began to desire Jeanne with a desperation in which sexual longing mingled with social aspirations. A decorous courtship began.

Father would pick her up from the French consulate every day and drive her home, sparing her the unpleasant crush of Tianjin public transport. They went for meals at exclusive hotel restaurants, danced at the country club and went to the movies. Tianjin boasted three cinemas, the Gaiety, Empire and Capitol, which showed romantic Hollywood films. He gave her at first flowers and chocolates; then pearls, jade and diamonds. The trinkets became increasingly expensive. Jeanne must have had a fairly clear idea as to where things were leading when she expressed a desire for a Russian sable coat costing four thousand taels of silver. Though Ye Ye voiced his objection in front of Jeanne and called it 'senseless extravagance', Father went ahead with the purchase and had the coat delivered three days later. That Father should have behaved in such an unfilial way

27

was a clear indication of his passion for Jeanne. Things started out as they were destined to continue, with Jeanne stating her terms and Father agreeing to meet them. As the Chinese saying goes: to Father, even Jeanne's farts were fragrant.

Father also made himself agreeable to her family. Jeanne's home was only a mile from Shandong Road. Mindful that her exquisite daughter was poised to enter a world far more luxurious than any she could ever provide, Mrs Prosperi encouraged the courtship. Father suspected that Mrs Prosperi came from peasant stock. In her rented, cramped apartment, conversation was limited to the basic to and fro of daily life. Her Mandarin was coloured by a heavy Shandong accent and her spoken French was very elementary. She could read or write neither language. Her eldest son had been in trouble with the police and had been sent away to labour camp in Hanoi. Her older daughter, Reine, had just married a sensible and educated Frenchman who worked for the United Nations. There were also two younger sons. Eventually, Father was to give the older boy, Pierre, a job in his company and send the youngest son, Jacques, to school in France.

When they became engaged there were diamond earrings, a diamond bracelet and necklace as well as a spectacular ring. In the face of tradition, Jeanne brought no dowry. The wedding ceremony took place at Notre-Dame des Victoires Catholic church. Father appeared nervous in his well cut tuxedo. Jeanne looked spectacular in a figure-hugging white satin dress trimmed with lace, resplendent in all her jewellery. None of us children attended. The Prosperi clan brought many guests, including a good many children. Aunt Baba said that she, Ye Ye and Grandmother felt somewhat uncomfortable at the lavish reception paid for by Father at the grand Astor House Hotel. Ye Ye found himself one of the very few male guests dressed in a long Chinese gown, matching satin *ma-gua* (short jacket), skull cap and cloth shoes. All the other men were in western suits and ties. The French guests called for endless toasts but the Chinese party were simply not used to drinking so much.

My aunt believed that she may have embarrassed Jeanne and her family because she had to retire to vomit more than once.

Afterwards Jeanne complained to Father that some of his Chinese kinsmen at the wedding banquet offended her delicate French relatives by being too loud and strident. However, her expression was sweet and demure when she said this. Father was utterly in her thrall, so much so that he began to adopt ambiguous notions about his own race. Growing up in the treaty ports, observing daily the symbols of western might, living within a foreign concession in his native country, ruled by extraterritoriality, he, like many Chinese, had come to see westerners as taller, cleverer, stronger and better. Although Jeanne was fluent in three languages, she could not read or write Chinese and was proud of this because it proclaimed, yet again, her western heritage.

Jeanne's taste reflected her mixed origins. She invariably wore western clothes and she wore them well. She liked to be surrounded by French furniture, red velvet curtains and richly textured wallpaper. At the same time, she collected antique Chinese porcelain, paintings and chairs. She liked plants and flowers to scent the hallway, living-room and her own bedroom. Like Grandmother, she smoked incessantly.

I think Jeanne was happy at first. Ye Ye and Grandmother welcomed the idea of Father's remarriage as it was not right for a young man to be without a wife. Aunt Baba, moreover, was partially released from her housekeeping obligations and might, in theory, have picked up the threads of her own life. Quite how my sister and brothers reacted to the marriage I cannot really say as I was only an infant when it took place. But a Chinese saying goes, if you are to have but one parent, choose your beggarwoman mother rather than your emperor father.

Father bought the house next door on Shandong Road as a present for his bride and the newly-weds moved in by themselves. The rest of the family and the servants remained in the old house, where Father still kept his offices. The family ate dinner together every evening. Father and Ye Ye continued to work downstairs side by side and business thrived.

Since my elder sister and brothers still spoke frequently of our own dead mother, whom they called 媽媽 Mama, Grandmother told us children to call Jeanne 娘 Niang, another term for mother. We, in turn, were given new European names by Niang. Overnight, my sister Jun-pei became Lydia, my three brothers Zi-jie, Zi-lin and Zi-jun were named Gregory, Edgar and James, and I, Jun-ling, was called Adeline.

Japanese troops, which already occupied Tianjin and Beijing, were now moving steadily southwards. They met surprisingly strong resistance in Nanking and, in retaliation, went on a terrifying spree of rape, looting and murder. Over 300,000 civilians and prisoners of war were tortured and killed during the Rape of Nanking in 1937 and early 1938 after the city was captured by the Japanese. Shanghai fell and Chiang Kai-shek fled westwards across China, up the Yangtse River, deep into the mountainous province of Sichuan. There he set up his wartime government in the town of Chongqing. It's not hard to imagine the tension and turmoil that these momentous political upheavals must have imposed on Chinese family life.

In 1939, suddenly and without warning, Tianjin was drowned in a great flood. The disaster was of staggering proportions. Ye Ye called it 'China's sorrow' and went to the Buddhist temple to burn incense and offer prayers for relief. Pro-Japanese newspapers printed in Tianjin blamed the catastrophe on Chiang Kai-shek while the Nationalist party (Kuomintang) press in Chongqing accused the Japanese. Dykes on the Yellow River had been deliberately dynamited and river water released to slow the advance of troops. The flood encompassed three provinces. All crops in its path were destroyed. Two million people became homeless. Hundreds of thousands died from starvation and disease. Schools were closed. Businesses came to a standstill. However, Father's lumber company kicked into high gear. The price of rowing boats soared from one hundred to eight hundred yuan. Oars were extra.

The flood caused Father to construct a high wooden platform connecting his two houses. Crossings were slippery and hazardous, particularly for Grandmother tottering on her small bound feet. Niang had just given birth to our half-brother, Franklin, and was still recuperating. Father virtually had to carry her across to the 'old house' every evening so that the family could eat dinner together.

Niang had little sympathy for all the difficulties the servants faced. Cook was expected to reach the market every morning, and return home laden with groceries, on a flimsy raft nailed together with planks. When Ye Ye pointed out the dangers inherent in these shopping expeditions, Niang simply replied that Cook was a good swimmer and she did not see fit to arrange for a rowing boat to be put at his disposal. When the waters finally subsided after forty days, Grandmother ordered that a solid and covered room be constructed linking the two houses. Lydia nicknamed it 'the bridge' and we used to play hide-and-seek there.

The youngest child of our generation, our half-sister Susan, was born in November 1941. Two weeks later, on 7 December, across the Pacific in Pearl Harbor, Japanese bombers attacked the American fleet. Japan was suddenly in league with Germany and at war with America and her European allies. At that precise moment (8 December in China), Japanese soldiers in armoured vehicles were ordered to roll over flimsy barbed wire barricades and take over the foreign concessions of Chinese treaty ports. Simultaneously, Japanese marines invaded Malaya and bombed Singapore. In one day, the Sino–Japanese conflict had merged with the war in Europe, expanded into Malaya, involved America and turned into the Second World War.

In Shanghai and Tianjin, British and American settlers, formerly almighty and invincible, were herded into Japanese concentration camps. The French Concessions were transformed overnight into malleable puppets at the mercy of the Japanese. All trading, especially that between China and the West, was being closely monitored by the new masters. The Vichy French law court presiding over Father's business affairs now found itself headed by a freshly appointed judge from the New Order in East Asia, a puppet government led by the traitor Wang Jhing-wei during the Japanese occupation.

The few American businessmen in Tianjin hurried to escape with their families and what they could salvage of their possessions. A robust eighteen-year-old peasant girl now came to us, introduced by one of Father's interned American colleagues. She applied to be a wet nurse for Susan and demanded three times the going wage, stressing that she had come from the employ of an American couple and was accustomed to the 'highest standards'. Her goal was to save up 500 yuan by the time Susan was weaned, buy an ox, return to her village and raise her own baby at the side of her husband.

It caused the most dreadful commotion. Niang was determined to hire this girl. No one else would do. She seemed to think that only a woman who had suckled a white American baby was good enough for her own daughter. Father acceded to her wishes, even though the new maid's thirty-yuan monthly salary infuriated all the other servants. Her wages were supposed to be secret but the entire household staff soon discovered the discrepancy. Franklin's maid demanded parity for herself and everyone else. Accusing Niang to her face of unfair discrimination, the spirited maid simply packed her belongings and left.

Aunt Baba was now entrusted with the additional care of two-year-old Franklin. She took on the task with reluctance but Grandmother pointed out that Franklin was as much a nephew to her as all the rest of us. So Franklin joined me and Aunt Baba in our bedroom. She used to buy us dragons' eyes to snack on. This was a summer fruit rather like lychees, said to make children's eyes grow large and bright.

Aunt Baba was unsparingly kind to both of us and started

teaching us elementary Chinese characters. Lydia was attending St Joseph's, from which school Niang had graduated in 1937. I was also enrolled there in kindergarten in the summer of 1941.

CHAPTER 5

一場春夢

Yi Chang Chun Meng
An Episode of a Spring Dream

My own memories of Tianjin are nebulous. Early photographs show a solemn little girl with clenched fists, pressed lips and serious eyes, dressed in pretty western frocks decorated with ribbons and bows. I enjoyed school and looked forward to going there. Lydia and I were pulled there and back daily in Grandmother's black, shiny rickshaw. It had a brass lamp on each side and a bell operable by foot. When I revisited Tianjin in 1987, I was surprised to find that it took only seven minutes to walk from our house to St Joseph's.

I remember Lydia as an imposing, rather intimidating figure. Between us there were three brothers and a gap of six and a half years. We were a world apart.

Lydia liked to exercise her authority and flex her muscles by quizzing me on my homework, especially catechism. Her favourite question was, 'Who made you?' To this, I always knew the answer. Like a parrot I would trot out the well worn phrase, 'God made me.' Then came the twister. A gleam came into her eyes. 'Why did God make you?' I never could answer because teacher never taught us beyond the first question. Lydia would then give me a resounding slap with her powerful right hand, and call me stupid. During our daily rickshaw rides, she liked to keep me waiting and was invariably late. On the rare occasions when I was delayed in class she simply rode the rickshaw home alone but would send the puller back to get me. She tended to be stocky, even as a child. Her physical deformity gave her a characteristic posture, with her semi-paralysed left arm hanging limply by her side and her face perpetually tilted slightly forwards and to the left. From my four-year-old perspective, she was a fearsome figure of authority.

My eldest brother Gregory had a sunny personality and the infectious ability to turn ordinary occasions into merry parties. His *joie de vivre* endeared him to many people. Being the eldest son in China meant that he was the favourite of Father as well as of our grandparents. I remember him, full of mischief, gazing with rapt fascination at a long, black hair blowing in and out of the right nostril of snoring Ye Ye one hot afternoon. Finally Gregory could no longer resist the temptation. Skilfully, he pinched the hair ever so tightly between his thumb and index finger during the next exhalation. There was a tantalizing pause. Ye Ye finally inhaled while Gregory doggedly hung on. The hair was wrenched from its root and Ye Ye awoke with a yell. Gregory was chased by Ye Ye brandishing a feather duster but managed, as usual, to escape.

On the whole, Gregory ignored James and me because we were too young to be interesting playmates. He was always surrounded by friends his own age. He did not enjoy studying but, like Grandmother, excelled in games of chance such as bridge. Good with numbers, he occasionally taught us younger ones neat mathematical tricks, roaring with laughter at his own cleverness.

Of all my siblings, it was Edgar I feared the most. He bullied James and me and used us as punchbags to vent his frustration. He ordered us around to perform his errands and grabbed our share of toys, candies, nuts, watermelon seeds and salted plums. He did not distinguish himself at school and was deeply insecure, though he possessed enough fortitude to maintain a passing grade.

My 三哥 *san ge* (third elder brother) James was my hero and only friend. We used to play together for hours and developed a telepathic closeness, confiding to one another all our dreams and fears. With him, I could discard my vigilance and I needed that haven desperately. Throughout our childhood, it was immensely comforting to know that I could always turn to him for solace and understanding.

We were both Edgar's victims, though perhaps James suffered more because for many years he shared a room with our two eldest brothers. He hated to make waves. When pushed around, he endured the blows passively or hid from his tormentor. Seeing me being beaten by Edgar he would skulk quickly away in blinkered silence. Afterwards, when Edgar was gone, he would creep back and try to console me, often muttering his favorite phrase '*Suan le!*' (Let it be!) . . .

Of Niang's two children, she openly favoured Franklin. In physical appearance he was the spitting image of Niang: a handsome boy with round eyes and a pert upturned nose. Susan at this stage was still a baby. But they were already special. I don't recall either Edgar or Lydia ever laying a finger on them. James and I were the ones singled out to do everyone's bidding. If we were not fast enough there was often a slap or a shove, especially from Edgar.

I always felt more comfortable with my friends at school than at home, where I was considered inferior and insignificant, partly because of the bad luck I had brought about by causing the death of my mother. I remember watching my older sister and brothers playing tag or skipping rope and longing to be included in their games. Although James and I were very close, he went along with the others and became 'one of the boys' when they wished to preclude me.

At St Joseph's, marks were added together every Friday and the girl with the highest total received a silver medal which she could wear pinned on her breast pocket for the entire week. Father immediately noticed when I wore the medal. Those were the only times when he showed pride in me. Father would say teasingly, 'Something is so shiny on your dress. It's blinding me! Now what could it be?' or 'Isn't the left side of your chest heavier? Are you tilting?' I lapped up his words. Soon I was wearing the medal almost continuously. At prizegiving at the end of 1941 my name was mentioned for winning the scholarship medal for more weeks than any other student in the school. I remember my pride and triumph as I climbed up the steps, which were so high and steep that I had to go up on my hands and knees, to receive my award from the French monseigneur. There was warm applause and delighted laughter from the audience, but no one attended from my family, not even Father.

At the beginning of 1942 the Japanese were taking uncomfortably closer looks at Father's books, insisting on an exhaustive audit and finally demanding that his businesses be merged with a Japanese company. Father could remain nominally in charge but profits would be split 50/50. This 'offer' was, in fact, an order. Refusal would have resulted in confiscation of assets, probable jail for Father and unthinkable retaliation against the rest of the family. Acceptance meant open collaboration with the enemy, immediate loss of independence and possible reprisal from the underground resistance fighters.

After many sleepless nights, made worse by elaborate luncheons during the day when the Japanese alternately cajoled and threatened, Father took a radical step. One cold day, he took a letter to the post office and never returned home.

Ye Ye carried on with this life-and-death charade for a few months. Those were chaotic days. Kidnappings, murders and disappearances were everyday events. He immediately went to the local police and reported his son missing. He placed advertisements in the newspapers offering a reward for knowledge of Father's whereabouts, alive or dead. It was a dramatic ruse and the price was high but ultimately it had the desired effect. Without Father at the helm, Joseph Yen & Company floundered. Many of the staff were laid off. Business dwindled. Profits plummeted. The Japanese soon lost interest.

Father, meanwhile, having managed to transfer part of his assets before his staged disappearance, made his way south to

Japanese-occupied Shanghai under an assumed name, 嚴洪 Yen Hong. He bought what was to become our family home on the Avenue Joffre. Soon afterwards he sent for Niang and Franklin, who travelled with a couple of trusted employees and joined him there.

For the rest of the family, stranded in Tianjin, life became oddly serene. Aunt Baba ran the household and encouraged us children to invite friends home to play and snack on various dim sums in a way Niang would never have tolerated. Mealtimes were informal and the adults talked and played mah-jong late into the evening. Ye Ye kept a skeleton staff in the office. By and large the Japanese left us alone. A chauffeur was hired and on Sundays we were driven to various restaurants to try out different cuisines, including Russian, French, and German. I remember drinking hot chocolate and eating pastries at the sparkling Kiessling Restaurant while a music trio played Strauss waltzes and Beethoven romances. Sometimes we were even taken to see suitable movies.

Father was keen that the rest of his family should join him in Shanghai. In the summer of 1942, Grandmother was persuaded to visit for two months but returned saying that Tianjin was now her home. She stubbornly refused to move and told Aunt Baba that the essence of life was not which city one lived in, but with whom one lived.

After dinner one stiflingly hot day, 2 July 1943, we were planning next day's menu with Cook. Aunt Baba suggested that we have Tianjin dumplings instead of rice. Freshly made with chives, ground pork and spring onions, these dumplings were a great favourite among us children. We were all shouting out ridiculously high numbers as to how many dumplings we could eat. Grandmother developed a headache from all the commotion. She went to her own room, lit a cigarette and lay down. Aunt Baba sat by her and narrated a story from *The Legend of the Monkey King*. Even though Grandmother knew many tales from the well-known Chinese classic, she found it relaxing to hear them told again and again by her daughter.

She removed the shoes, stockings and bindings from her tiny damaged feet before soaking them in warm water to relieve the constant ache, giving a sigh of contentment. Aunt Baba left her and was taking her own bath when Ye Ye hammered on the door. Grandmother was twitching, frothing at the mouth. Doctors were called but it was too late. Grandmother never regained consciousness. She died of a massive stroke.

I remember waking up in the sweltering heat of a Tianjin summer morning. Aunt Baba was sitting at her dressing table and crying. She told me that Grandmother had left this world and would never come back; her life had evaporated like 一場春夢 yi chang chun meng (an episode of a spring dream). I recall the sound of cicadas humming in the background, while street-hawkers clicked wooden clappers to announce their presence, chanting their wares melodiously on the pavement below: 'Hot beef noodles. Stinky bean curd. Fresh pot stickers.' I wondered how it was possible that life could go on being so much the same when Grandmother was no longer with us.

Grandmother's body was placed in a coffin in the living-room. Her photograph sat on top and the coffin was elaborately decorated with white flowers, candles, fruits and banners of white silk covered with elegant, brush-stroked couplets memorializing her virtues. Six Buddhist monks came to keep watch, dressed in long robes. We children were told to sleep on the floor in the same room to keep her company. We were all terrified, mesmerized by the shaven, shining heads of the monks chanting their sutras in the flickering candlelight. All night I half feared and half hoped that Grandmother would push open the lid and resume her place among us.

Next day, there was a grand funeral. We mourners were all dressed in white, with white headbands or pretty white ribbons. We followed the coffin on foot to the Buddhist temple, accompanied by music and chants provided by Buddhist priests. Along the way, attendants threw artificial paper money into the air to appease the spirits. My brother Gregory took the place of chief mourner in the absence of Father, who was still hiding. He walked directly behind the coffin, which was placed on a cart and pulled by four men. Every few steps he would fall on his knees and start bewailing the loss of Grandmother at the top of his voice, banging his head repeatedly on the ground to make obeisance. We followed Gregory silently, marvelling at his performance.

Finally we arrived. The coffin was placed at the centre of an altar, surrounded by white floral arrangements, more silk banners and Grandmother's favourite dinner. There were about sixteen dishes of vegetables, fruits and sweets. Incense heavily scented the air. Prayers were chanted by monks. We were instructed to kowtow, kneeling and repeatedly touching our foreheads to the ground. The monks brought paper effigies of various articles which they thought she might need in the next world. There were masses of 'gold' and 'silver' ingots, a very intricate cardboard automobile resembling Father's Buick, an assortment of furniture and appliances, even a mah-jong set. These effigies were all burnt in a large urn. This delighted us children, and we eagerly helped stoke the urn by dropping in the effigies, forgetting in the excitement the purpose of the occasion and fighting over the paper car, which was very ingeniously made and covered with bright tin foil. Years later, Aunt Baba informed me that all of it, including the eulogizing banners, monks, flowers, musicians and effigies, were chartered from a speciality shop which arranged for such 'happenings' and supplied the appropriate props.

I remember watching the various paper images burning furiously and the smoke curling up and believing it would all regroup somewhere in the sky in the form of articles for the exclusive use and pleasure of Grandmother.

Our relatives and friends then followed us home and a lengthy and elaborate meal was served. Afterwards, we children were sent out to the garden to play. Lydia set up a makeshift urn. We manufactured paper stoves, beds and tables and began our own funeral for Grandmother. Soon the urn, which was a wooden flower pot, started to burn. Ye Ye came out in a fury, turned on the faucet and drenched us and our funeral pyre. We were sent to bed, but the incident helped to dissipate the dread and gloom of the last two days, and we felt that Grandmother was going to be happy in the other world.

Far away in Shanghai, Father grieved deeply. He could not accept that his beloved mother had died when she was just fifty-five. From then on, he wore only black neckties in honour of her memory.

The funeral marked the end of an era. We did not know it, but the carefree years of childhood were over.

CHAPTER 6

家醜不可外揚

Jia Chou Bu Ke Wai Yang
Family Ugliness Should Never be Aired in Public

One day in August 1943, about six weeks after Grandmother's death, Lydia, Gregory, Edgar and I were taken to the railway station with our bags. There was a long line of carriages waiting at a platform with the placard 'To Shanghai'.

In a first-class compartment marked 'Soft Beds', we found Father dressed in black, sitting by himself next to the window. We were very much surprised because though we knew he was 'missing', none of us had been told that he had returned. His eyes were red, and he had been crying.

Father had come specially to escort us to Shanghai. Ye Ye, Aunt Baba and Susan would remain in Tianjin for two more months to observe the traditional Buddhist hundred-day mourning period for Grandmother. James, who was recuperating from measles, would stay behind too and travel with them.

The train journey from Tianjin to Shanghai took two days and one night. Along the way, we stopped at numerous stations where Father bought snack food from hawkers who flocked around. We feasted on tea eggs, barbecued chicken wings, smoked fish, *man tou* (steamed bread) and fresh fruit. It was extremely hot and humid. Father left all the windows in our compartment open. I slept in an upper bunk above Father's bed and at night dreamt of being sucked out of the window. I woke up crying for Aunt Baba as our train rushed southwards.

On arrival, Father took us to the house he had purchased. It was situated in a 'long tang' (a complex of houses), deep in the heart of the French Concession. Our long tang consisted of seventy closely packed residences built in the same style, surrounded by a communal wall. On each side, three narrow alleys opened on to a central main lane ending in bustling Avenue Joffre, now called Huai Hai Road. Our three-storeyed home was built in the 1920s. It had Bauhaus features and a simplicity which evoked Art Deco lines. There was a roof terrace as well as a small garden in front, enclosed by a seven-foot wall. Guests entered through a wrought-iron gate into the garden. This was neatly landscaped with a small lawn, flowering camellia bushes and a magnolia tree with wonderfully fragrant blooms. Tucked away in one corner was the wooden dog house in which Jackie, Father's ferocious German shepherd, slept. Against the wall was a picturesque well where watermelons held in string baskets tied to a rope were cooled and stored in summer.

Stone steps led up to French windows which opened into the living-room on the ground floor. This room was formally furnished with Burgundy-red velvet couches, matching velvet curtains and a Tianjin carpet partially covering a teak parquet floor. The wallpaper was striped with a raised velvet napping to match the couch and drapes. White lace antimacassars covered the headrests and the arms of the chairs. In the centre of the room was an imitation Louis XVI coffee table.

The dining-room to the left had large bow windows and a pleasant view of the garden. It was furnished with an oval dining table surrounded by cane-backed chairs. There was a sideboard and a refrigerator.

At the rear of the house were the kitchen, bathroom, servants' quarters and garage. We children were required to enter and leave the house through the back door, which opened on to an alleyway formed on one side by the walled gardens of neighbouring homes.

Upstairs on the first floor, Father and Niang occupied the

best room. Besides a large double bed and an ornately carved dressing-table and mirror, it contained an alcove which over-looked the garden and served as a sitting area. James was to nickname their bedroom the 'Holy of Holies'. It was separated by a bathroom from the 'antechamber', Franklin's and Susan's bedroom, which opened on to a balcony from which Franklin often threw food or toys down to Jackie prowling below.

When we first arrived from Tianjin, we, the 'have-nots', were relegated to the second floor. Ye Ye had his own room with a balcony. Aunt Baba and I shared a room, my three brothers another. It was tacitly understood that we, the second-class citizens, were forbidden to set foot in the antechamber or the Holy of Holies. However, 'they', the first-floor residents, roamed our quarters at will.

In the beginning, Lydia was also assigned to 'our floor'. Later she was given a room on the first floor, 'their floor', and went over partially to 'their side'.

My new school, 聖心 Sheng Xin (Sacred Heart) primary school, was one and a half miles from home. On the first day, Cook took me on the handlebars of his bicycle on the way to market. Ye Ye and Aunt Baba had not yet arrived from Tianjin. In their absence, no one remembered to pick me up.

When school was let out, I saw all the other first-graders being greeted by their anxious mothers at the gate. I remember the interminable wait and my mounting panic as I watched my classmates disperse from sight, each clutching her mother's hand. Finally, I was the only one left. Too embarrassed to return to school, I hesitantly strode into the Shanghai streets. The further I wandered, the thicker the crowds became. The pavements swarmed with pedestrians, coolies carrying large loads on bamboo poles, hawkers, stall-holders and beggars, some of them legless, blind and grotesquely deformed, banging tin cups on the ground for a hand-out. Everyone was going somewhere. Everyone had a destination except me. I wandered desperately for miles in search of a familiar landmark. I was hopelessly lost. I did not know my home address.

In those lawless days, children were often kidnapped and disappeared into the bowels of Shanghai. They were sold as *ya tou* (girl slaves), sometimes to brothels. As darkness fell, hunger and fear gripped me. I found myself hovering in front of a brightly lit dim sum shop, drooling over the dumplings, noodles, roast ducks and barbecued pork displayed in the window. The proprietress came out, glanced at my brand new school uniform and asked, 'Are you meeting your mother here?' Too terrified to answer, I lowered my head. 'Come in!' she said, and I followed.

Suddenly, out of the corner of my eye, I saw it: my lifeline! The telephone! Our new Shanghai phone number had stuck in my mind: 79281. My brother Gregory had a knack for numbers. He had taught me to play with the number the previous week, backwards and forwards, attempting to end up with the number thirteen. The restaurant was very noisy and crowded. Nobody noticed when I lifted the receiver and dialled. Father answered the phone. 'Where are you?' he asked quite calmly. No one had missed me. 'In a restaurant somewhere. I am lost.' Hearing the racket in the background over the telephone, he asked to speak to the proprietress. She gave him directions and soon he came alone to fetch me in his big black car. He drove in silence, lost in thought. When we arrived home, he patted me on the head and said, 'You wouldn't be lost if you had taken a map with you and studied the location of the school and your home.'

I learned from this experience to rely on myself. I realized that without Aunt Baba, there was no one looking out for me. That evening, I asked Gregory to teach me how to read a map. I never got lost again.

Two months later, Ye Ye, Aunt Baba, James and Susan arrived from Tianjin. I was ecstatic. Niang had been separated from her daughter since the spring of 1942, when Susan was only a few months old. By the time they were reunited in Shanghai, Susan had grown into a beautiful little toddler with big round eyes, chubby cheeks and thick black hair. To meet her mother, Aunt Baba had dressed her in pretty pink trousers with a matching padded jacket. Her hair was plaited and stood up on each side. She looked adorable as she rushed around the sitting-room, examining an occasional ornament and running back to show Aunt Baba. Then Niang went over and attempted to pick Susan up. To my two-year-old sister, her mother was a complete stranger. Susan wriggled and fought and resisted with all her might. Finally, she burst into tears screaming, 'I don't want you! I don't want you! Aunt Baba! Aunt Baba!'

No one dared say a word. All conversation ceased as we watched Susan kick and struggle in Niang's arms. Finally, to my horror, Niang forced her child down on the couch beside her and gave her a stinging slap across the face. Susan only cried louder. Exasperated and by now no longer in control, Niang began a vicious beating of her daughter, her slaps landing on Susan's little cheeks, ears and head. Everyone in the room cowered.

I was totally bewildered. I could not understand why Father, Ye Ye or Aunt Baba did not intervene to stop this torture. I wanted to leave, but my feet seemed rooted to the floor. I knew I should keep silent, but words choked me and I felt compelled to spit them out. Finally, forgetting who I was or where I was, I blurted out in a trembling voice, 'Don't beat her any more! She's only a baby!'

Niang turned around and glared fiercely, her large eyes seeming to pop out of their orbits. For a moment, I thought she was going to come after me. Aunt Baba gave me a warning look to say no more. Even Susan was barely whimpering. My protest had interrupted Niang's frenzy but I had become the target of her fury.

In those few moments, we children saw and understood everything: not only about her, but also about Father and Ye Ye and Aunt Baba. We had witnessed another side of her character. With Grandmother gone, she alone was in total control.

My apprehension mounted as she glowered at me. A torrent of words escaped her clenched lips. 'Get out!' she screamed. 'Get out of my sight at once! How dare you open your mouth?' As I hurried out of the door, she added with calculated menace, 'I shall never forget or forgive your insolence! Never! Never! Never!'

This was how our family became reunited in Father's Avenue Joffre house in Shanghai during October of 1943.

Our lives changed drastically after our move. Father sent us all to private missionary schools where lessons were in Chinese, and English was taught as a second language. While I was at Sheng Xin, my three brothers were enrolled at St John's Christian Boys' School and Lydia attended Aurora Catholic Middle School. Father began an austerity programme to teach us the value of money. We received no pocket money and had no clothes except for our school uniforms. We were also required to walk to and from school daily. For the boys, this was a three-mile trek each way. They had to get up at six thirty in order to be at school by eight. Lydia's school adjoined mine and was one and a half miles from our house. Trams ran almost from door to door.

After Ye Ye's arrival from Tianjin, we shamelessly begged him for the tram fare and were each given a small sum every evening. Parallel tram lines ran along the centre of Avenue Joffre, ending at the Bund along Huangpu River. My tram stop was immediately outside the entrance to our lane. On mornings when I was lucky, a tram would be just approaching in the correct direction. The fare was twenty fen for adults and ten fen for children. At the tram's approach, everyone pushed and jostled to get in. No one ever bothered to queue.

The first tram stop was Do Yuen Gardens. Two years later, when the Japanese lost the war and Father and Niang flew to Tianjin to reclaim his businesses, Ye Ye would take James and me for picnics there. This was a rare treat because under Niang's regime, we children were forbidden to leave the house outside school hours. Cook packed us wonderful sandwiches: thick layers of eggs flavoured with garlic, onions and Yunan ham, within two slabs of crisp, fresh, French bread. Amidst towering trees, green lawns and tidy flower beds, Ye Ye practised t'ai chi early in the morning while James and I played hide-and-seek or pretended to be historical characters from our favourite Chinese folk-tales. Sometimes there would be a professional storyteller sitting in the pavilion spinning wonderful yarns.

The second stop was the Cathay Cinema. How I yearned to see those wonderful movies! Their titles, stills and photographs of the film stars were posted on the walls outside the cinema which at night was lit up like a palace. As soon as the war ended, Hollywood movies swept across Shanghai like a prairie fire. Clark Gable, Vivien Leigh, Laurence Olivier and Lana Turner became household names. *Gone with the Wind*, cleverly translated into just one Chinese character, 飄 *Piao*, a rather romantic word meaning to float or drift, was a big hit in 1946. At school, we shared film magazines and cut out photographs of American film stars. One day a girl two years ahead received a photograph of Clark Gable, reputedly sent all the way from a film studio in Los Angeles. Mr Gable had even signed his name at the bottom of the picture! During recess, all the girls flocked around her, wanting to catch a glimpse of the famous actor, as if she had become a celebrity herself.

The third stop was at the street corner leading to the Sheng Xin and Aurora schools. Along the way was a variety of small food shops selling fresh fruit, dim sum, noodles, French bread, cream cakes and sundry pastries. It was often agonizing for me to walk past these establishments because hunger was my constant companion and my pockets were always empty. Gone were the days in Tianjin when we could order anything we fancied for breakfast provided we gave Aunt Baba advance notice: bacon and eggs with toasted French bread; fried noodles with ham and cabbage; steamed dumplings; sweet glutinous rice balls with sesame paste; hot chocolate. Now we were allowed to have only one kind of breakfast: the right kind of food for growing children according to Niang. We were given *congee*, a soupy gruel made of rice and water, and pickled vegetables. Occasionally on Sundays we were each served one hard-boiled, salted duck egg.

Austerity did not stop with us, the stepchildren. It included Ye Ye and Aunt Baba. In Tianjin, Father and Ye Ye had a joint account, and Ye Ye signed all the cheques as chief financial officer. On his return to Shanghai in 1943, Ye Ye trustingly transferred all of the Tianjin funds into Father's Shanghai bank accounts opened two years earlier under Father's new, assumed name, Yen Hong. With one stroke of the pen, Ye Ye, like King Lear, signed away his entire fortune. The only other signatory on this new account was Niang. Ye Ye and Aunt Baba now found themselves penniless and completely dependent on the largesse of Father and Niang, even for the most meagre purchase.

Initially Ye Ye had a small amount of cash in his wallet which he had brought with him from Tianjin. We were in the habit of asking Ye Ye for pocket money and he would often slip us an extra coin or two just to see the joy in our eyes. Ye Ye supplied us with our daily tram fares to and from school until his money ran out.

About two months after school started, the subject of tram fares was raised at dinner one evening. Dinner was almost over and we were peeling our fruit when Aunt Baba started the ball rolling by saying that she had decided to return to work as a teller at Grand Aunt's Women's Bank. We could see from the pursed lips of Niang that she was annoyed. 'You have everything you need here,' Father said. 'Why do you wish to go to work?'

Aunt Baba politely answered that there was too much free time during the day with all of us away at school and so many maids to do the housework. She did not mention what was on everyone's mind: that the salary would give her some measure of independence.

Father turned to Ye Ye. 'Do you think this is a good idea?' he asked. 'She will be out of the house most of the day. If she stayed at home, she would be more of a companion to you.'

'Let her do what she wants,' Ye Ye said. 'Besides, she likes to earn a little extra money to spend on this and that.'

'If you need money,' Father said grandly, addressing Aunt Baba, 'why don't you come to me? I have told you both before, any time you want money just come to me and ask. And if I'm at the office, Jeanne is always available to write you a cheque.'

A shiver went down my spine at the thought of anyone, let alone my gentle Ye Ye, going to Niang, his young French daughter-in-law, to ask for money.

Ye Ye cleared his throat. 'I've been meaning to mention this before. The children need a little pocket money now and then.'

'Pocket money?' Father said, turning to Gregory and Lydia. 'Why do you need pocket money?'

'Well,' Lydia answered, 'first there is the matter of the tram fare to and from school.'

'Tram fare?' Niang asked. 'Who gave you permission to ride the tram?'

'It's so far to St John's,' Gregory piped up. 'If we had to walk, it would probably take us all morning. No sooner would we get there than we'd have to start back home again. We might as well not go to school at all, and just go for a long walk everyday for exercise.'

'胡説八道! *Hu shuo ba dao!* (Don't talk nonsense eight ways!)' Father exclaimed. 'You're always exaggerating. Walking is good for your health.'

Gregory muttered under his breath. 'I hate walking! Especially in the early morning. It's a waste of time.'

'Are you contradicting your father?' Niang thundered. 'Your father works day and night to support all of you in this house. If he decides you should walk to school, then you walk to school. Do you hear?'

Dead silence greeted this outburst. We turned to Ye Ye for support. Finally Lydia said, 'Ye Ye has been giving us tram fares now for two months. We're used to going to school that way.'

'How dare you go behind your father's back and trouble Ye Ye for money?' Niang demanded. 'From now on you're forbidden to go to anyone else for money! All of you! Your father works hard and sends you to expensive schools so that you can have a decent education. He certainly does not want you to grow up to be spoilt kids and good-for-nothings.'

Even though her critical remarks were addressed to us, we all knew they were meant for Ye Ye and Aunt Baba.

'No one else in my class walks to school,' Lydia protested. 'Most of my friends come in chauffeured cars.'

'It's your father's wish that you should walk to school! Your father and I want you to know that you will no longer bother Ye Ye or Aunt Baba for money. If you think you need money, come directly to me. Money doesn't grow on trees. Right now you think all you have to do is to stretch out your palm and money will be placed in your hand. We're going to teach you some facts of life . . .' She paused. 'We're not saying we'll not give you your tram fares. But we want each of you to come to us individually. Apologize for your past behaviour. Admit that you've been spoilt. Turn over a new leaf. Come to us and beg for your tram fare and we might give it to you, but you have to learn that a tram fare is not a birthright. We'll only give it if you show enough repentance.'

All of us held our breath. The maids busied themselves handing each of us a small hot moist towel to wipe our mouths and hands. Finally it was approaching the end of dinner. We waited expectantly for Ye Ye or Aunt Baba to say something, anything. There was only silence. Was there nothing they could do? Was Ye Ye's half-foreign daughter-in-law now the matriarch of our family?

Then Niang added, looking directly at Ye Ye in her sweetest and most cajoling tone. 'Have you tried these tangerines? They are so juicy! Here, do let me peel one for you.'

So Aunt Baba began working at the Women's Bank. And we all started walking to school and back. We were enraged by Niang's insinuation that Ye Ye was wrong to spoil us by giving us tram money. All of us understood that the whole issue of tram money was a power struggle within the family. By walking, we were pledging our loyalty to Ye Ye whom we still regarded as head and protesting against Niang's usurpation. (In reality, of course, Niang had wrested command as soon as Grandmother had died. Years later, when I asked my aunt to tell me about my mother, she revealed that shortly after Grandmother's funeral, Father had had all photographs of my mother destroyed.)

Lydia was the first to give in. Her classes started and ended one hour later than mine, so we did not leave or return together. Within two weeks, I noticed that she was home only fifteen minutes after me. I knew that she had defected.

My brothers held out for two months. St John's was really far away. As winter deepened, they were getting up in the dark to get to school on time. Every afternoon, following soccer practice or basketball, they still had to face the long, exhausting walk home, sometimes in the dusk. One by one, they succumbed.

Somehow, throughout the years I lived in Shanghai, from 1943 to 1948, I could never make myself go to Niang to beg for my tram fare. Days became weeks. Weeks became months. Months became years.

From time to time, both Ye Ye and Aunt Baba would urge me to go downstairs to negotiate. I never did.

Often, on a Sunday afternoon, we would suddenly hear Father or Niang call out: 'Time for your weekly tram fare distribution! Come and get it!' On hearing this, I would be gripped by a spasm of acute agony. Aunt Baba would nudge me. 'Go on! Go get your share! Go downstairs and talk to them. All you have to say is "May I please have my tram fare too?" and you will get your portion just like the rest of them.'

Occasionally, when Aunt Baba had an early morning business meeting, she would wake me a little later. I would leave the house first, run out of our lane, and wait for my aunt a few yards up the road on Avenue Joffre. She would hail a pedicab from the row for hire parked by our lane, pick me up and drop me off at Sheng Xin.

In June or September, when rain cascaded down and wind howled through the streets, I would curse Niang as I struggled along the seemingly endless Avenue Joffre, carrying my heavy book bag and sloshing through water at times ankle deep, clinging desperately to a wind-blown umbrella. I also endured the mocking taunts of schoolmates as they gingerly picked their steps along puddle-avoiding wooden planks into waiting cars and whispered among themselves that I boarded my own private 'number eleven tram' daily to school, meaning that my legs carried me.

Day after day, twice a day, morning and afternoon, walking to and from school, I chased my shadow in the sun and steadfastly avoided cracks in the pavement. I also made up fairytales and indulged in an imaginary wonderland. It was one way of passing the time. In my serialized stories which continued from one day to the next, I was really a little princess in disguise, thrust into this cruel Shanghai household by accident. If I was truly good and studied very hard, one day my own mother would come out of the sky to rescue me and take me to live in her enchanted castle. Eventually I became so absorbed in these fantasies that I actually began to look forward to my obligatory walks. I confided to my Aunt Baba that I held a key in my head which enabled me to enter a magic land. Nothing in Shanghai was so mysterious and exciting as this secret kingdom which I could visit at any time. High up in the mountains amidst the clouds, this place was full of tall bamboos, twisted pines, odd-shaped rocks, wild flowers and colourful birds. Best of all, my mother also lived there and every little child was wanted and welcomed. On evenings when I had no homework I used to scribble it all down on paper in my room. Back at school it thrilled me to show my stories to my giggling classmates and watch them pass my attempts at creative writing illicitly from desk to desk.

Once, one of the girls objected to my using her surname to portray a villain. She crossed it out and replaced it with my surname, Yen. When I indignantly reinserted her name back, she started to cry. Telling her it was only make-believe while writing down an entirely different name, I began to recognize the awesome power and responsibility of the pen.

On my way home, I was always specially glad as I approached Do Yuen Gardens. In a large plaza outside the park, hawkers assembled on fine days to market their wares. Among the regulars was an elderly, scholarly-looking man who staked out his portable bookstall at the far end. His booth resembled a set of wooden shutters which could be unfolded, displaying rack upon rack of dogeared, tattered, paperback Kung Fu novels for sale or loan. For fifty fen, paid in advance by Aunt Baba, I was allowed to borrow up to five books per week. These were printed in black and white on cheap paper and much loved by Chinese schoolchildren. Each book related tales of heroes and heroines skilled in martial arts, fighting battles on behalf of the weak and oppressed. Many stories were based on fables as pivotal to Chinese culture as the legends of King Arthur and Robin Hood are to western culture. After desperate struggles, right would triumph over might, and victory invariably went to the champions of the underdog. These books gave me hope.

Father's austerity programme extended to every aspect of our daily existence. Lydia and I were not allowed to have long hair or perms, only sensible, clean, old-fashioned haircuts. For the three boys it was much worse. They were forced to have their heads shaved completely bald. This was Father's idea, to impress upon us that life was not a frivolous affair. My brothers became the laughing stock of their entire school, nicknamed (after each fresh head shave) 'the three light bulbs' because of their shiny scalps.

Lunch was the cheapest canteen meal we could get at school. When America won the war against Japan in 1945, we at Sheng Xin were given US army surplus C-rations for our noonday meal. We ate tinned ham, beef stew, hard biscuits, cheese and chocolate until the rations ran out. Before every meal we prayed and thanked our American allies for winning the war and giving us C-rations.

Dinner was our only decent meal, and was a formidable affair. Promptly at seven thirty the dinner bell would sound and we would file downstairs to the dining-room. There, around an oval table, we settled into our assigned seats. Ye Ye, token master of the house, presided at the head facing the garden, with Aunt Baba to his right, and Father and Niang to his left. Gregory and Edgar sat next to Aunt Baba. James and I were relegated to the foot of the table. In those Shanghai days, Franklin and Susan did not eat with us.

We presented ourselves nightly in our school uniforms with our hair combed, bladders emptied and hands washed. We sat upright in our seats: anxious and stiff, hoping to be un-noticed. We, the stepchildren, never spoke at the dinner table, not even to each other. Whenever my name was called, an oppressive fear invariably gripped my whole being and my appetite would vanish. Without fail, an unpleasant scene would follow.

There were always six or seven tasty dishes. Two maids brought in the food: pork loin, roasted chicken, steamed fish, Shanghai crabs, sautéed vegetables, ending with a steaming tureen of hot soup. Father genuinely loved to see his children eat during dinner. We were encouraged to have as many bowls of rice as we wished. It was frowned upon to leave behind any scrap of food, even one grain of rice, in our bowls.

James and I both had an aversion to fatty meat. We were forced to eat it and soon developed ingenious methods of hoarding chunks of it in our pockets, socks, trouser cuffs, or sticking it to the bottom of the table. Sometimes we would make a dash for the bathroom with our cheeks bulging with fatty meat which would be flushed down the toilet. When all else failed, we swallowed it whole.

Fresh fruit was always served after dinner. When Father had guests, we ate the leftovers. Though there was less food, we liked to eat by ourselves. It reminded us of the good old days in Tianjin. We did not have to hide the fatty meat. We were free to laugh and talk and be ourselves again.

A governess was engaged to look after Franklin and Susan, a supposedly educated woman called Miss Chien. Their meals were served separately in their room, and they ordered what they fancied from the kitchen. Austerity apparently ceased on the first floor. They were served bacon and eggs, toast and cereal, fresh strawberries and melons for breakfast. Franklin's hair was fashionably cut by the best children's hair stylist in Shanghai. Susan wore brightly coloured dresses trimmed with lace and ribbons. They often outgrew their elaborate costumes before they had a chance to wear them. They received lots of toys and played on their own private balcony. Every afternoon they had tea with finger sandwiches, chocolate biscuits, sweet buns, cakes and pastries.

Though she was ostensibly Franklin's tutor, Miss Chien also acted as a spy and informer, reporting back the activities and conversations of those from the second floor. Ingratiating and obliging, Miss Chien never overstepped her boundaries. She and Lydia became friends. Lydia was the only one of us ever to have afternoon tea with them, on the first floor in the antechamber.

We resented the double standards. Lydia held a series of meetings on the second floor. Various strategies were proposed. Hunger strike? Rebellion? An interview with Father alone? An anonymous letter pointing out the injustices? We whispered and complained and felt very conspiratorial. There were many plans. None was carried out. One Sunday afternoon, James got up to go to the bathroom in the midst of a fantasy plot and found Niang eavesdropping outside the slightly open door. They stared at each other for a few dreadful seconds. Then Niang placed her fingers on her lips and waved him on. James realized that the game was up. He stayed in the bathroom for a long time, fearing the showdown. Finally he returned. Niang had gone. The door remained ajar. Lydia was still plotting. There was a stunned silence when James revealed his discovery. We were terrified. When the dinner bell sounded, the meeting ended abruptly and we filed down to the dining-room in silence. But dinner came and went and nothing was mentioned. We began to doubt James's story and his sanity, but not for long.

Niang's new strategy was to divide and rule. A few days later Lydia was summoned down to the Holy of Holies (Father and Niang's bedroom), and told to move to a spare room on the first floor. She was given her very own writing desk, a chest of drawers and a brand-new lacy white bedspread with matching curtains. We had to knock on her door before we could enter her domain. We were full of envy.

From then on Lydia straddled the two floors and the two sides of our lives. Like Miss Chien, she too carried tales back to Father and Niang. She gossiped not only about the three boys and me but also about Ye Ye and Aunt Baba. She was rewarded with special favours: candies, treats, pocket money, new clothes, outings with her friends. In time, she developed an air which distinguished her from the rest of us, making us constantly aware of her 'special' status.

Sometimes, when going up or down stairs, I would catch a glimpse of Lydia at the doorway of Franklin's and Susan's room, begging for a slice of chestnut cream cake or a sandwich. Her wheedling posture invariably made me cringe with revulsion. I could hardly bear to listen to her whiny voice, beseeching and badgering the wily Franklin for the 'smallest little taste' of goodies. I would bounce past her with averted eyes wishing that I could become invisible. James once commented that he would rather starve to death than plead for food from Franklin.

At school Lydia excelled in English but performed poorly in maths and science. Father asked her to help Gregory with his English homework. Armed with the authority of a teacher, she became increasingly domineering. Uncowed, Gregory fought back. Their English lessons quickly deteriorated into shouting matches.

'You are ignorant, lazy and dumb. I told you to study these English verbs last week!'

'And you're an idiot! Imagine not knowing how to do fractions and getting a zero on your maths test! 大零蛋! *Da ling dan* (Big fat zero egg!) That's what you got!'

Enraged, Lydia gave Gregory a resounding slap, forgetting that Gregory had grown taller and stronger. Gregory stood up and gripped her healthy right arm. 'If you do that again, I'm going to knock you down with my fist. Now get out of my room.'

Lydia went to report to Niang. When Father came home, Gregory was reprimanded and told to stand in a corner with his face to the wall for thirty minutes. Gregory muttered that he was doing better in English than she was doing in maths. Besides, anyone could see that his face was all swollen from Lydia's slap. Gregory claimed that she packed a right as powerful as the American champion boxer Joe Louis, the strength in her right compensating for the weakness in her left.

After this incident, there were no more English lessons. Lydia's maths did not improve. When report cards were handed out at the end of each term, her average often hovered dangerously close to a fail. The only one of us who scored lower was Franklin, but Father considered his brain not yet mature enough for serious study. Lydia was reprimanded by Father in the Holy of Holies and told to concentrate on her maths. She came out with red eyes and a streaming nose and loudly wailed to the world at large that she had tried her best, but maths was so much more difficult at Aurora than it had been at St Joseph's in Tianjin.

At St John's the boys learned to play bridge from their

schoolfriends and they taught me the game because they needed a fourth, though I was only seven years old. One Sunday, Lydia found the four of us playing bridge. After watching for a while, she became resentful and felt ignored because we were so absorbed in the game. Suddenly she ordered me off my stool because she wished to play. The score was close and competition was keen. Gregory, by far the best bridge player, had chivalrously chosen me as his partner. He took his bridge seriously and would rant and rave whenever I played the wrong card or wasted a trump. Though I disliked being called dumb and ignorant, I accepted the abuse because Gregory's reasoning was always logical and his skills superior. Now Lydia became Gregory's partner. The game was more complicated than she had bargained for. Quick mathematical calculation and assessment of probabilities were not her forte. To the delight of Edgar and James, the new partners began to lose hand after hand.

Unwilling to accept Gregory's criticisms delivered in ever higher decibels, Lydia threw down her cards in a huff and stomped downstairs, swearing that she never wished to play with Gregory again. To this Gregory replied that he would rather take me, Franklin or even three-year-old Susan as his partner than Lydia. That evening at dinner, Father reprimanded Gregory for being disrespectful to his older sister.

The special treatment of Lydia grew apace. One of my vivid memories is Lydia bounding up the stairs one Sunday afternoon, dressed in a pretty pink western dress and matching shoes, singing snatches of a song from the latest Hollywood movie, jingling some loose change in her pocket. Without breaking her stride, she disdainfully placed the exact tram fare for the week in front of each of my brothers, carefully avoided my gaze and hurried back downstairs. Silently the boys counted their coins while her song receded into the background: 'You are my sunshine . . .'

She entered the antechamber; the door banged shut behind her, and silence filled the hallway. Finally Gregory growled contemptuously, 'Showing off!'

Undeniably she had become a member of Niang's élite world.

In Shanghai, Aunt Baba was not having an easy time. She no longer enjoyed the informal yet respected place she held in Tianjin. Niang had demoted her, making her feel like a superflous spinster.

Aunt Baba was always like a mother to me. Now we drew even closer. She paid the greatest attention to everything about me: my appearance, my health and my personality. Most of all, she cared about my education, probably mindful of the fact that her own had been curtailed. She checked my homework every evening. On days when I had a test, she woke me at five so that I could set off for school with my head crammed with last-minute revisions. She was determined that I should eventually gain a college degree . . . the ticket to escape, independence and limitless achievement. Some things she did not say but I understood. I knew that I was the least-loved child because I was a girl and because my mother had died giving birth to me. Nothing I did ever seemed to please Father, Niang or any of my siblings. But I never ceased to believe that if I tried hard enough, one day Father, Niang and everyone in my family would be proud of me.

So I studied hard, not only to please my aunt but also because this was the only time I could lose myself, forget my fears and momentarily escape from this home so full of sinister manoeuvrings and hidden machinations.

At school I gained the nickname 'genius' because I came top in every subject except art. My classmates sensed my vulnerability and yearning for acceptance behind the irritatingly perfect scholastic record. They must have realized that there was something pathetic about me. I never mentioned my family. I possessed no toys, trinkets or pretty clothes. I had no money to spend on sweets or excursions. I refused all invitations to visit anyone outside the school and never asked anyone to my home. I confided in no one but went to school every day carrying inside me a terrible loneliness.

At home, I did my homework, invented my own solitary games and read Kung Fu novels.

It must have been awkward for twenty-three-year-old Niang to acknowledge the presence of five stepchildren in front of Father's friends. We suspected that she often denied our existence and intentionally gave the impression that little Franklin and baby Susan were Father's sole offspring. We were therefore pleasantly surprised one day when one of Father's colleagues came to visit and brought a gift in a large box in which we found, to our delight, seven little ducklings. As usual, Franklin and Susan chose first. Lydia, Gregory, Edgar and James then took their pick. By the time it came to my turn, I was left with the smallest, scrawniest and weakest little bird with a tiny head but soft, fluffy, yellow feathers. I fell in love with it at once and named it Precious Little Treasure, or PLT for short.

PLT soon meant everything to me. I must have been about eight. I used to race home from school to take PLT in my hands and lovingly carry her from the roof terrace into the bedroom I shared with my aunt. I did my homework with PLT waddling between the beds. Aunt Baba never complained about helping me shampoo PLT's feathers or clean up after her occasional mishaps.

Sometimes, I explored the garden to hunt for worms for PLT's dinner. One Saturday, I must have come too close to the domain of Jackie, Father's ferocious German shepherd. He rushed over, barked his terrifying bark and bared his sharp teeth. I tried to calm him by reaching out to pat his head, whereupon he sank his teeth into my outstretched left wrist. I got away and ran up to my room. I was washing off the blood when Aunt Baba entered. At the sight of her, I burst into tears.

Aunt Baba held me and rocked me, dried my tears and understood. Jackie was *their* favourite pet. It would be best to say nothing, cause no trouble, draw no attention. She dressed the wound with mercurochrome, cotton wool and a small bandage. We then comforted each other in our usual way: by looking at all my report cards from kindergarten to the most recent times. In these records lay our secret weapon, our ultimate plan. One day, I was going to be a famous writer? Banker? Scientist? Doctor? Anyway, a famous 'something'. And the two of us would leave and set up house on our own.

Meanwhile we had to have good grades. Aunt Baba was inordinately proud of my success at school. She pored over each card, touchingly enraptured. 'Oooh! Look at this! A in four subjects and B+ in drawing! We'll top the class again this year, I'm sure.'

She made me believe I was brilliant. Her pride in my small achievements was truly inspirational. She filed each report diligently in a safe deposit box and wore the key around her neck, as if my grades were so many priceless jewels impossible to replace. When things were bad, she consoled us by taking them out and looking at them. 'See this one? First grade and all of six years old and getting As in everything already. My! My!' Then 'I'm certain nobody going to university could have a more perfect record.' Or 'We'll be the most successful banker yet, just like your Grand Aunt, and we'll work together in our own bank.'

That Saturday as we read our report cards together I forgot the pain in my wrist and we were happy . . . until dinner-time.

It was a warm, humid summer evening and Father decided that we should cool off on the lawn in the garden. Jackie had been receiving obedience training lessons from a German dog trainer, Hans Herzog. Father wanted to check on his progress.

'After dinner,' Father announced, 'let's all go sit in the garden and test Jackie on one of those ducklings that was given to the children.' Then, as my appetite vanished and horror gripped me, Father turned to my oldest brother. 'Go and fetch one of the ducklings from the pen for my test,' he instructed. Immediately I knew that the doomed duckling would be mine.

Gregory ran up to the roof garden and came back with PLT. He avoided my eyes. (Afterwards, he told me in private: 'The sacrificial duckling had to be the one with the weakest patron. Nothing personal, you understand?')

Father placed PLT on his palm and strode into the garden. A wave of nausea swept over me. PLT looked so fragile and alive. Jackie greeted his master joyously. It was a beautiful night. The moon was full. The stars were bright. Father sat down on a lounge chair, flanked by Niang, Aunt Baba and Ye Ye. We children squatted on the grass. I shuddered as Father positioned PLT gingerly on the lawn and felt my heart breaking.

Jackie was ordered to 'sit' about six feet away. He panted and strained and fidgeted but he sat. PLT suddenly spotted me. She chirped softly and moved towards me. At that instant, Jackie sprang. In one powerful leap, Jackie had PLT's left leg between his powerful jaws. Father rushed over, enraged by Jackie's disobedience. Immediately, Jackie released my duckling, but the damage had been done.

I ran over and picked up my pet. Her leg was dangling from her body, her tiny webbed foot twisted at a grotesque angle. A desolation swept over me more intense than any I had ever known. Without a word, I carried her back to my room, placed her gently on my bed, wrapped her in my best school scarf and laid down next to her. The night I spent with PLT was a night I never forgot. I lived through a crushing sadness of which I was unable to speak about to anyone afterwards. There was just no one who could possibly have understood, not even my aunt.

PLT refused to eat or drink and died early the next morning. Aunt Baba gave me an old sewing box for a coffin. James and I buried her together under the magnolia tree with all its flowers in full bloom. Even today, I'm unable to smell the sweet fragrance of magnolia blossoms without experiencing the same awful sense of loss. We arranged a bouquet in a milk bottle in front of her grave, as well as a shallow dish containing a few grains of rice, some water and the worms PLT used to love.

As we stood side by side mourning her, James glanced at my tear-stained face and murmured sympathetically, 'It won't be like this all the time. Things are bound to get better . . . *Suan le!'*

I was grateful but found it difficult to thank him. Instead I replied, 'It's Sunday and everyone is still sleeping. I don't know why, but right now it feels like the two of us against the whole world!'

The wound on my wrist healed, but the scar lingered like a memorial to a beloved fallen friend, accompanying me wherever I went, whatever I did.

When I was ten years old, two events occurred within a few days of each other which substantially worsened my relationship with Niang. One of my classmates invited me to go to her birthday party, which happened to fall on a Catholic feast day: a special holiday for the nuns at Sheng Xin but not for the other schools. Though I knew I was forbidden to visit my friends in their homes, I thought I could avoid detection if I planned it very carefully.

On the morning of the party, I dressed in my school uniform and carried my book bag as if I were going to school. Aunt Baba had given me a silver dollar which I carefully saved. I placed it in my pocket, intending to buy my friend a birthday present after lunch. We met at her parents' house, a short walk from my home, and spent a wonderful morning playing with her enormous collection of dolls. Noon soon arrived. (By then, American C-rations had run out and I was expected to go home for lunch. I was given a tram fare but only for the round trip at noon.) I told my playmates I had to rush home for an errand but would be back within the hour. They asked for my home phone number, and I gave it to them without thinking.

I ran home in high spirits and bounded into my bedroom. There, unexpectedly, I came face to face with Niang. What she was doing there, I never did find out.

She was startled and caught off guard, as I was. 'Why are you home so early?' she asked.

'Well, I got off a little early,' I lied, adding stupidly, 'from school, I mean.'

'Come here!' she commanded suspiciously. I remember my

64

heart pounding as I approached her. She was flawlessly coiffed, immaculately dressed: a panther about to pounce for the kill.

She searched me and found the silver dollar Aunt Baba had given me. 'Where did *this* come from?' She asked.

I lied and squirmed and felt like a worm. I would not, could not, implicate Aunt Baba. The inquisition went on and on.

She slapped me hard. Once, twice, three times. The inquisition continued interminably.

'From whom did you steal this?' No reply.

'Did you sell something you stole from the house?' she asked.

I was considering admitting to theft as a way out when we both noticed the new maid timidly standing at the door.

'Sorry to interrupt you, 嚴太太 *Yen tai tai* (Mrs Yen),' she said. 'There is a telephone call for her . . .' She pointed at me.

I suddenly remembered my friends waiting for me to continue our game. They must have become impatient and decided to phone me. Niang hurried to the phone at the stairwell landing, and I could hear her voice, now transformed into a sickeningly sugary tone.

'Adeline's busy right now. This is her mother. Who is calling, please?'

Slight pause . . .

'I'll tell her you are waiting for her. What are your names and where are you waiting?'

Another pause . . .

'But don't you have to be at school today? . . . I see. What's the occasion? A holiday! How nice! And what are you all doing?' Then the ominous, the inevitable, 'Adeline won't be able to return to your house this afternoon. I'll tell her you called but don't wait any more.'

She came back and glared at me. 'You're not only a thief and a liar, but manipulative as well. The problem is that you have bad blood from your mother. Nothing will come of you! I don't think you deserve to be housed and fed here. I think you belong in an orphanage!'

As my world crashed around me, she added, 'Stay in your room until your father comes home. You'll have nothing to eat until this matter is settled.'

Frightened and miserable, I sat alone in our room on the second floor looking down at Jackie restlessly pacing the lawn in the garden: back and forth, back and forth. The sound of tinkling plates and laughter rose from the first-floor antechamber where afternoon tea was now being served. Soon Franklin appeared on his balcony carrying a plate of assorted goodies. Nonchalantly, I saw him tossing chestnut cake, sausage rolls and chicken sandwiches over the railing while a delighted Jackie jumped to catch the delicacies between his powerful jaws. And I remember wishing fervently that I could become Jackie, if only for a few hours: so carefree, merry and well-fed.

Later, Father came into my room in a sombre mood, carrying the dog whip Hans, the dog trainer, had given him the Christmas before. When he questioned me about the silver dollar, I could not lie.

He ordered me to lie face down on my bed, and he whipped my bottom and my thighs. As I lay there trembling with pain and shame, I saw a rat scurry across the floor, its pointed ears alert and its long tail flicking from side to side. I wanted to scream out my terror, but remained silent throughout the beating.

Father then looped the whip over his arm and announced that Aunt Baba was a bad influence and that we would have to be separated. The thought of such a possibility filled me with unspeakable dread.

Two days later, while I was still under a cloud, the second catastrophe occurred. After having topped my class for the past four years, I was elected class president. On the afternoon of my triumph, I walked home from school elated, momentarily forgetting my troubles. A large group of my classmates, led by my campaign manager, numbering perhaps twelve girls, had decided secretly to follow me home to give me a surprise celebration party. Five minutes after I entered the house, the doorbell rang. The maid opened the door to a bevy of high-spirited, giggling little girls dressed in identical uniforms, all clamouring to see me. Aware of my home situation and my state of disgrace, she hesitated, then admitted them to the formal living-room and quietly climbed the stairs to the second floor.

I no longer remember the maid's name, but I recall distinctly the expression of alarm on her face as she whispered to me, 'A crowd of your little friends has come from school to see you. They've asked for you.'

I blanched with consternation. 'Is Niang home?'

'I'm afraid so. So is your father. They are in their bedroom.'

'Can you tell my friends that I am not at home?' I asked desperately.

'I'm afraid not. I tried to say something to that effect when I first opened the door, but apparently they followed you home and saw you enter the house. They want to give you a surprise party for winning the election for class president. They mean well.'

'I know.' I had no choice but to go and greet my friends. As I crept slowly down the stairs behind the maid, I could hear the unsuppressed merriment of a dozen ten-year-old girls echoing through the whole house.

The next few minutes are a blur in my memory. My class-mates were too happy and excited to notice my white-faced silence. They surrounded me, shouting out their congratula-tions, full of joy and laughter. My stomach churned. 'I'm only ten years old.' I told myself. 'I didn't ask them to come here. Surely Niang can't kill me for this.'

At that moment, the maid reappeared in the doorway. 'Your mother wants to see you *now*.'

With great determination, I forced my face into the semb-lance of a smile. 'Excuse me,' I muttered, adding with a shrug, 'Now I wonder what *she* wants.'

67

I slunk up the stairs and stood in front of the closed door of their room, the Holy of Holies. My mind was blank and my eyes were blurry as I knocked on their door. They were expecting me. They sat, side by side, in the little alcove overlooking the garden. Through the sparkling bay windows, I could see Jackie prowling among the bushes, chasing a bird.

I knew it was going to be terrible as soon as I entered. As I attempted to close the door after me, Niang said, with grotesque sweetness, 'Leave the door open. There are no secrets in our home.'

I stood in front of my parents. In the silence all we could hear were the squeals of merriment wafting up the stairs.

'Who are these hooligans downstairs in the living-room?' Niang demanded loudly, seething with anger.

'They are my friends.' I clenched my fists and felt my nails dig into my palm. I was determined not to cry.

'Who invited them here?'

'No one did. They came on their own to celebrate my winning the campaign for class president.'

'Is this party your idea?'

'No, Niang. I had no inkling of it.'

'Come here!' she screamed. Slowly, reluctantly, I approached her chair. She slapped my face so hard that I was knocked off balance. 'You're lying!' she continued. 'You planned it, didn't you, to show off our house to your penniless classmates. You thought we would not be home.'

'No, Niang, I didn't.' I could no longer hold back the hot tears coursing down my cheeks.

'Your father works so hard for all of you. He comes home to have a nap and there's not a moment of peace. This is intolerable! You know very well that you're not allowed to invite any of your friends home. How *dare* you invite them into the living-room?'

'I've already told you that I didn't invite them! My friends know that I'm not allowed to go to their homes after school, so they probably decided to come here. They did not know it is forbidden.'

She slapped me again, this time with the back of her hand across my other cheek. 'Liar! You planned it all to show off! I'll teach you to be so sneaky! You go downstairs right now and tell those hooligans to leave our house this minute. And tell them never to come again. Never! Never! Never! They are not welcome!'

I left their room and trudged down to face my friends. An ominous silence had replaced their revelry. I wiped my streaming nose and eyes with the back of my sleeve and saw blood. To my horror and shame, I realized that Niang's slaps had caused a nose bleed, and my face was stained with a mixture of tears and bloody mucus.

I must have been quite a sight when I stepped back into the living-room to face my campaign supporters. Stripped of my defences, obviously unloved and unwanted by my own parents, I could not look them in the eyes, and they could not look at me. They knew that I knew they had heard every word. My friends had had no idea of my family situation. Towards the outside world, I was desperate to present the façade of being part of a loving family. Now, my carefully preserved guise had been stripped away, exposing the pathetic truth.

I tried to gather a little dignity and said, to no one in particular, 'I'm sorry. My father wishes to sleep. They ask me to tell you to go home.'

My campaign manager, Wu Chun-mei, a tall athletic girl whose father was an American-educated doctor, took out her handkerchief and handed it to me. Unnerved by this kind gesture, I attempted to give her a smile of thanks, but somehow found it impossible when I saw the loving compassion in her red-rimmed eyes. With tears now streaming down, I told them, 'Thank you all for coming. I shall never forget your loyalty.'

They filed out, leaving behind their gifts. Wu Chun-mei was the last to go. As she passed the stairway, she suddenly shouted upwards, 'This is unfair! You are cruel and barbaric! I'll tell my father.'

I collected my presents and mounted the stairs. Their bedroom door was wide open. Father summoned me in and ordered me to close the door. We three were alone.

'Your Niang and I,' Father began, 'are very upset at your behaviour and your attitude. You invited your little friends here this afternoon, didn't you?'

I silently shook my head from side to side in denial.

Father looked at my armful of gifts, some of them wrapped festively in brightly coloured paper and ribbons.

'Put them on the bed,' he ordered. 'Open them.'

I hastily complied. We gazed at the motley collection: a Kung Fu novel, some comics, a Chinese chess set, packages of treats: beef jerky, preserved plums, watermelon seeds, sweet ginger slices, salted limes, peanuts, a sheet of calligraphy paper with the word 'victory' boldly and childishly stroked out with brush and ink, a skipping rope.

'Pick up the whole lot and throw them in the wastepaper basket.'

I hurriedly carried out his command.

'Why should your friends come here and give you gifts?' Niang asked.

'I suppose it was because we won the election today. I'm now class president. We worked hard at it . . .'

'Stop bragging!' Niang screamed. 'How dare you! No matter what a big shot you think you are at school, you are nothing without your father. Nothing! Nothing! Nothing!'

Father said quietly, 'Your Niang and I are specially upset that you tried to turn all your friends against us and plotted for them to come here to insult us.'

'But I did nothing of the sort.'

'Stop contradicting your father! You're getting altogether too conceited! What are you? A princess of some sort that all your classmates should come here to pay you tribute?'

'五妹! *Wu mei!* (Fifth Younger Daughter!)', Father added sadly, 'we really have no choice. 家醜不可外揚 *Jia chou bu ke wai yang* (Family ugliness should never be aired in public).

You've violated the trust we placed in you when you asked your friends to insult us.'

'What's going to happen to me?' I asked fearfully.

'We're not sure,' was Father's cruel reply. 'Since you're not happy here, you must go somewhere else.'

'But where can I go?' I asked. I saw myself wandering aimlessly along the streets of Shanghai. I had seen abandoned babies wrapped in newspapers lying on the roadside and children in rags searching for food scraps in garbage cans. Some of the poor foraged the streets of our neighbourhood, the elegant Avenue Joffre, and were reduced to eating the bark stripped off the sycamore trees lining the boulevards. I was terrified.

I dropped to my knees in front of them, hoping to soften Father and mollify Niang. Instead, he said, 'In these uncertain times, you should be grateful you have a home to return to and rice in your bowl every night.'

'I am, Father.'

'Apologize to your Niang.'

'I apologize, Niang.'

'You don't know how lucky you are,' Niang said. 'You will move out of Aunt Baba's room. You really should not speak to her again. She is an evil influence. She has spoiled you and nourished your arrogance and taught you to lie and cheat by giving you money behind our backs. Meanwhile, we will find you an orphanage until you are old enough to go to work and earn your own living. Your father has enough to worry about without bothering with the likes of you. That's all.'

'Thank you, Father. Thank you, Niang.'

I got up from my knees, cast a long glance at the wastepaper basket and went up to the room I shared with Aunt Baba, perhaps for the last time.

My eyes fell on the textbooks which I had laid out on my desk before I was summoned by the maid. There were compositions, history, maths, English and calligraphy to be done. With great determination, I set to work . . . and began to escape into my school world where the rules were simple. unchanging and fair, and Niang was not there to lord it over me.

My anguish subsided as I began to write. My nose stopped bleeding. My face no longer hurt. I saw only black words and numbers on white sheets of paper. The problems challenged and beckoned. The solutions soothed and gratified. I was in control of my own destiny. The completion of each assignment satisfied an emptiness within.

That night, after a dinner filled with foreboding and during which Father and Niang neither glanced at nor spoke to me, I went straight up to my room. Aunt Baba was out playing mah-jong. My homework was finished and I could think of nothing else to do. Despair began to creep in. Niang was about to wrench me away from the only person who loved me.

Hour after hour went by. I could not sleep. I crawled out of bed and sat on the top stair in the dark, listening for Aunt Baba's footsteps. It was after eleven. Surely she would be home soon? I thought of running away and taking a train to the distant Sichuan Province, on the borders of Tibet. From my Kung Fu novels I had learned of Buddhist monasteries in the fabled E May mountains where monks prayed and practised the martial arts. Perhaps one of them would take me as an apprentice. I saw myself suddenly skilled in wu-shu, judo and karate, jumping over rooftops with ease, avenging the wrongs dealt out to those without hope . . .

I must have dozed off in the darkness, huddled against the banisters. I awoke in pain. The hall light was on. The hulking shape of Edgar towered over me. On his way to the bathroom, he had stumbled over my sleeping body. He was very angry.

'What are you doing here in the middle of the night?' he demanded. 'You almost made me fall! You idiot! You're always getting in my way.'

Sleepily, I rubbed my eyes. I thought safety lay in silence.

'Hey, stupid! Answer me!'

Still I said nothing. Slowly, I started to get up. Viciously, he bent down, grabbed my arm and twisted it fiercely. I bit my lip to keep myself from crying. I stared at him defiantly, determined not to make a sound. 'Answer me!' he repeated as he twisted my arm even harder.

At that moment, James emerged from their room. Silently, looking straight ahead as if he had neither seen nor heard, he rushed past us into the bathroom; relieved himself without fully closing the door and went back to bed.

Edgar pushed me on to the floor and kicked me again and again. After he swaggered off, I ran into the bathroom and locked the door. One of his kicks had landed on my nose which was haemorrhaging briskly. I stared at my bruised and bloody face in the mirror, and suddenly began weeping uncontrollably while trying desperately to stifle my sobs so Edgar would not have the satisfaction of knowing that he had made me cry. Gradually the injustice of it all took hold and an all-consuming fury seized me. Finally, I heard Aunt Baba's footsteps. It was almost one in the morning.

She only had to glance at me to understand everything. As I poured out my tale of woe, I could see from her expression that the evening had not gone well for her either. She was in a mildly depressed mood, usually brought on by an evening of steady losses at the mah-jong table. I told her I was planning to take the train to Sichuan Province and asked her to lend me money for the journey.

'What a mixture of sense and nonsense! Sometimes I forget how young you are.'

I was in deadly earnest. 'Trust me!' I told her. 'I won't waste your money! I'll learn everything and come back and make everything right. I'll look after you and Ye Ye.'

'Stop dreaming! You've been reading far too many Kung Fu novels. If you board that train you'll most likely be kidnapped and sold as a *ya tou* (girl slave). Ye Ye and I will never be able to find you. Even here in Shanghai the police once found thirty missing children chained to the wall of a tin factory, half-starved and almost beaten to death. If they survived their childhood, they would be sold to brothels. 五妹 *Wu mei* (Fifth Younger Daughter), you have to separate fact from fiction. Concentrate on the things you're really good at. Get yourself the best education you can. Forget the Kung Fu masters and martial arts and all that foolishness.

'As for your Niang, go to her tomorrow and swallow your bitterness. Knock on her door. Beg for her mercy. Tell her everything she wishes to hear. You know as well as I what you should say. What can we do? She has the money and the power. If necessary kneel on the floor and kowtow to her. Humbly beg her for your tram fare. If you do that, everything will be all right, you'll see. Now get under the covers and go to sleep. You've got school tomorrow.'

I went under the covers but did not sleep. I could not bring myself even to think of surrendering. I soon heard Aunt Baba snoring gently. As the night wore on I became more and more determined not to give in, no matter how cruel the torture. Defenceless and armed with nothing but my resolve, I knew only that I had to do it this way while hoping that Niang would possess no weapon powerful enough to vanquish me.

CHAPTER 7

緣木求魚

Yuan Mu Qiu Yu

Climbing a Tree to Seek for Fish

At the age of sixty-five, Ye Ye found himself without a penny to his name. Father made it clear that Ye Ye and Baba were to negotiate with Niang for their allowance. This was unheard of in a society where fathers-in-law hardly deigned to speak to their sons' wives, let alone ask them for money. Besides breaking the Confucian bond of filial piety, Father was undermining Ye Ye's self-respect. Gently but firmly, Ye Ye declined, telling Baba he had no intention of 緣木求魚 *yuan mu qiu yu* (climbing a tree to seek for fish).

Instead, father and daughter visited Grand Aunt at the Women's Bank and Aunt Baba asked for her old job back. In the formal dining-room of Grand Aunt's sixth-floor flat, they were treated to a scrumptious dinner featuring Ye Ye's preferred Ningpo delicacies. The menu included steamed crabs and yellow fish noodles, shark's fin dumplings and fresh shrimps with peas, tender bamboo shoots and anise-flavoured pork. This was followed by three well-loved desserts: glutinous rice balls with sesame paste, 'eight precious' pudding and crab-apple mousse. Mellowed by cups of warm rice wine, brother and sister sang some arias together from their favourite operas. Since escaping from Tianjin twenty months earlier, Father had been hiding out from the Japanese by secretly ensconcing himself in Grand Aunt's penthouse during office hours. Many of his financial coups were carried out through her bank in her name. She knew better than anyone else how much money Father was making. She now extolled his accomplishments to Ye Ye and Aunt Baba. Fearing a loss of face, Baba did not mention the true reason behind her request. To protect his son from public censure, Ye Ye had bidden Aunt Baba never to reveal the truth.

Between father and son, the subject of money was never discussed again. Aunt Baba returned to work. On pay days, she took her salary in cash and placed half the bank notes in the upper left drawer of Ye Ye's writing desk. This was the only money Ye Ye had at his disposal to make his modest purchases of candies, tobacco and Chinese herbs, to visit a doctor, have a haircut, eat at a restaurant or buy his grandchildren an occasional toy.

They lived in an atmosphere of constant uneasiness. Niang made it all too clear that they were there on sufferance. For the sake of appearance she always showed them a smiling face but they sensed the contempt beneath the mask. Far from enjoying a dignified and peaceful retirement, Ye Ye was given a roof over his head, three meals a day and nothing else. Father never visited the second floor. When Niang entertained at home, Aunt Baba and Ye Ye were expected to stay upstairs in their rooms, just like the rest of us stepchildren. The servants took their cues from the mistress of the house: those favoured by Niang turned bold and insolent.

For Ye Ye, life became increasingly lonely. Although visits from friends were not forbidden, Niang succeeded in making them feel so uncomfortable behind a veneer of politeness that they gradually ceased coming altogether.

He spent his time reading and practising calligraphy. Once he wrote the character 忍 *ren* (endure). He instructed Aunt Baba to study the word. 'Divide 忍 *ren* (endure) into its two components, top and bottom. The top component, 刀 *dao*, means knife, but it has a sheath in the centre of the rapier 刃. The bottom component, 心 *xin* means heart. Combined together, the word is telling us a story. Though my son is wounding my heart, I shall ensheath the pain and live through it. To me, the word 忍 ren (endure) represents the epitome of Chinese culture and civilization.' Aunt Baba looked at the word and saw the pain and fury evident in each stroke of the brush. Ye Ye did not display his beautiful calligraphy on the wall for fear of offending Niang.

My elder sister Lydia did not excel in school. With her handicapped left arm, her prospects were not promising. Father and Niang feared for her future. They decided to arrange an early marriage. On their next visit to Tianjin they took Lydia and introduced her to Samuel Sung.

Samuel was the younger son of our family doctor in Tianjin. He was a graduate of the University of Tianjin with a degree in engineering. He taught for a few years and then obtained a master's degree from Purdue University in Indiana. In 1948, he returned from America and was looking for a wife. He was already thirty-one years old, three years older than Niang. He was five feet three inches tall, had a large, rapidly balding head, small, shifty eyes and eyebrows that pointed upwards, giving him a somewhat sinister appearance. His lips were tilted lopsidedly in a perpetual half grin. Though not exactly an oil painting, he was soft-spoken and well educated.

I remember Lydia talking happily about her impending marriage to Samuel and doodling her future married name of Mrs Samuel Sung over and over on a sheet of paper, in English and Chinese.

Many years later, Lydia gave this version of events leading to her engagement which painted a very different picture.

When I was seventeen Father called me to their bedroom to have a long talk with me. They told me to go in front of the mirror and look at myself. When I did not understand what they meant (because I looked every day at the mirror and did not find anything unusual), they asked me to look closely at my left hand, which was deformed due to Erb's palsy and which I thought was not my fault.

Father said, 'You are now reaching the age of marriage and we have found a very good man for you. It is really for your own benefit for the future, because now is a good chance, and if you do not get married when you are still young, you will certainly be another spinster in the family and we will not let such a thing happen. And this is final.'

Their words were like a thunderbolt to me and I felt terrified, miserable and at a loss as to what to do or think. For I had never even thought of marriage at seventeen. Instead, I admired some of my classmates who were going for further studies abroad. I could do well because my English was good. Nobody ever told me anything about sex or love. But I was to do what I was told or else I would be sent to a convent to become a nun for the rest of my life. I can still remember Niang's cold voice in my ears: 'I'm not going to keep another old maid in my house! What do you expect? We'll certainly send you behind closed doors in a convent if you do not act as you're told. And we'll be good to you if you obey!' This made me realize that I was really surplus and unwanted. When I looked in the mirror I saw that I was truly not very good-looking with a handicapped hand. Though I was then unaware that every child has rights which include that of education and the choice of her own spouse, still I had a strong impulse to rebel against their selfish tyranny. I went to Ye Ye and Aunt Baba for help. They told me they could do nothing because first of all I was Father's child and secondly they themselves were dependent on Father for a living.

At the age of seventeen, I was naive and puerile and trusted Father entirely, thinking that his decisions must be best for my future. Only later when he sent all my brothers to England to study did I realize that I had been a fool. I felt so wretched and depressed for having submitted to their mean plot of shifting their burden to someone else. I hated them for discriminating against me when all the time I had trusted Father completely. Looking back, I think Father had the feudal idea of male supremacy.

According to Lydia, Niang practically forced her to marry Samuel by reminding her that Father had seven children to support and she was the oldest. Since it would be difficult to get a job with her crippled left arm, there was no point in wasting money on a college education. 'If you marry Samuel,' Niang told her, 'Father will give you a dowry.' Under this pressure, Lydia gave in.

They had a big wedding in 1948 with over five hundred guests, all Chinese. Two popular radio comedians were engaged as masters of ceremony. Months before the wedding, gifts arrived at our house and were carefully sorted out. The best ones were kept by Niang.

My three brothers were ordered to have their heads cleanly shaven for the occasion. They were dressed in long, traditional Chinese gowns. Franklin wore a well cut, tailor-made western suit and his hair was fashionably styled and waved. Susan attended in a frilly lacy satin dress.

During the ceremony and for days afterwards my brothers, the three light bulbs, were mercilessly teased by their peers. Father's friends remarked on the unequal treatment of the two sets of children by his two wives.

As promised, Lydia was given a dowry of 20,000 US dollars, an enormous sum in those days. She and Samuel moved directly to Tianjin after the wedding and lived with Samuel's parents. I was not to see them again for thirty-one years.

After Japan lost the war, Father reclaimed his businesses and properties in Tianjin. He and Niang were frequently away visiting them. The boys increasingly asserted themselves during our parents' absences. I remember them flirting with some girls who lived immediately behind us across the alleyway, using rubber-banded slings to catapult 'airmail letters' wrapped around hard candies from the rear window of their bedroom.

Gregory was tired of his daily breakfast of congee and preserved vegetables. One Sunday morning, when Father and Niang were away, he strode purposefully into the kitchen. As *shao ye* (young master) of the house, he demanded eggs for breakfast. Cook demurred, protesting that there were not enough eggs. Whereupon a determined Gregory searched the larder for himself. He found sixteen eggs which he deliberately and systematically broke, one by one, into a large bowl. He then made himself a giant sixteen-egg omelette for breakfast, relishing every bite until his plate was empty.

Chasing an errant ball one afternoon while my brothers were away at a school function, I crept under Gregory's bed and found a lidless box containing school stationery, seal and ink. James later confided that Gregory had solved his cash-flow problems by printing fictitious invoices for small sums on school stationery. Gregory had befriended a clerk at the accounting office, who would 'refund' in cash for any 'over-payments'. This gave him a steady stream of pocket money and a happy life.

Meanwhile, Ye Ye started to notice that from time to time, banknotes were disappearing from the upper left drawer of his writing desk, where Aunt Baba regularly placed half her monthly salary. Ye Ye suspected that the culprit was one of us, but did not make an issue of it. Disagreeing with Father's austerity programme and sympathetic to our plight, he kept his counsel and never reported the periodic losses. His was an awkward predicament because he approved neither of stealing nor of the circumstances which led to it.

Things came to a head one day in 1948. Inflation was rampant and Chinese money was worth less and less. As a valued employee, Aunt Baba was being paid in US currency and silver dollars (called big heads because of the imprinted profile of Yuan Shih-kai, a Qing dynasty general who had proclaimed himself Emperor of China for eighty-three days in 1916). As usual, she placed half her salary in Ye Ye's desk.

Chinese currency depreciated so fast that the central bank in Shanghai could not print money fast enough. Soon one US dollar was being exchanged for two million Chinese yuan. Huge bundles of banknotes changed hands for the simplest purchase.

The thief, who happened to be Edgar, had taken a few American dollars from Ye Ye's drawer and changed them on the black market. He was given an enormous sackful of local currency. Now he was in the terrible dilemma of having so much money that he had no place to hide it. There were just too many banknotes to slip under the mattress. Besides, the three boys shared a room.

Edgar dug a large hole in the garden and buried all the money. He thought his secret was safe, but he had forgotten Father's dog, Jackie.

Next day, while we were away at school, Jackie dug up the small patch of earth with his paws and sniffed out the stacks of cash. Soon banknotes were flying everywhere all over the yard. Meanwhile, the maids found a foreign exchange slip in Edgar's trouser pocket in the laundry basket.

Niang instructed the servants to pick up all the money and tidy up the garden. Not a word was mentioned until dinner had been served and eaten. Then, instead of the usual fruit bowl, the maids brought out a large platter stacked with soiled banknotes, a veritable mound of local currency.

Father was as much taken aback as everyone else. He launched into a terrible tirade. After interminable threats and much fulmination, Niang revealed what she had known all along: that Edgar was the culprit. Father followed with another of his diatribes about dishonesty, untrustworthiness, bad blood from our dead mother and a doomed future for all of us, especially Edgar, who would bring nothing but shame to the Yen family name. He insinuated that Ye Ye and Baba had over-indulged us to such an extent that we were all worthless. Finally, he took Edgar upstairs and thrashed him with Jackie's whip.

We second-class residents gathered in Ye Ye's room. We could hear the sounds of the lashes and Edgar's whimpers. Ye Ye, Baba, Gregory and I winced at every stroke, but James merely shrugged his shoulders and nonchalantly suggested a game of bridge to 'pass the time'.

Throughout our childhood, James was the only stepchild

never singled out for punishment. He survived by detaching himself emotionally. We were very close and shared many confidences but never did he come to my defence. Once he gave me this piece of advice: 'Don't trust anyone. Be a cold fish. I hurt no one. And no one can hurt me.'

Franklin and Susan were the pampered ones, the empress's son and daughter: favoured and privileged. To us on the second floor, the antechamber seemed like paradise. But paradise turned out to be Franklin's own private garden of Eden.

He used to bully Susan, grab her toys, pull her hair, slap her face, twist her arm. Niang chose to ignore this. Every night she came into the bedroom to kiss Franklin goodnight. She sat on the edge of his bed and cooed and teased and talked to him without even acknowledging Susan's presence. On those evenings when Franklin was away with his French cousins or friends, Niang did not bother to visit their room at all.

Ye Ye and Father were overjoyed when the Japanese Occupation finally ended after America dropped the atom bombs in 1945. However, civil war recommenced almost immediately between the Nationalists (Kuomintang) and Communists. In the next three years, they were increasingly alarmed to see the balance of power shifting towards the left. Mao Zedong, the Communist leader, and his armies were on an inexorable march.

Newspapers those days were full of stories of atrocities committed by the Communists against landlords and merchants. There were daily reports of fresh barbarities and appalling savagery. The prevailing impression, goaded on by Chiang Kai-shek (ruler of China since the death of Sun Yat-sen in 1925) and his Kuomintang press, was that if Shanghai should fall into Communist hands, there would be a bloodbath.

By 1948 a colder wind tempered the economic climate for businessmen like my father. In a last-ditch effort to stabilize the currency, the Nationalist government had just announced the issue of a new form of currency called the Gold Yuan Certificate. This measure was necessary because the people had lost all confidence in the old currency, called Fa Bi or legal tender. Rampant inflation had escalated to the point where one US dollar was being exchanged for eleven million Chinese yuan: even more than Edgar got for his stolen dollars.

Official announcements called for all Chinese to turn in their old banknotes, their personal caches of gold and silver and their foreign currency by 30 September 1948. Gold Yuan Certificates would be given in exchange, supposedly backed by gold and worth four to each American dollar. Immediately there was a gold rush as most private depositors withdrew their precious metals and foreign currency from local banks. No sane mind believed that there was any gold to back those certificates. Big capitalists like my father spirited their wealth abroad to Hong Kong, the United States and Europe. Small wage earners such as Aunt Baba were obliged to obey government instructions. The value of the Gold Yuan Certificates fell with each Communist victory until they became as worthless as the old currency which they replaced. By obeying Chiang Kai-shek's orders, Aunt Baba lost all her savings.

Father was making all sorts of contingency plans and it was simply a matter of time before he made his move.

It must have been the Sunday immediately following my classmates' disastrous visit when Father suddenly appeared alone at the doorway of Ye Ye's room. He summoned Aunt Baba and ordered me to go and play on the roof terrace. He seemed preoccupied, but attempted a semblance of respect towards his father and sister. Aunt Baba reflected sadly that this was the first time the three of them had spoken alone together since the family moved back to Shanghai five years earlier. For a short while a sort of intimacy was restored. Father started talking about the civil war, and the possibility of Shanghai being occupied by the Communists. He and Niang had decided to move to Hong Kong. Would Ye Ye and Baba go with them?

It dawned on Aunt Baba that besides leaving her friends she would have to give up her job at Grand Aunt's bank and revert to being the spinster living on charity under Niang's critical eye. She wondered if life under the Communists could really be any worse than a life under Niang. She decided to remain in Shanghai.

Meanwhile, beads of sweat had appeared on Ye Ye's brow and his face had turned white with fear. Tremulously, he accepted his son's invitation to move to Hong Kong and together risk their chances under British rule.

'Surely we don't have to leave right away?' he asked. 'Maybe Old Chiang (Kai-shek) can still pull it off with the help of the Americans.'

'Of course we don't have to go immediately,' Father replied. 'We still have a few months at the very least. Jeanne and I plan to fly to Tianjin next week and sell off as much as possible. It looks as if Beijing and Tianjin will fall before Shanghai. I will convert all my funds into Hong Kong dollars and take them with me to Hong Kong.'

Father now asked Ye Ye to show him where he kept his money, stressing that it should always be locked away. He meandered on distractedly about how wrong it was for children to be put in the way of temptation, turning to my aunt and accusing her of favouring me over my siblings. Aunt Baba dismissed the notion, adding that she would have given a silver dollar to any of his other children if they, too, had reached the top of their class. She reminded him that children needed to be rewarded if they excelled in their endeavours.

Father began a litany of my deficiencies: my small stature and thinness; my poor appetite, no doubt due to secret snacks between meals provided by Aunt Baba; my arrogance and aloofness. He demanded that Aunt Baba write down every fen she had given me over the past year and was sceptical when my aunt insisted that the silver dollar was all that I had received. He marched her into her room and demanded that she open up her small box of snack foods which she was in the habit of keeping, making a list of its contents:

Salted preserved plums:	2 packets
Pork jerky:	1 packet
Beef jerky (sweet):	½ packet
Beef jerky (spicy):	2 packets
Roasted peanuts:	1 four-oz bag
Peanut candy:	1 eight-oz jar
Dried melon seeds:	1 packet

Ye Ye and my aunt watched in astonishment as he made this inventory. Father then began a harangue about my worthlessness, my want of moral fibre, my excessive consumption of snack foods and my monstrous behaviour. Aunt Baba tried to defend me, telling him that I was just a little girl who never knew her own mother, but Father waved her protests aside.

Aunt Baba asked whether Father had made any provision for us children. Lydia was living with Samuel and her in-laws in Tianjin. Father's inclination was to leave his three teenaged sons in their Shanghai schools until graduation, then send them to university in England. Franklin and Susan were to go to Hong Kong with our parents. There was a short pause.

'That leaves 五妹 *wu mei* (Fifth Younger Daughter),' Ye Ye said. 'What do you intend to do with her?'

Father picked up the 'food list' and scoured it. 'Lately she has become very rebellious. Her successful performance at school has given her a high opinion of herself. You have both spoilt her by giving her too much praise. We have decided to discipline her.'

Ye Ye was startled. 'What has she done to deserve this?' he asked. 'She is only a little girl in primary school. What are you punishing her for?'

'This is the problem!' Father replied. 'The two of you are entirely too protective. It is not exactly what she has done or not done. She must be taught to be obedient and modest. She should know her place and realize that her opinions and desires count for nothing. After all, she is nothing without her Father and Niang. We have decided to remove her from this cocoon of permissiveness. When we go to Tianjin next week, we are taking her with us. We plan to place her as a boarder back at St Joseph's. She is to be left there on her own. I forbid you to write or mail her food packages like these!' He started waving the list in Aunt Baba's face. 'She will not be allowed to send or receive letters. The nuns will be instructed to keep her locked behind gates until she graduates.'

'The Communists! What about the Communists?' Aunt Baba asked, 'The newspapers report intense fighting in Manchuria. Hundreds of thousands of refugees are pouring into Tianjin. Don't you remember reading about those university students fleeing south? They were demonstrating in Tianjin for food and shelter when they were actually fired on by Kuomintang troops. Is it safe for her to go to school there now?'

'This must be stopped at once!' Father shouted, brandishing the list. 'She must be separated from you two.' Still clutching the list he rushed from Aunt Baba's room, slamming the door behind him.

'What's all this about?' Aunt Baba asked Ye Ye in a shaky voice. 'The child has done nothing. He behaves as if he wants to destroy her. He knows it will 傷心 *shang xin* (wound her heart) to be taken away from us. Can you make any sense of it?'

Ye Ye knew. 'His child has done no wrong. But every day her presence is like a thorn in their side: she annoys them by simply being around. They're sending her away because they want to be rid of her.'

Those were uncertain times. Every other family with property, Kuomintang ties or even western professional training agonized over what to do next: to stay or to go. For established businessmen with homes, offices, families, friends, and *guanxi* (connections), the choice was particularly hard. Time was running out. Chiang Kai-shek's army lost city after city. Were the Communists really as bad as all that? Could anyone be certain how things would evolve under the new regime? Many did not stay to find out. Everyday, trains, planes and boats were loaded with refugees heading for Taiwan and Hong Kong.

In later years Father would relate the fate of an acquaintance who wavered at the very last minute. He was actually on his way to Shanghai airport with his wife and son. He could not believe that he was a big enough player to be singled out for persecution. He stopped at the house of his cousin. They exchanged places. The cousin flew with wife and daughter to a life of prosperity in New York. Father's friend stayed and was eventually stripped of everything he owned. His son was imprisoned for criticizing Jiang Qing, Mao's wife. His wife committed suicide during the Cultural Revolution.

Father, Niang, Franklin and Susan left for Hong Kong in December 1948. Grand Aunt could not bear to leave her bank. She decided to stay and throw in her lot with the new rulers. Ye Ye's departure was heartrending. He loved his home town and doubted if he would ever see it again. The sights, smells, sounds and memories of Shanghai were irreplaceable. He dreaded the life stretching before him in Hong Kong but knew that he had to flee. Up to the last he tried to change Aunt Baba's mind. This she simply could not do. Thirty years later, my aunt was unable to describe their final parting without anguish.

One by one, the cities fell: Luoyang, Kaifeng, Jinzhou, Chanchun, Mukden. In December 1948 Beijing was surrounded by Communist troops. The city was under seige. In January 1949 the die was cast when the Battle of Huai Hai was finally won by the Communists. Over 300,000 Kuomintang soldiers were taken prisoner. On 21 January 1949, Chiang Kai-shek resigned as President of the Republic. The People's Liberation Army crossed the Yangtse River in April. In less than a month, they took Nanking, Soochow and Hangchow.

The Red Army entered Shanghai in triumph on 25 May, 1949. Young, zealous and disciplined PLA troops were seen marching up and down Nanking Road. They cheerfully helped residents and shopkeepers clean up the sandbags and other impediments put up by the Nationalists. They were courteous and well fed. There was no looting.

For my aunt, there now followed a period of unprecedented peace and happiness. Within a matter of days Grand Aunt's bank reopened. The Communists bent over backwards to maintain law and order. Shops and restaurants resumed business as usual. Inflation was finally halted. Gold Yuan Certificates were changed into Jen Min Pi, the new currency of the People's Republic. Prices of commodities stabilized and supplies became once more available. Public services such as transportation, mail delivery and street cleaning seemed better managed than before. The new regime repeatedly assured the populace in newspapers and radio broadcasts that properties and businesses of Chinese and foreign merchants would be for ever protected, and their religions respected.

Aunt Baba was in charge of the household, supervising my three brothers who were still at school in Shanghai. She spent her bank salary for her own needs and collected the monthly rental income from Father's properties to run the house. She trimmed the domestic staff down to two maids and Miss Chien. She was profoundly moved when she heard Chairman Mao's broadcast from Beijing on 1 October 1949, proclaiming the founding of the People's Republic of China. All her fellow employees gathered around a radio to hear Mao announce, 'The Chinese people have arisen.'

Her days were calm and orderly. After breakfast, she saw the boys off to school before going to work herself. They ate dinner together as usual at seven thirty and the boys were encouraged to bring their friends home. Each was given a fair weekly allowance so that they could take themselves off on outings from time to time. The Communist interference did not extend beyond the compulsory registration of everyone in the abode, including Franklin's governess, Miss Chien. A *hu kou* (residents' committee) was set up for administrative purposes. Later these committees became government tools to control and account for the movements of every inhabitant in Shanghai.

Miss Chien was a spinster in her mid-thirties. After the departure of Franklin and Susan, she had no obvious function and feared that she would be dismissed. Her education had ceased at the age of fourteen and she was now unable to teach the boys in any subject. She tried to curry Aunt Baba's favour by preparing regional delicacies from her home town. When the weather turned cold, she warmed Aunt Baba's bed with hot-water bottles and brought up thermos flasks of hot water for Aunt Baba's nightly bath. She spent her days reading the newspapers, gossiping with the two remaining maids, writing letters and knitting tirelessly. Aunt Baba was amazed at her seemingly endless supply of good-quality wool which was becoming impossible to procure in the neighbourhood stores. Many imported commodities were in short supply as westerners were leaving in droves and foreign firms were closing down. Generously, Miss Chien gave many of her hand-knitted cardigans to Aunt Baba and the boys as gifts.

Gregory graduated from middle school in 1950. Under Father's instruction, he and Edgar went by train to Tianjin and had some western-style suits custom-made by Uncle Pierre's tailor. Travel in those days was still free and easy. They left Tianjin by boat for Hong Kong with their new clothes. Three weeks later, they were sent to England for further studies.

James remained at school for another year during which Aunt Baba lavished loving care on him. The maids were told to cook his favourite dishes. He took expensive riding lessons, entertained his friends at home and went on excursions to neighbouring cities. Gallant and witty, he proved a good companion to my aunt. They often read Ye Ye's letters together and James was coaxed into writing weekly to Father and sometimes to Ye Ye as well. He enjoyed considerable freedom in

Shanghai; so much so that when word came from Father for him to leave for Hong Kong in 1951 he was reluctant to go. Aunt Baba pleaded James's case with Ye Ye but to no avail. Ye Ye replied that the two of them must have taken leave of their senses. He thought it unwise to even show their letter to Father.

By the time James left in July 1951, travelling restrictions had tightened. Accompanied by Third Uncle, Frederick (our own dead mother's youngest brother), they travelled by train to Canton. A special pass was needed to cross the border into Hong Kong which they lacked. They were finally smuggled across in a leaky boat in the dead of night. Luck was with them and they sailed peacefully into Hong Kong harbour. Back in Shanghai Aunt Baba was now left alone with the two maids and Miss Chien.

CHAPTER 8

一視同仁

Yi Shi Tong Ren
Extend the Same Treatment to All

Father and Niang took me north to Tianjin in September 1948 at the height of the Civil War. Province after province was being lost to the victorious Red Army. Most people were fleeing in the opposite direction.

Following the collapse of the Kuomintang army in Manchuria, refugees were arriving at the rate of 600 a day, bringing with them pestilence and squalour. Tianjin's population swelled by 10 per cent within a matter of months. City services, already desperately strained, simply could not cope. Soon the refugees were kept out by force and housed in primitive camps. Dysentery was rife.

Against this backdrop Niang enrolled me as a boarder at St Joseph's. There were only about a hundred pupils left. I was one of four boarders; the rest were day girls. Classes were sporadic because attendance was erratic. Over the next few weeks, the number of girls dwindled. Soon we were gathered together into one classroom, ranging in age from seven to eighteen. No Chinese was spoken during school hours. Indeed, while I was there, no Chinese was taught at the school. We had to converse with each other in English or French.

I was miserable. Chinese had been the language of instruction at my primary school in Shanghai. English was a second language; French was never taught. I was lonely and longed to return to Aunt Baba, James and my friends in Shanghai. I poured out my wretchedness in long letters, begging for a few kind words from home. Day after day I waited expectantly for my name to be called when mail was distributed. No letter ever came. I did not know of my parents' instructions to the nuns that I was to receive no visitors, no phone calls and no mail.

Sealed in a hermetic world behind convent gates, I was totally unaware that meanwhile the Communists, having captured Manchuria, were sweeping past the Great Wall and moving steadily towards Beijing and Tianjin. Kuomintang and Communist troops fought pitched battles for the control of North China. Many students and their families fled to Taiwan and Hong Kong. Formal classes were abandoned. We spent our time reading English books of our choice. I steeped myself in the English–Chinese dictionary. During an informal conversation class one day, our teacher asked us each to name one favourite book. Everyone laughed when I said mine was the dictionary. And if I could have one wish granted what would it be? To receive a letter addressed to me. Just one letter. From anyone.

More and more girls left the school as the Communist armies approached. Inside St Joseph's there were no more farewell parties. Girls simply failed to appear at class. The nuns seemed distraught and preoccupied. They were being advised by their superiors in France to leave Tianjin and save themselves from persecution.

I spent every Sunday and every holiday by myself in the school, including Christmas and New Year. All the other boarders would go home to their families. I was not allowed to accept any invitation from my friends. The nuns did not know what to do with me. I wandered like a ghost from classroom to classroom, spending much time reading fairy tales in the library. My memory of that Christmas is sitting by myself in the enormous refectory, eating ham, potatoes and plum pudding and pretending I hadn't a care in the world. Outside, I could hear the sweet refrain of 'Silent Night' piercing the air as I stoically avoided the solicitous glances of kindly Sister Hélène, rushing in and out while I ate my Christmas dinner alone.

On 31 January 1949, victorious Communist troops marched into Beijing without a shot being fired. Next day Fu Tso-I, the Nationalist general, surrendered with all his armies and rich military supplies. He was rewarded with the post of Minister of Water Conservation of the People's Republic. Tianjin was taken by the Communist general, Lin Biao, about the same time.

My eldest sister, Lydia, was actually living in Tianjin with her husband Samuel and his parents during the time I was incarcerated in the convent. They neither visited nor enquired after me. When they fled from the Communists to Taiwan in January 1949, they left me behind without having made contact.

Day after day I sat alone in the library wondering what was to become of me. My school routine had disappeared. There were no more classes and every day was a 'free' day. My teachers appeared at a loss as to how to educate one solitary child who spoke little English or French. The mood at the convent was one of barely controlled panic, relieved only by Roman Catholic rituals.

Suddenly one morning Niang's elder sister, Aunt Reine, appeared in the lobby of my school. I was overjoyed because I had had no visitors since my admission. Though we hardly knew each other, I wept when I saw her. She was preparing to leave Tianjin with her husband and two children when she remembered that I was stranded at St Joseph's. On her own initiative and without consulting anyone, she took me out of school.

Tianjin had just been liberated. On the streets, I saw Communist soldiers dressed in padded winter uniforms and peaked caps. They were removing sandbags, pill boxes and fortifications set up by the Nationalists to block the passage of enemy vehicles and troops. Recently melted snow had reduced the sandbags to muddy blobs. The streets were eerily quiet. There

93

was hardly any traffic. We walked the short distance to Father's two houses on Shandong Road.

Everything was strange and baffling to me that day, not least being back in the home where I had stored away a bank of fond memories. There I met Uncle Jean Schilling (who worked for the United Nations) and their two children, Victor and Claudine. I was shy but they were kind and made me feel at ease. Victor, who was my age, invited me to play in his room. We made paper airplanes and flew them all over the house. Aunt Reine, noting my tongue-tied nervousness, placed her arm around me and whispered, 'Don't worry, I will 一視同仁 *yi shi tond ren* (extend the same treatment to all) three of you.'

Over dinner Uncle Jean explained that my parents were in Hong Kong and we were to join them as soon as possible. The day before, Communist soldiers had attempted to enter and commandeer Father's two houses to use as General Lin Biao's temporary headquarters. Uncle Jean raised the United Nations flag to protect the houses and prevent them from being occupied by force.

At that time, all Niang's relatives were living in Father's Tianjin houses. Her mother had passed away. Lao Lao, her unmarried Chinese aunt, was living with Niang's older brother Pierre in the 'old' house, together with a skeleton office staff. Pierre was still the managing director of Father's Tianjin businesses but was soon to flee to Morocco. Reine and her family lived in the 'new' house. Father had sent the youngest brother, Jacques, to Paris and was financing his education at the Sorbonne.

A few days later, the Schilling family and I boarded a ship for Hong Kong.

The island of Hong Kong (香港 Fragrant Harbour) was ceded to the British in perpetuity after China's defeat during the First Opium War in 1842. At the conclusion of the Second Opium War (1858–60), Britain was 'given' the tip of the peninsula of Kowloon, south of Boundary Street, as her permanent possession. In 1898, Britain made further demands and extracted a ninety-nine-year lease on the rest of the Kowloon peninsula north of Boundary Street. This area was known as the New Territories and was to be returned to China on 1 July 1997.

Aunt Reine had succeeded in smuggling Niang's diamonds out of Tianjin. She covered the stones with cloth and sewed them as buttons on to her winter coat. The unveiling was dramatic. As each precious gem escaped from Reine's scissored fingers to glitter magnificently on the coffee table, Niang became so overjoyed that her mood lifted noticeably and my unexpected presence did not cause the immediate fury I had anticipated.

Father, Niang, Ye Ye, Franklin and Susan were living in a rented second-floor flat on Boundary Street in Kowloon, across the street from Maryknoll Convent School. In 1949, this British colony was a far cry from the bustle and sophistication of Shanghai; nor did it have the tradition and culture of Tianjin. It was a sleepy, tidy, rather provincial city with clean streets, bright red double-decker buses, orderly traffic and a magnificent harbour. Cantonese was the prevailing tongue. English was spoken only at first-class hotels like the Peninsula.

Day after day Niang took the Schilling family sightseeing in the chauffeur-driven car. I was left behind with Ye Ye and the servants. Politely, Niang would ask Ye Ye whether he wished to accompany them. He always declined. I was never invited. It was automatically assumed that the excursions did not include me.

Secretly I was very pleased. It was wonderful to be with my Ye Ye. I accompanied him on short walks. His eyes were failing and I read the newspapers to him every morning. We played Chinese chess and he would generously swap me a horse (knight) for a chariot (castle). These games were competitive and he seemed to enjoy them, analysing the end result regardless of who won or lost. He told me stories from *Legends of the Three Kingdoms*, accompanying the tales with snatches of

Chinese opera when he was in a good mood. He taught me the magic and mystery hidden in many Chinese characters, illustrating them with brilliant examples which filled me with wonder and delight. Once he pointed out that the words 買賣 (business) held the secret to all the riches in the world. '買 means buy, 賣 means sell,' he said. 'The two words are identical except for the symbol 土 (dirt or land) on top of sell. The essence of 買賣 (business) is buy–sell; and its most important ingredient is 土 (dirt or land). Always remember this.' Often we would just sit quietly together, content to be in each other's company, with Ye Ye peacefully smoking his pipe.

At Sunday breakfast, Niang suggested that we all have lunch at the luxurious Repulse Bay Hotel on Hong Kong Island. Everyone piled into Father's large car. It was a very tight squeeze. I was the only one left behind, standing forlornly at the kerb with the servants.

Victor spoke up. 'It's not fair, Maman,' he said to Aunt Reine in French. 'Why does Adeline never get to go anywhere with us?'

Impatient to depart, and not understanding French, Father asked Victor in English, 'Do you need to use the bathroom?'

Niang interrupted in French, 'Adeline does not get to go because the car is too crowded. There is no room.'

'Then what about yesterday and the day before, and the day before that?' Victor demanded in French.

'Get in the car, Victor!' Aunt Reine ordered. 'You're delaying everything. You can see there's not enough room in the car today.'

'It's just not fair,' Victor persisted. 'Why is she always the one left behind?'

'Because that's the way it is,' Niang exclaimed rather sharply in French. 'You either come with us now or you can stay home with her.'

'In that case I think I'll keep Adeline company.' Victor climbed out of the Studebaker and stood by my side as the car drove away. I have never forgotten his chivalry.

Uncle Jean and his family soon left for Geneva, where he was being posted by the United Nations.

Father had rented an office on Ice House Street in the main business district on Hong Kong Island, known simply as Central. Every morning, the chauffeur drove him to the Star Ferry terminal for the seven-minute boat ride across Victoria Harbour from Kowloon to Hong Kong. Once there, it was a short walk to his office.

Father quickly adapted to business life in the British colony. First he set up a flourishing import–export company. Then he astutely traded in stocks, commodities and foreign currencies. He launched a property company, Mazman, which was later listed on the Hong Kong stock exchange. Mazman bought choice pieces of land at government auctions and built residential units as well as industrial buildings. He obtained the right to dispose of the loose gravel, stones and earth when Stubbs Road was lengthened and widened through the heart of Hong Kong's exclusive 'Mid-levels' location, halfway between the Harbour and the Peak. He created a temporary quarry and sold the excavated materials to eager builders. He became a member of many of the most prestigious clubs in Hong Kong and was known as a successful entrepreneur from Shanghai.

Father and Niang rose to prominence among the small westernized circle of Hong Kong's high society. In those days few Chinese businessmen spoke English or felt at ease among westerners. In contrast, Father and Niang were comfortable in both worlds.

Elegant and photogenic, Niang was no stranger to the society columns of local newspapers and magazines. She employed a famous illiterate chef from the Park Hotel in Shanghai who carried all the recipes in his head and reputedly knew one hundred different ways of preparing chicken. Spectacular dinners were held at home. Invitations were treasured because of the quality of the food and Niang's cosmopolitan guest list. During these parties, Ye Ye and we stepchildren (on those occasions when we were home) were never mentioned or introduced. It was understood that we should keep ourselves hidden in our rooms, and not embarrass anyone by our presence, especially when there were westerners.

Two days after the departure of the Schilling family, Niang ordered me to pack my belongings. I was being taken away.

I remember that Saturday afternoon with vivid clarity. Father was at the office. Susan was attending a birthday party. Ye Ye was taking his afternoon nap. Niang, Franklin and I sat side by side in the Studebaker behind the chauffeur. The car was saturated with the scent of Niang's expensive perfume, making me dizzy with premonition.

To my amazement, the car stopped in front of the elegant Peninsula Hotel. Apparently, Franklin fancied afternoon tea. Inside the cool, high-ceilinged lobby-restaurant, elegantly decorated with potted palms, whirring overhead fans and rattan furniture, I sat gingerly in a large bamboo chair. A chamber orchestra struck up the 'Blue Danube' waltz. Franklin wanted an ice-cream sundae and Niang ordered finger sandwiches while I nervously scanned the extensive menu. A wave of nausea seized me. I longed to escape to the bathroom but sat glued to my seat, wondering if she was about to carry out her threat to abandon me in an orphanage. Was this to be my last meal before her *coup de grâce*?

Niang's piercing voice suddenly interrupted my gloomy thoughts. 'Adeline!' she was saying impatiently. 'You can order anything you want, understand? But *do* hurry up!'

CHAPTER 9

人傑地靈

Ren Jie Di Ling

Inspired Scholar in an Enchanting Land

The Sacred Heart Convent School and Orphanage, run by the sisters of Canossa from Italy, was situated on Caine Road, Hong Kong Island, perched at Mid-levels facing the sea. After crossing the harbour by ferry from Kowloon later that afternoon, our car climbed past the dense financial Central district where Father had his office, upwards towards the Peak Tram Terminal. Immediately below the Botanical Gardens, we turned right by the Governor's Mansion with its white uniformed sentries and lush green lawn, travelling westwards for half a mile before stopping directly outside the Convent's narrow entrance to the north. A flight of steep stone steps led up to the courtyard lobby where, after a short wait, we were greeted by Mother Mary and Mother Louisa.

In 1949, Sacred Heart was one of the very few Hong Kong Catholic schools which took in both boarders and orphans. The two groups were dressed in distinctly different uniforms and not allowed to socialize with one another. The orphans did not attend regular classes but were taught 'practical skills' such as sewing, laundering, cooking and ironing. During mass, they sat in a special section of pews. After school, while the boarders played games, received private lessons in art and music, or read in the library, the orphans were assigned to help out in the laundry, kitchen and garden. They were expected to leave the convent at sixteen and get jobs as waitresses, maids and shop girls.

Girls were a cheap commodity in China. Unwanted daughters were peddled as virtual slaves, sometimes by brokers, to unknown families. Once sold, a child's destiny was at the whim of her buyer. She had no papers and no rights. A few lucky ones became legally adopted by their owners. Many more were subjected to beatings and other abuses. Prostitution or even death were the fate of some child slaves.

I did not know what Niang's intentions were but my future was in her hands. Accompanied by Franklin, she conferred with the two nuns in a private room for what seemed like an interminable period. Meanwhile I was left outside to peruse the brochures describing the school and orphanage. I learned that the vast majority of the 1200 students at Sacred Heart were day girls, arriving at eight and leaving at three thirty. The waiting was horrible. I sat there in trepidation, recalling Niang's threats the year before in Shanghai . . .

Finally they emerged. Astonishingly, Niang smiled and patted me fondly on the head in front of the nuns. This was the first and last time she ever touched me, aside from slaps, during my childhood. 'How lucky you are!' she exclaimed. 'Mother Mary has agreed to admit you to the boarding school during the middle of the school year!'

When I was enrolled there were sixty-six boarders. Throughout my years there, I never entirely overcame the very real fear of being transferred to the orphanage section. I would then cost my Father nothing.

On admission as boarder, each child was assigned an identification number. From then on, all our belongings were stamped with that number. Our day started at five forty-five. A loud bell aroused us from bed. Daily mass was compulsory. My friend Mary Suen, who was not an early riser, used to complain that it was 'just like being a nun, whether you wish to be holy or not'. The only legitimate excuse for escaping mass was serious illness, pretended or otherwise. All through mass most of us would have just one thought : getting out of the chapel as soon as possible and rushing into the dining-room for breakfast. Seating was prearranged and could not be altered; they placed us according to our age. Mary sat to my immediate left.

We were each given a pigeonhole in a huge cupboard prominently displayed in the dining-room. Each boarder would store her provisions from home in her allotted space, duly numbered. The abundance or scantiness of your very own food supply was readily visible to all the girls. It was a barometer of the degree of affection accorded to you by your family. During my entire stay at Sacred Heart, my pigeonhole was perpetually empty.

Eggs had special significance. They had to be brought from home and were stored in the refrigerator in the kitchen. Before handing them over, each boarder was required to paint her number in indelible ink on the shells.

For breakfast we each had two slices of bread, a pat of butter and a portion of jam. For those lucky ones whose parents paid an extra fifteen dollars per month, there was hot milk into which you could stir your own supply of chocolate or Ovaltine from your pigeonhole. Some girls brought out anchovy paste, Marmite, chicken liver pâté or canned tuna to spread on their bread. Mother Mary would then bring in a huge vat of piping hot, freshly boiled eggs. She used to pick up the eggs one by one and place them in individual egg cups, reading out the numbers as she worked. You walked up to her when you heard your number and retrieved your egg.

Those eggs became symbols of rare privilege. They were cheap and readily available in the markets, but having your number called by Mother Mary meant that someone from home loved you enough to bring you eggs so that you would eat a nourishing breakfast. Just because your family was rich did not mean that you automatically received an egg. You could not charge eggs to your account like milk or piano lessons. The breakfast egg, more than anything, divided us into two distinct and transparent groups: the loved ones and the unloved ones. Needless to say, I remained eggless throughout my tenure at Sacred Heart.

After breakfast, we rushed to pick up our books from the study room and join the day girls in the playground. Classes started at eight. Lessons were in English but we spoke to each other in Cantonese. To my surprise, the months I had spent at St Joseph's had given me sufficient grounding to keep up with my studies.

At noon, the school broke for lunch. We boarders were summoned by a bell into the dining-room. There we found a plate of spaghetti and meat balls, or macaroni and cheese. On good days, we were served pork chops and rice, and sautéd vegetables with mashed potatoes. 'So called western food!' Mary muttered under her breath. 'Give me a bowl of wonton soup any day.'

Afternoon school was from one thirty to three thirty. Tea was served in the dining-room at four. It was the only meal you were free to partake of or not. This was the hour when the haves could really show off to the have-nots. Besides the usual bread, butter and jam, out came the goodies brought in during Sunday's visiting hours: chocolates, biscuits, candies, beef jerky, preserved fruits, assorted nuts. On birthdays, the birthday girl was allowed to change out of her uniform into a pretty dress. Decked out in dainty lace, ribbons and bows she dispensed largesse to the rest of us while parading next to Mother Mary behind an enormous birthday cake ablaze with the appropriate number of candles. We sang 'Happy Birthday'. The cake was sliced and arranged on a platter. Mother Mary and the birthday girl then went around the room from boarder to boarder, serving or withholding a piece of cake as she wished. After this little game of discrimination, the birthday girl would open her presents while we oohed and aahed over them.

My habit was to go to tea a little later, wolf down my bread, butter and jam as fast as possible, then bolt out of the door. I knew that there would never be a birthday celebration for me. At no time could I ever reciprocate in kind or buy anyone a birthday present. My friend Mary and I did not speak to each other about any of this, but I often found some treats from her laid out on my plate: a few coconut candies, a packet of preserved plums, a piece of fruit.

Mary was not considered academically clever. She had difficulty with maths and often asked me for help. She used to sit by my side as I worked on her assignments, saying, 'It's so obvious now. Why didn't *I* think of it?' I would bask in her admiration and try even harder.

In other ways Mary was wise beyond her years. When Daisy Chen was first admitted as a boarder, I noted that she had a Shanghai accent and was curious about her background. I must have asked a few too many questions. Daisy became vague and evasive. Afterwards Mary said to me, 'Don't ask such questions. Girls like us who end up here usually come from unhappy homes. It's better not to ask. Her story'll come out in the end anyway.' I kicked myself for being insensitive and boorish.

After tea, there was an hour of recreation. We were free to play with our dolls, read novels, skip rope, practise the piano, roller skate, compete in softball or shoot a few baskets. I usually visited the library.

It was a large square room tucked away in one corner of the boarders' wing. Its floor-to-ceiling shelves were lined with books. Most of them were in English. A few were in Italian or Latin. There were no Chinese books.

Oh, what magic it held for me to walk into this treasure trove where the written word was king! The windows were small. The lights were dim. Because of this, the room was dark and forbidding. There was no librarian. Many of the volumes were reference books or magazines which could not be removed. The rest was a kaleidoscope of every subject under the sun. We were allowed to check out as many books as we wished. Mother Louisa was in charge and locked the doors promptly at five. Since tea was from four to five, I was usually the only one there. Often I encountered Mother Louisa on my way out, my arms loaded with the latest batch of reading material. I became such a familiar sight that she often looked out for me before locking up. 'Is the "scholar" out of her lair?' she would joke, jangling her keys. 'Or is she spending the night in here?'

She gave me that nickname because a maths problem I had helped Mary solve proved to be more correct than the one in her textbook. It was probably just a printing error but the story made the rounds and reached the other boarders. Many came to me when they had problems with their homework.

They started to overlook my one and only Sunday dress which was too short, too tight and too small for me, my worn shoes with holes in the soles, my empty pigeonhole and even my egglessness.

Sundays were designated visiting days. Between the hours of ten and twelve in the morning we boarders, dressed in our prettiest street clothes, with hair combed and shoes polished, waited downstairs in the courtyard lobby for our parents. Chairs were placed in clusters for family groupings. We did not intrude on the relatives of our fellow boarders.

In the beginning I used to be caught up in the excitement of the Sunday visit and prepare for my family with as much anticipation as everyone else. Invariably I had no visitors. It was difficult to ignore the scathing comments and pitying glances Sunday after Sunday. Among all the boarders it was clear that I was the only truly unwanted daughter.

Finally I solved the embarrassment by removing myself from the scene. On Sunday mornings, when the girls were prinking themselves in the mirror, I would pick up a pile of books and quietly slip into the lavatory. There I stayed until I heard the steady trickle of chatter and giggles as my friends came back upstairs, laden with edibles and treats, comparing gifts, exchanging food, and trying on new clothes and shoes. After I judged them all to be back I used to tuck my books under my uniform and nonchalantly saunter out. Tactfully, no one ever mentioned my Sunday morning disappearances.

Often, late at night, when everyone was asleep, I would be awakened by an attack of acute anxiety, filled with gloomy thoughts about my future. In winter, when the weather was cold, I burrowed under the blankets and read my favourite books by flashlight so that the nuns could see no shadows flickering on the ceiling. Invariably my inner turmoil would be dispelled by the trials and tribulations of the make-believe characters as I drifted slowly off.

Between April and September the weather was oppressively hot and humid. During the turgid summer vacations I was one of the very few boarders left behind; sometimes the only one. In the dead of night, I developed a technique of rolling myself under the empty beds and emerging silently on the other side, where French windows opened on to a balcony overlooking the harbour. There I used to creep on to the cool balustrade lining the verandah under a star-studded dark blue sky, and gaze out at the giant ships dotting the bay. I loved to sit hugging my knees and staring at the vision below, my dreams floating miles and miles into the distance.

Sometimes, one of the ocean liners would emit a low-pitched hoot signalling its departure. How magical it was for me to listen to that evocative sound! Longingly my eyes would follow the receding vessel as it faded quietly into darkness. I saw myself standing at the bow of the giant ship gliding through still, dark waters, carrying me on an entrancing journey to those fabulous lands: 英國 *Ying Guo* (Heroic Country) and 美國 *Mei Guo* (Beautiful Country)! These words, meaning England and America, conjured up vistas of ivy-covered college buildings, citadels of learning in the shape of baronial castles and holy cathedrals. As described by the Tang dynasty poet, Wang Bo, these were the mythical places I truly longed to visit and be transformed into an 人傑地靈 *ren jie di ling* (inspired scholar in an enchanting land).

For ever afterwards, whenever I hear the forlorn hoot of a foghorn at night, I feel once more the poignancy of those late-night hours, the sound haunting me like a call from an oracle across the ocean of time, beckoning towards a land of dreams.

CHAPTER 10

度日如年

Du Ri Ru Nian
Each Day Passes Like a Year

Ye Ye's long Chinese gowns, embroidered jackets and shaven scalp appeared even more old-fashioned in Hong Kong than they had been in Shanghai. He remained a strict Buddhist. He spoke neither English nor Cantonese and felt totally alien in this southern city. He had no friends and could hardly communicate with the maids. His only pleasures were his daily meals, his after-dinner cigar, and writing and receiving letters from Aunt Baba. Of his remaining grandchildren, Franklin was insolent and Susan was too young to interest him. So he turned more and more to James and me. On the three occasions I was allowed to go home (twice for Chinese New Year and once to recuperate from pneumonia), a cot was placed in Ye Ye's twin-bedded room which he shared with James.

In order to make small purchases such as cigars or stamps, he had to ask for money from Father. I remember Ye Ye looking old and sad, quietly reading the morning papers in the living-room.

In his last years Ye Ye developed diabetes. He had a sweet tooth, so it was a great hardship to be deprived of one of his few pleasures. Father administered his insulin injections daily. From time to time Ye Ye helped himself to an occasional chocolate or biscuit. Niang always found out about these small infractions. When Father came home, there was invariably a yelling session. Ye Ye would be reduced to a cowering, shrunken old man, confessing that yes, he did eat the chocolate. Yes, he knew that it was forbidden and bad for his health. No, he did not wish to die. It usually ended humiliatingly with Father administering an insulin shot.

Father decided to change Ye Ye's diet. He cut out the rice wine, the roast pork, the fried yellow fish in sweet and sour sauce, the salted vegetables, the fermented bean curd. On some English doctor's recommendation, Ye Ye was given a single plate of food. Each item was carefully weighed out by the maids. There were some carrots, a piece of boiled fish, a pile of boiled potatoes and a small mound of steamed rice. The same food was laid out for him three times a day, seven days a week. He no longer ate with us. His repasts were served punctually at eight, noon and six. He was not allowed to snack on anything in between.

When Ye Ye protested, he was told that these were 'doctor's orders'. During my rare visits home I remember sitting with him as he ate. It was painful to see his anguish as he swallowed his monotonous diet, obviously loathing every mouthful.

Father probably believed that this deprivation was in Ye Ye's best interests. Otherwise, how could he have withstood the despair in Ye Ye's very posture at those awful meals? Lydia told me years later that Ye Ye rebelled and demanded to move out and live on his own. He announced one day that he intended to remarry and wished to consult a marriage broker. They categorically refused. There was nothing Ye Ye could do. A deep depression settled over him. He wrote to Aunt Baba that he wanted to return to Shanghai and spend his last years with her (though he knew this was impossible because of his capitalist past); that life was so unhappy in Hong Kong that he could see no way out but suicide. Aunt Baba showed these letters to Lydia before they were destroyed by the Red Guards during the Cultural Revolution.

In the summer of 1951 I developed pneumonia and was admitted to hospital. James, who had recently come out of

Shanghai, recalled how Ye Ye became extremely concerned when he heard the news and decided to visit me. Niang was using the car for her weekly bridge game. She told him not to go because it was inconvenient and futile since I was already being treated by the 'best doctors that money could buy'. But this time Ye Ye insisted. He asked James to accompany him because he was unfamiliar with the roads, the buses and the ferry from Kowloon to Hong Kong.

Ye Ye changed into his best Chinese gown. It started to rain. He could not wear his comfortable cloth-soled shoes from Shanghai. He was unable to locate his leather-soled loafers. Finally. after much searching, Franklin found them. Apparently they had been in the hallway closet all along, even though both James and Ye Ye had looked for them there. They set out in the pouring rain, with James holding the umbrella and Ye Ye leaning heavily on his arm. The pavements were wet and slippery. As they left, Franklin said, 'Niang told you not to go. Don't blame me if you slip and fall in the rain.'

Ye Ye fell with a heavy thud even before they turned the corner from Boundary Street to Waterloo Road to catch the bus. They had to abandon the trip. Ye Ye was slipping and sliding with every step. As they approached the apartment, Ye Ye could see Franklin prancing and gesticulating on the balcony in the rain, shouting with laughter and excitement. 'See, I told you that you would fall! I was right! I was right! Niang told you not to go. She told you not to go.'

Ye Ye recounted all this to me when I was discharged from hospital and allowed to convalesce for a few days at home . . . quietly, sadly, apologizing for his failure to visit me during my illness. 'The frightening thing,' Ye Ye related, 'was the complete absence of filial piety in Franklin's demeanour. When I fell, my loafer came off. I picked it up from the gutter and noticed that the sole was greasy. When I went home, I examined my shoes. The soles were covered with a whitish greasy substance which smelled like Darkie toothpaste.' (Darkie toothpaste was a well-known brand of toothpaste made in

Hong Kong. The owners of the company lived below us in the Boundary Street apartments. They generously supplied us with samples.) Ye Ye was too gracious to accuse Franklin directly. He could sense my sorrow and rage. 'You have your whole life ahead of you. Be smart. Study hard and be independent. I'm afraid the chances of your getting a dowry are slim.' I nodded. 'Don't end up married off like Lydia. You must rely on yourself. No matter what else people may steal from you, they will never be able to take away your knowledge. The world is changing. You must make your own life outside this home.'

Towards the end of 1951 Father moved his family into a secluded villa on Stubbs Road at Mid-levels on Hong Kong Island. Stubbs Road was a major highway with cars hurtling down at breakneck speed. There were no shops within the vicinity and walking was hazardous. A car was needed for the simplest purchase. Ye Ye's letters to Aunt Baba became more and more despondent. 'All of us cling so tenaciously to life,' Ye Ye wrote, 'but there are fates worse than death: loneliness, boredom, insomnia, physical pain. I have worked hard all my life and saved every cent. Now I wonder what it was all about. The agony and fear of dying, surely that is worse than death itself. The absence of respect around me. The dearth of hope. In this house where I count for nothing, 度日如年 *du ri ru nian* (each day passes like a year). Could death really be worse? Tell me, daughter, what is there left for me to look forward to?'

Ye Ye died on 27 March 1952 from the complications of his diabetes. In the last three months of his life, he wrote to Aunt Baba mainly about the past. The ten-course feasts prepared by his own father for Chinese New Year at their tea-house in the old, walled city of Nantao; horseback riding with Grand Aunt as a boy when much of Shanghai was still rural; watching his sampans as they sailed up and down the Huangpu River; the many happy days he spent with Grandmother when Aunt Baba and Father were little. He apologized for not having arranged a suitable marriage for Aunt Baba. 'If I erred, I erred because I cared too much,' he wrote. 'Somehow, no one was ever quite good enough for you. I felt you needed someone special to look after you. Perhaps no such person exists, except in my mind.'

When Ye Ye died, Father was too busy to inform Aunt Baba himself. Instead, she received the news second-hand, from a letter written by one of Father's employees.

CHAPTER 11

自出機杼

Zi Chu Ji Zhu

Original Ideas in Literary Composition

My illness in 1951 was during the summer vacation. Most of the girls had gone home. I started coughing up blood, developed a fever of 104 degrees and had difficulty breathing. After two days I was admitted to hospital. At first the doctors thought I was going to die. They informed my family.

I was lonely and afraid. No one came from home. Mary, my best friend from boarding school, was my one and only visitor. Her father kept a concubine. She lived with her mother in a separate house within walking distance of the hospital. She told me she had nothing better to do. I was deeply grateful for her trouble, whatever the reason. As my condition improved she brought me little treats: fresh sweet mangoes, roasted peanuts, Dairy Farm ice cream, dried persimmons. We played cards, drew pictures, solved puzzles and shared the food she brought. The fever abated. The cough diminished.

One day, at lunch-time, Father suddenly appeared. Mary had gone home to eat. He walked brusquely into my room unannounced, dressed impressively in a dark blue suit. He stood by my bed looking anxious.

'How are you feeling?' he asked. I wanted to reassure him. 'I'm feeling fine, Father. I'm much better.' The combination of pleasure, fear and surprise rendered me tongue-tied and I could think of nothing else to say.

Apparently neither could he. He watched me for a few minutes until our mutual silence became awkward. Touching me vaguely on the forehead to gauge my temperature, he muttered, 'Take care,' and left.

A nurse and Mary walked in at that moment. 'Who was *that?*' the nurse asked.

I answered proudly, 'That's my father.'

She looked at me, astonished. 'We thought you were an orphan.'

'Almost an orphan, but not quite.' I looked at Mary, wondering if I had said too much.

'Me too,' Mary told the nurse. 'I'm in the same general category.'

'In fact,' I added brightly, 'you can find about fifty of us in the same general category at the Sacred Heart.'

'But only among the boarders,' chirped Mary and we giggled hysterically. The nurse left. At that moment I felt very close to my schoolmate. The thought suddenly struck me that here I was, yearning for my family to visit, day after day. Yet, when my father actually came, we had nothing to say to each other. Why should I force myself on my parents when there were loyal friends?

Mary and I began to make plans to escape from Hong Kong and live in college hostels somewhere far away: London, Tokyo or Paris.

When I returned to school after a week of rest at home, I found myself the only boarder because the holidays were not yet over. There was no one to talk to and nothing to do. I spent a lot of time in the library, flipping through books and magazines. In one of these journals I stumbled upon an announcement of a playwriting competition open to all English-speaking children aged between ten and nineteen. Buried in that library and with time on my hands, I set to work. My play was called *Gone with the Locusts*. It was about the ravages wrought by those insects in Africa. Time passed quickly and I was rather sorry when the play was completed. I sent off my entry and soon forgot all about it. School resumed and all the girls came back.

One Monday, months later, I was playing basketball in the lunch-break when Sister Valentine (nicknamed 'Horseface') interrupted our game and told me that my family chauffeur was waiting for me. Ye Ye had died and was to be buried that day.

I was driven directly to the Buddhist temple in my school uniform and saw Ye Ye's photograph placed on top of his coffin. I started to cry and the tears would not stop, though I could see that no one else was crying. Father and Niang, James, Franklin and Susan sat stony-faced in front of the maids, the cook and the chauffeur. There were no other mourners.

I wept throughout the ceremony, inundated with a tremendous sense of loss. As we walked out of the temple, I was still sobbing, not realizing that my tears were increasingly irritating Niang.

'What are *you* crying about?' she suddenly whispered angrily.

Miserably, I looked up at her with my swollen red eyes and running nose, bracing myself for a cutting remark.

It came. She turned to Father. 'I do think Adeline is getting uglier and uglier as she grows older and taller. Just look at her!'

We returned to the house after the funeral, and Niang called me into the living-room. She wore a smart black suit and her long nails were painted scarlet. The powerful scent of her perfume caused me to feel faint. She stared at my shabby school uniform, straight, unpermed hair and stubby, bitten fingernails. I felt small, plain and worthless.

'Sit down, Adeline,' she said in English. 'Would you like some orange juice?'

'No. No, thank you.'

'I noticed you crying just now at the funeral,' she said. 'You are growing up. You really should spend some time grooming yourself. Make yourself presentable. No man wants an ugly bride.'

I nodded, telling myself that this was not what she had called me in to tell me. I clenched my fists and waited.

'Your father,' she said, 'has seven children to support. Thank goodness Lydia is safely married off. However, there are still six left. It is not too early to be thinking of your future. What plans do you have?'

Thinking of my report card studded with A grades, I glanced at the menacing presence in front of me. I knew that if she could, she would see to it that I never had a future.

Terror-stricken, looking at my feet, I muttered something about hoping to attend university like my brothers, preferably in England.

'Your father,' she interrupted, 'does not have an endless supply of money. We have decided that you should learn shorthand and typing and find yourself a job.'

I was fourteen years old when Ye Ye died. James was going to London to continue his studies that summer. My teachers had told me that the best universities were in Europe and America. Back in my convent school I wrote letter after letter to Niang and Father, begging them to allow me to go to London with James, enclosing report cards filled with commendations, prizes and awards. There was no reply. I seriously considered running away to join Aunt Baba in Shanghai to continue my education. I was determined to go to college.

One Saturday afternoon about a month later, Mother Valentino came to me again with the news that the family car was waiting for me. I wondered who had died this time. The chauffeur assured me that everyone was healthy. Then I asked myself what I had done wrong. I had dread in my heart all the way home.

At last, my luck had changed. I did not know it, but I had been nominated first-prize winner of the play-writing competition I had entered seven months earlier. The review board wrote to the Hong Kong educational department which released it to the newspapers. The announcement was given great prominence and carried as a front-page insert. My name, age and school were mentioned as well as the fact that the competition was open to students from all over the English-speaking world. Father was going up in the lift to his office that Saturday morning when an acquaintance nudged him and showed him the news article. 'Would the winner, Adeline Jun-ling Yen, be related to you?' he asked. 'You have the same uncommon last name.' Father, elated and bursting with pride, read and re-read the article. That afternoon, he sent for me.

Arriving home, I was told to go immediately to the Holy of Holies, a room I had never been in before. Niang had gone out and Father was alone. I could see that he was in a happy mood. He showed me the article in the newspaper. I could hardly believe it! I had actually won! Father wanted to talk to me about my future.

My heart began to beat wildly. 'Father, please let me go to England to study. Please let me go to university.'

'Well, I do believe you have potential,' he replied, 'and might even possess 自出機杼 *zi chu ji zhu* (original ideas in literary composition). Tell me about your career plans. What subjects do you wish to pursue?'

I was silent for a long while. I had no idea what I wanted to study. Going to England was all I dreamt of. It was like going to heaven. Did it matter what you did after you entered heaven?

Father was waiting for a reply. Flushed with the thrill of my recent triumph, I said boldly, 'I think I'll study literature. I shall become a writer.'

'A writer!' he scoffed. 'What sort of a writer? And what language are you going to write in? Your Chinese is very elementary. As for English, don't you think the English people can write better than you?'

I readily agreed. Another of those awkward silences followed.

'I've thought about it,' Father announced. 'I'll tell you what the best profession is for you.'

I was relieved. I would do whatever he advised.

'You are to go to England with James to study medicine. After you graduate, you will specialize in obstetrics, just like Grand Aunt's best friend, Dr Mary Ting. Women have babies and someone has to deliver these babies. Women patients prefer women physicians.'

That night I was allowed to stay at home. James and I talked late into the night. We were full of plans. The future seemed limitless. Then I started to worry. Suppose the English should discriminate against us? What about eating English food daily? Would we be the only Chinese in our English schools and be considered rare or odd? At midnight, we were searching the dictionary, with James proclaiming that we would be called 'rare' if the English liked us, and 'odd' if they did not, when the door opened and in walked Niang.

Father and Niang had been out to a dinner party. She was dressed in a black sequinned evening gown with diamonds flashing at her throat and matching jewellery on her ears and fingers. Her long nails were polished black. She did not look pleased. 'What are you two doing wasting electricity and laughing at this time of night?' she demanded. 'It's bad enough that you do nothing but eat and sleep during the day. It's intolerable that you should continue to waste your Father's money and joke around until all hours of the night!' With that, she switched off our light and left the room, slamming the door after her.

We climbed quietly back into our beds. I tried to comfort James. 'At least she didn't forbid us to go to England,' I told him.

'No matter how bad it is in England,' James declared, 'no matter how much they discriminate against us, no matter what names they call us, just remember, it can't be worse than this!'

CHAPTER 12

同床異夢

Tong Chuang Yi Meng
Same Bed, Different Dreams

In January 1949, Lydia fled from Tianjin to Taiwan with her husband Samuel and his parents. Samuel's father, our family doctor in Tianjin, soon established another medical practice in Taipei. He started an affair with a younger woman and brazenly established her as his concubine. The situation became unbearable for Samuel's mother. After a bitter quarrel, she left and returned to Tianjin in 1950.

Taiwan in the 1940s was a semi-tropical island with an economy based on agriculture and fishing. There was hardly any industry. Jobs were scarce and living conditions primitive. Samuel was unsuccessful in obtaining suitable employment. After the birth of a daughter, they decided to follow Samuel's mother and return to Tianjin.

Father tried to dissuade them from going back to mainland China. Repeatedly he warned them of the hardships and tyranny under Communist rule.

A few months after their return in 1950, Samuel was arrested and accused of being a counter-revolutionary. Samuel's uncle had been a well-known political figure in the Kuomintang government, a prominent member of the 'exploiting class'. Though this uncle had defected to the Communist side in 1949, Samuel's background was considered tainted and his past required to be examined. During his imprisonment, Lydia and their daughter Tai-ling lived with Samuel's mother. The two women did not get along.

When Samuel was released after six months, his mother informed them that they had to get lodgings elsewhere. Husband and wife now remembered Father's two houses on Shandong Road. Of the two houses, one was occupied by Father's employees, the other by Niang's Aunt Lao Lao. Lydia and her family decided to move in with her.

When Niang found out they were living there, she was furious and told Father to write and threaten them with eviction if they did not move out immediately. Samuel and Lydia counterattacked. They warned Father that they had found evidence showing that Father's staff had illegally dealt in foreign exchange and precious metals all through the late 1940s and even after liberation. If Father tried to evict them, they would denounce him and his employees to the authorities. They then demanded and received a sum of money. They remained in Father's house but he never forgave them.

For Lydia the hardship of the years under Communism was exacerbated by this family estrangement. She became more and more embittered, blaming all her misfortune on her husband. She began to loathe him, and though they continued to occupy the same bed, they certainly did not share the same dreams: 同床異夢 tong chuang yi meng (same bed, different dreams).

Later, after our departure for England, Franklin dominated the household. Niang indulged his every whim and gave him large sums of pocket money while Susan was not given a penny.

One day, when he was thirteen, returning home from a birthday party, the chauffeur drove past a field of fresh strawberries. Franklin spotted a stall piled high with boxes of the freshly picked fruit. He stopped the car and bought two large boxes. On the long drive home, he ate every single strawberry.

A few days later, he developed a sore throat and a slight fever. Father was at work and Niang was attending a social function. He put on his roller skates and went outside under the hot afternoon sun. Half an hour later he slumped into the house complaining of a severe headache. He asked Susan to get him a glass of water and then flopped into bed. When Susan brought the water, he took one swallow, complained that it was not cold enough and threw the glass at her. Susan picked up the glass and left the room.

Three hours later, when Niang came back, Franklin was delirious and made strange sounds at the back of his throat. They admitted him to Queen Mary's Hospital by ambulance. Professor McFadden (Lo Mac or Old Mac to his students) was consulted. By then Franklin could not swallow. He kept asking for water but when he attempted to drink, the water came out through his nostrils. Lo Mac took my parents aside and gave them the diagnosis. Franklin had contracted bulbar polio: a most dangerous variety affecting the brain stem. He had probably caught the virus from eating those unwashed strawberries. Chinese farmers fertilized their fields with human manure, a known method of transmission of the polio virus. Lo Mac said there was no specific treatment for the disease, only supportive measures. They made a hole in his trachea and placed him on a ventilator. His condition waxed and waned. Father visited him every day. Niang practically lived in his hospital room. Susan was kept at home to prevent her from catching the disease. Gradually, Franklin appeared to improve.

John Keswick, the taipan of Jardine Matheson, was giving a ball which was *the* social event of the season. Niang very much wanted to go and consulted Lo Mac. He told her that her social life should not cease because of Franklin's illness. Besides, her son's condition appeared to be stable.

It was a glittering occasion. Niang was dancing the night away in a green silk dress and matching jade earrings when she was urgently called to the telephone. It was Professor McFadden himself. He sounded tired and distressed. He said he felt duty-bound to give her the bad news himself. Franklin had suddenly taken a turn for the worse and had died.

Niang never got over his demise. Whatever love she was capable of perished with her son. Afterwards, she did not turn to Father, nor to her only remaining daughter.

Father was also devastated by the loss of his favourite son. He engrossed himself with work and did not complain, though it became increasingly obvious that he was happier at the office than at home.

Susan was growing into a ravishing beauty, tall and willowy, with thick black hair, long-lashed dark eyes and snow-white teeth. She was headstrong, outspoken and intelligent. Father adored her. Niang did not relish the pleasure they took in each other's company. She felt supplanted by her own daughter.

Father and Niang began to drift apart. Whenever the two of them had an argument, Niang would sulk and refuse to leave her bed. Father had to sleep in the guest room. He would return from his office and try to cajole and placate Niang, who once remained in her bed continuously for two months.

Father started taking Susan everywhere with him, obviously proud of his pretty daughter. Their close relationship further aggravated Niang.

CHAPTER 13

有何不可？

You He Bu Ke?
Is Anything Impossible?

In August 1952, James and I sailed together to England on the giant P & O liner *SS Canton*. I could hardly believe my good fortune, recalling those countless nights on the balcony of my boarding school dreaming of just such a voyage. Throughout the month-long ocean voyage, I was suffused with elation.

We were at last on a wonderful journey of discovery and independence. Life shimmered with hope. James quoted me the well-known couplet 山高水長、有何不可？ *shan gao shui chang/ you he bu ke?* (mountains are high and rivers are long/ is anything impossible?). We made friends with the small group of Chinese students on board. They nicknamed us Hansel and Gretel because we were inseparable.

After we docked at Southampton, an agent employed by Father's travel service met and transferred us on to a train bound for London. I had studied photographs of London in my school library but was unprepared for the grim bleakness of England's capital city, still scarred from the ravages of the Second World War. Bomb craters dotted renowned city sites.

In London, we met Gregory and Edgar and caught up with their news. At first Gregory was miserable. He was the only Chinese in his school and he hated the wretched weather and tasteless food. It seemed to be mutton every day, gristly and rank. When he noticed that his Jewish schoolmates were given baked beans or eggs whenever ham or bacon was served at breakfast, he hatched a plan and went to see the headmaster.

'Sir, I wondered about this concept of religious tolerance in England. Does it apply to all religions?'

'Naturally! In our country we do not discriminate.'

'I think that is admirable, sir. I wish we had religious tolerance in China. Unfortunately, we only have barbaric intolerance. I hate to inconvenience the kitchen staff but it is against my religion to eat certain foods.'

'Oh! My dear boy! We certainly have to rectify this situation. And what might these foods be?'

'Well, the chief one is mutton: in any form or shape!'

'I am so sorry to hear this. Let me notify the kitchen at once. And what does your religion permit you to eat when the boys are served mutton?'

'To make it easy on the kitchen staff, bacon and eggs will be fine, sir.'

'Certainly, certainly. By the way, what is the name of your religion?'

Gregory had the answer all thought out. 'It's a very rare and remote sect which comes from a region between Tibet and Mongolia.' He mumbled some Chinese words which meant 'Anti-mutton-eaters' Affiliation'. Like Somerset Maugham, Gregory believed that, in order to eat well in England, he had to consume three breakfasts a day.

Gregory and Edgar found few science courses offered at their respective schools and enrolled after a year at a London tutorial college for a dose of cramming. When we arrived, they were living in bedsitters in Earl's Court. Eventually, Gregory entered Imperial College to study mechanical engineering and Edgar was to become my contemporary at medical school.

At college, Gregory's main interest was bridge. He became captain of the bridge team. The day came when he decided he would much rather devote the rest of his life to bridge than to engineering. He wrote a six-page letter to our parents asking permission to give up his studies for bridge. He was convinced he would be happier as a professional bridge player than as an engineer. After all, was not the pursuit of happiness the final goal?

Back came Father's reply in a short but succinct telegram. 'WHY DON'T YOU BECOME A PIMP INSTEAD?'

Gregory stayed on to graduate.

Father had enrolled me at a lay Catholic boarding school in Oxford called Rye St Anthony. During the month-long voyage on the *SS Canton*, I was befriended by the American widow of a Methodist missionary. She insisted I call on her English sister-in-law who had retired to Oxford after living in Shanghai for many years. In due course I telephoned Lady Ternan and, after chatting about her sister-in-law, was invited to tea.

Lady Ternan was also a widow and lived alone in an imposing Edwardian manor. I was admitted by a uniformed maid and appeared to be the only guest. Tea was served.

'Likee more tea and cakee?' she asked in pidgin English.

At first I thought it was a joke. On the phone, she had spoken in standard English. Across the table my Chinese features must have sparked off an old, buried, conditioned reflex. I had a wild desire to laugh. To humour her, I answered in my own version of pidgin English made up on the spot. As I spoke, I began to grasp that to Lady Ternan, this dialect placed me where I 'belonged'. By speaking pidgin, she reaffirmed her own superiority, establishing with every rounded vowel and clipped consonant that we were not equals. Needless to say, we never met again.

Although recommended to my parents as a proper girls' school with high academic reputation, Rye St Anthony was actually a finishing school. No science courses were offered. Instead of physics, chemistry and biology, we learned music appreciation, dancing and riding. I transferred myself to the convent school of Our Lady of Sion in Notting Hill Gate, attended a tutorial school over the summer vacation and fulfilled my entrance requirements for medical school. At the age of seventeen, I was admitted to University College in Bloomsbury where my brother Edgar was also enrolled.

Of my three older brothers, Edgar was the least favoured physically. He had a squarish face and bulging forehead, accentuated by a receding hairline. His eyes were small and closely set. His lips were thin and pressed tightly together, giving him a look of dogged determination.

Edgar had neither Gregory's charm nor James's good looks and intelligence. He was sandwiched in the middle and was nobody's favourite. When we were children he vented his frustration on me, the most insignificant member. It galled him to witness Father's pride at my academic successes. Initially, he had been one year ahead of me in medical school. However, he failed his first attempt at the second MB examination and we ended up taking some classes together. He took this as a personal insult. Gradually, his resentment turned into pathological hatred.

At college, he refused to admit that we were brother and sister, or even related. To our schoolmates, he claimed he did not know me. Father and Niang were well aware of our mutual antagonism, though neither made any effort to mend our differences. On the contrary Niang seemed pleased by our reciprocal animosity and would fuel our rivalries. She would be pointedly nice to me when she wanted to hurt Edgar, driving the wedge ever deeper between us.

In the 1950s racial prejudice was much in evidence in England. Chinese students were few and far between and there was a layer of reticence between my English classmates and myself. Most of them had never been in such close proximity to a Chinese. Some felt uncomfortable around me. A few showed barely disguised contempt. Others were patronizing, making a show of their liberal acceptance. Condescending reference would be made to China, or Shanghai, or chopsticks – usually about a subject highlighting the glaring differences. The underlying assumption was the superiority of the West.

I found that not all English words conveyed what they depicted. In a social context, words like 'exotic' or 'interesting' hid subtler shades of discrimination. 'Exotic' meant 'possibly considered decorative in China, but very strange indeed and certainly not my cup of tea'. 'Interesting' meant 'let me give you my valuable attention for the time being, while my eyes stray around in hopes of meeting someone worthwhile'.

British liberalism and magnanimity were flaunted at school functions where my professors would single me out to show that they even accepted female Asian students into medical school. While they patted themselves on the back, I would be left standing like a prize sample, steadfastly maintaining a frozen smile of amiability suitably deserving of their attention.

Female medical students consisted of less than 20 per cent of the class. By and large, we were a studious and earnest bunch. The boys resented our 'constant swotting' and good grades. They called us DARs (damned average raisers). Some pronounced quite openly that *all* female medical students were ugly. Others proclaimed that we were capriciously 'robbing' qualified males of entry into medical school and those on scholarships and grants were 'wasting' government-subsidized educational funds.

It was sometimes hard to ignore the racial and sexual slights encountered along the way. Not infrequently, I sat and ate lunch by myself in the college cafeteria while my classmates grouped themselves cosily around neighbouring booths. Once when I picked up enough courage to join them and brought my lunch tray to their table, a boy came and grabbed the last seat. Somewhat self-consciously, I carried over an adjacent stool. Dead silence fell around me. Everyone wolfed his food down at record pace and made for the exit. I found myself alone, surrounded by dirty dishes and empty chairs.

My dissection partner, Joan Katz, and I were in the habit of going into the anatomy lab on some weekends to work on the 81-year-old male corpse assigned to us. We nicknamed him Rupert. Apparently our extra zeal provoked discontent among our male peers. One Saturday morning we eagerly descended into the dark and forbidding workshop to begin our dissection. Behind the heavy doors, the room was pitch black and smelt strongly of formaldehyde. Joan reached up to pull the cord controlling the light switch and gave a blood-curdling scream. The light went on. There was raucous, hysterical laughter from a group of boys who had been lurking in the dark. They had severed Rupert's penis and secured it to the light cord. A few cameras clicked and Joan was caught with her upraised hand clutching a penis and an incredulous expression on her face. The boys circulated her picture among themselves for many days afterwards with the caption 'Awarded First-Class Honours in Human Anatomy'.

Despite these problems, it was a wonderful period of my life. The whole world of science was opening up to me. I could not wait to get to classes every morning. Physiology, biophysics, pharmacology and biochemistry were like pieces of a giant jigsaw puzzle depicting the mystery of life. Experiments reminded me of intricate chess games. My opponent was the great 'unknown', about to be unmasked. Along the way, there were tantalizing clues.

Consistently, I studied hard and gave my best effort. I dreamt of returning to Hong Kong with the highest academic honours and making a name for myself in my father's city so that he would be proud of me.

Many of my non-Chinese friends at medical school were Jews. They treated me as an equal, invited me to their homes and never made stereotypical remarks. We discussed our studies, played chess and ate at Chinese restaurants. I felt as if real life had begun at last. I never suffered the bouts of depression that sometimes affected my classmates. They called me Pollyanna but I didn't mind. How could they understand the exaltation I felt to be at last free of Niang's looming shadow?

I stayed at Campbell Hall, a hostel two blocks away from University College. The Chinese Students' Union was in nearby Gordon Square. The London University Students'

Union was across the road. Later on, Hong Kong House was founded at Lancaster Gate about three miles away. Father sent me an annual stipend of five hundred pounds, one hundred pounds less than my brothers because I was a girl. We were expected to be our own stewards of the money, which was to last the entire year. My life revolved around medical school and the students' unions. I joined the table-tennis team and played chess for my college. James had been admitted to Cambridge University to study civil engineering. I often visited him on Sundays. We spent pleasant afternoons drinking coffee and talking in his medieval rooms at Trinity College, intoxicated by our new-found freedom. It gave me a thrill to trot along on cobblestones after my tall and handsome big brother, dressed in his flapping black college gown and Cambridge scarf, while all around us church bells rang out their chimes for evensong.

The carapace that shielded me from the wounds of prejudice and injustice also served as a secret shelter into which I could retreat. It enabled me to form and develop a friendship which would have astonished all my peers and alarmed a few of them had they known of it.

Karl Decker was one of my lecturers. To my seventeen-year-old eyes, he was the ideal man: intelligent, sensitive, tall and handsome. Passionate about his work, he spent long hours in the lab. He was a thirty-four-year-old German who spoke with a stutter and a pronounced accent. Assigned to his tutorial group, I first noticed Karl because of his earnestness. He used to write long columns of corrections in the margins of my essays and I was touched by the trouble he took over my efforts. Sometimes I saw that his annotations had been erased and then painfully rewritten in his meticulous handwriting.

He started to comment on my clothes and appearance. 'That's a pretty blouse,' he would remark as I entered his class. And I would suddenly become tongue-tied and self-conscious.

For months I refused to admit, even to myself, that Dr Decker admired me. I found it hard to believe that this brilliant scientist could be seriously interested in a teenage Chinese medical student freshly out of convent school.

He spent hours discussing his experiments with me, laboriously showing me all the important articles related to his field. On cold days he showed me how to heat coffee over a Bunsen burner in his lab, and we would drink it together afterwards out of tall glass beakers.

Most of all, he wrote to me. Those scribbled notes in the margins of my essays were replaced by lengthy pages of self-revelation. I read about the death of his mother when he was ten, the remarriage of his strict and autocratic father, the bleak and fragmented memories of his emotionally disturbed adolescence. He wrote about a mysterious illness called schizophrenia which afflicted him as a young medical student in Prague; of shadowy voices, eerie convictions, frightful torments.

Guileless and inexperienced, flattered and moved by these extraordinary disclosures, I became enmeshed without realizing that I was treading on dangerous ground. He was full of fears, doubts and restraints but, to me, he projected an air of sensitive refinement tinged with gentle melancholy which captivated my imagination. Part of his appeal no doubt originated from my deep-rooted Chinese reverence for learning, age and wisdom.

His letters began to assume a central role in our emotional lives. He wrote about poetry, music and philosophy; his thoughts, moods and fears; his loneliness and yearning for me. Underlying it all was the solitude of his bleak day-to-day existence and the taboo of a budding interracial romance between teacher and pupil.

Karl was both self-sufficient and self-centred. He had no friends. He lived for his work, routinely spending fourteen-hour days in his lab, including Saturdays and some Sundays. He ate all his meals at the college cafeteria, hardly knowing or caring what he ate.

His was a stark, ascetic life, devoid of frills and indulgences.

We rarely went out anywhere together. Neither of us wished to be seen in public. Couples of mixed race were still a rarity in those days. Besides, we made an incongruous pair. To the outside world we did not look as if we belonged together.

He didn't want his colleagues to know that he was seeing one of his female students, a Chinese girl at that. I also didn't want my Chinese friends to find out, in case gossip reached my family.

Because of this our meetings were intensely private. Karl's lab at University College became our haven. It was one of the few places where we were not stared at by prying eyes and felt completely safe.

It was strange for me, gauche and socially incompetent, to see my esteemed professor, a man twice my age, so timorous and uncertain before me. When we were alone his fumbling manner, his shy stutter and his intense longing swept away my defences.

One of my Chinese friends, Yu Chun-yee, a pianist from Singapore, was giving a recital at Wigmore Hall. Knowing that I wished to support his efforts, Karl bought eleven tickets at the box office, split into two batches of eight and three. He gave me eight tickets so that I could invite my Chinese friends. He himself went to the concert with his American post-doctoral fellow and the fellow's wife. The three of them sat by themselves seven rows behind us. None of my Chinese friends knew that Karl had arranged this, but throughout the performance, I sensed his presence behind me.

It was an impossible situation and yet it went on and on. We were so different, but the affinity was immense. I was both attracted and repelled by the fanatic dedication with which he attacked his work to the exclusion of all else. He told me that he needed to fill his time with science in order to defeat the demons.

At times, his emotional instability baffled and frightened me. 'It's all so sad and difficult,' he would say, adding, as he looked at my puzzled countenance, 'of course, you shouldn't be spending time with me. You! You who are so full of life and hope!'

He never took sufficient time off from his experiments to understand the Chinese cultural values which moulded my personality. He never understood what he thought of as my obsession with food, calling my incessant search for the 'perfect neighbourhood Chinese restaurant' a hopeless quest for the Holy Grail. He failed to appreciate how central the sharing of food is to Chinese celebrations. Most of all, he could not comprehend my persistent refusal to consummate our relationship. Besides my youth and Catholic upbringing, I was ingrained with the Confucian belief that, for a woman, loss of virginity outside marriage was a fate worse than death.

For his birthday one year, I spent a whole week preparing a special dinner, planning and shopping for the best seasonal ingredients, buying fresh flowers and fruits, cleaning his sparse and dusty flat. He ate the six-course meal without comment in forty-five minutes: fresh broccoli soup, stewed goose with leeks, sautéd cauliflower with ginger, curried chicken, peas with mushrooms and steamed rice. He kept glancing at his watch, itching to return to some experiment at his lab. I washed up the dishes after he had dashed out, telling myself it was a wasted effort.

On rare evenings, after Karl's experiments were finished, his test tubes washed and dried, his frogs fed and my homework completed, we would sit perched on lab stools and talk deep into the night. There were moments when we reached a depth of intimacy and mutual understanding which was everything that anyone could wish for between a man and a woman.

Karl insisted that he was no good for me and that I should allow myself to be courted by the Chinese boys I met at the Chinese Students' Union. Just to compound my emotional confusion, these outings would often be preceded or followed by a long letter from Karl, full of anguish and regrets, letters which tore me apart.

※

My Chinese friends were an important part of my life. Among them, I could drop my defences and be myself. I needed to speak my own language and relax with people who could laugh at the same things. Now and again we would gently poke fun at some of the mores of our host country. There were Chinese students not only from China and Hong Kong, but also from Singapore, Malaysia, Indonesia, Mauritius and elsewhere, bringing an international dimension to our mini-Chinese world.

The grandparents or parents of many of these South-Asian Chinese students had emigrated from the Chinese coastal provinces of Fujian or Guandong because of hardships at home. Though my Singaporean friend Yu Chun-yee had never set foot in China, he had read the same Chinese novels, loved spicy Sichuan dishes and held many of the same cultural values. In many ways he was more Chinese than a Chinese.

Three of my fellow boarders from Hong Kong were also attending university in London. We all came under the influence of C. S. Tang, president of the Chinese Students' Union.

C. S. was originally from Shanghai. His family was in the shipping business. He was very handsome and was working for a Ph.D. at Imperial College. C. S. had leftist leanings. Unlike the rest of us, he fully intended to return home to serve the people of mainland China. He was our big brother.

At weekends, C. S. organized rowing excursions on the Serpentine in Hyde Park or ice-skating at Queensway. He arranged dances and pot-luck dinners with dishes full of peppers and garlic. He rented Chinese movies portraying Communist freedom fighters outsmarting corrupt Kuomintang officials and landlords. We felt very progressive and idealistic watching them, dreaming of returning to China one day to contribute our skills to the glory of our motherland.

C. S. had nothing but contempt for Chinese students dating westerners. 'Traitor!' he would mutter under his breath. 'Consorting with the enemy!' Once, at a Chinese restaurant near Leicester Square, our group ordered the house speciality,

Peking duck served with spring onions, plum sauce and wafer-thin pancakes. The waiter told us that the last duck was already in the oven, about to be served to a white man with his Chinese girl seated a couple of tables away. C. S. draped one arm around the waiter, a diminutive young Cantonese from Hong Kong called Little Chang, and said that for many years our great country China had been bullied by the barbarians. He repeated the story of the notice in the Shanghai park forbidding entrance to dogs and Chinese.

'Here you see a barbarian taking the last duck to share with that pretty Chinese girl. You simply cannot allow this to happen! Barbarians don't know their Chinese food. They can't tell a live duck from a live chicken, let alone when the bird is dead and roasted. Why don't you give him something else tasty, put a bunch of plum sauce on it and just call it Peking duck? It won't be difficult to fool a barbarian.'

So I ate the duck along with the rest, but inside I felt uneasy about C. S.'s attack on the 'barbarian'. Towards the end of the meal, I blurted out, 'When you talk about fooling barbarians, isn't it a sort of reverse racism?'

C. S. cocked his head and pondered. He ran his fingers boyishly through his thick glossy hair. He called me by my Chinese name. 'Junling, you ask the most difficult questions. How do I answer without sounding like an idiot? I suppose in everyone's life there are priorities. Mine are, in the following order: my country, my leader Chairman Mao, my family, parents, siblings, Chinese friends. My professor, schoolmates and other barbarian friends. Finally, everyone else. I can't help it if I feel kinship towards my own people like our waiter Little Chang here. Apparently Little Chang feels the same way about all of us.'

During that period in England, roughly between 1955 and 1963, most of us were proud of the way China had risen in the eyes of the world. However, we did not share identical hopes for the future of our nation. Some wanted China to blaze in a gleaming capitalist society like that of North America. Others hoped to see Mao's revolutionary policies of collectivism and socialism take an even firmer grip. Few were as evangelical as C. S. with his pamphlets and propaganda movies showing plump and rosy-cheeked children, happy workers, giant new factories and incredible and ever-increasing production figures: the whole of China on the move. I believe most of us, at some time or other, saw ourselves as a group of skilled university graduates trained in the latest disciplines of western technology, dreaming of going home to serve our motherland and right the wrongs of long ago.

In the lab, I tried to convey to Karl the pride and elation carried over from my life at the Chinese Students' Union. Karl would dampen my excessive zeal. 'I've lived through this patriotic nonsense in my own country during the Second World War. Believe me, reality is not like that. So everyone in China is now an angel because Mao Zedong has liberated the country! Overnight nobody is for himself any more. No more envy, hatred and malice. Only kindness, love and universal justice! Do you really believe that, you little fool?'

CHAPTER 14

一琴一鶴

Yi Qin Yi He

One Lute, One Crane

H. H. Tien was a postgraduate student in applied mathematics at Imperial College. He was of medium height, slender, wore thick glasses and, although not considered handsome, possessed warmth and charm. Kind and generous to a fault, H. H. was a natural leader and seemed to embody all that was most hopeful for the future of China. We looked up to him, not because of his logic or persuasive arguments, but because of the magnetism of his personality. His wealthy banker father had married for love and had spurned mistresses or concubines, which was unusual among Chinese men. In the 1930s, Mr Tien had been active in the Anti-Japanese Boycott Association and fought with the heroic Nineteenth Route Army in defence of Shanghai against Japan before joining the underground Communist Party. He welcomed the liberation of Shanghai in 1949 and wrote an eight-page letter to his son H. H. in London preaching the dawn of a new China. However, to hedge his bets, he pragmatically opened another bank in Hong Kong and moved there in 1951.

One evening, soon after the Hungarian uprising in 1956, I went out with H. H. to a concert at the Albert Hall. Earlier that week, Karl had been perturbed by reports on BBC radio that Russia had sent troops into Budapest. H. H. and I had a heated discussion, during which I echoed many of Karl's misgivings. H. H. described Russia's actions as the protective embrace of a big brother to prevent chaos within a branch of the same political family.

'How can you be sure that China will become a great country?' I argued. 'If there was so much greed and corruption under Chiang Kai-shek, why should a mere change of government alter the nature of every Chinese?'

We had arrived at my hall of residence in Tavistock Square. Reluctant to end the evening, we walked round and round Campbell Hall. H. H. suddenly chuckled. 'Know what they call Chiang Kai-shek?' he asked in English. 'Cash my cheque, Chiang Kai-shek.' He reverted to the Shanghai dialect in which we usually conversed. 'Seriously, if leadership is corrupt and inept such traits will permeate downwards to the masses. Under Communism, China is entering a new era of radical reform. Mao and his generals have made great strides and brought China into the world arena. Instead of kowtowing to General MacArthur, they forced America into a ceasefire in Korea. As Chairman Mao said, "China has finally stood up."'

Under the dim street lights his eyes were bright with fervour and hope. How I admired him! It started to rain. I raised the collar of my coat against the blustery chill. H. H. took off his warm college scarf and wrapped it around my neck. It felt so safe and comfortable to be in his company. In dribs and drabs I had confided in him parts of my painful childhood: information seldom disclosed.

'I'm almost eight years older than you,' H. H. was saying. 'Sometimes I wish you were older. There's so much I want to tell you. You had such a rough time with your stepmother. You need someone like me to defend you and look after you for the rest of your life.'

'I have to get back now,' I told him, suddenly flustered and confused. 'My brother Gregory said that a boy and a girl getting together is like taking a bus. You end up on a particular bus because the right number comes along at the right time. I've been thinking about that ever since.'

I unlocked the front door and handed H. H. back his scarf. I watched him as he wound his way around the puddles. Before he turned the corner, he waved and shouted, 'Let me know, am I the right number? Are you ready to board the bus?' Then he was gone.

Inside the hall it was dark and warm. On my way up, I noticed there was a letter in my letterbox. It was from Karl.

Dear Adeline,

It would be nice, and perhaps more than that, if we could meet after your tutorial on Wednesday. But I agree with you that we should not risk messing things up. Naturally, because of your youth, your concerns compared with mine are more substantial: to do with parents, grades, face, Chinese friends, your future and China (now the Big Thing). I have merely been trying to identify another biophysical problem and am now attempting to solve it. Of course, there will be no rewards, perhaps not even a paper at the end; and yet the enterprise seems so important. Would I be able to keep my position at the university if my feelings for you were to become known? It would be so wonderful to have you on my team permanently, but that is quite out of the question, and you are only eighteen.

So I don't expect to see you alone soon. However, if you feel there is a chance, remember that I can manage Wednesday almost any time. Maybe we might have something meaningful to say to each other. Or, we may just be happy together, as we were in the last few months, sometimes . . .

Do not be seduced by rhetoric. Communism appeals to men and women yearning for Utopia. It will not work. Conflict, envy and malice will always be in the breast of man no matter which government rules. It stands to reason. Don't be lured into adopting a particular religion because you happen to like the priest.

My little girl! My *femme fatale*! I have written little of what I meant to say. Thinking of you fills me with disturbing emotions I hesitate to transcribe. Suffice it that you have erased from my heart a bleakness I was happy to discard. Though I know I should probably step aside, please remember that wherever you go, I shall be waiting for you here in my lab, at all times.

Karl

Oh! The melting melody of his words! I never went out with H. H. again.

The Cold War was at its height during the 1950s and 1960s. A few of my most idealistic contemporaries were asked to leave Britain in 1961 by the immigration authorities for being 'undesirable'. Kim Philby had recently been revealed to be the third man behind Burgess and McClean: a circle of English spies spawned during their undergraduate years at Cambridge university in the 1930s. British authorities charged that Beijing was infiltrating secret agents among Chinese student circles in London, turning us into fledgling Communists.

C. S. married a Singaporean Chinese girl. He took her back to Shanghai and then taught and did research at the Academy of Science in Beijing. They were to suffer greatly during the Cultural Revolution. By the time I next saw him and his wife in 1980, C. S. had lost his hair and his patriotism. He no longer talked about rebuilding China but asked if I could help him obtain a post-doctoral fellowship in America. What concerned him most were education plans for his children and a pleasant retirement spot for himself and his wife. Not once did he complain about his decision to return to China. He remained warm, generous, honest and kind.

Others were less fortunate. H. H. was thirty-three and still single when he was told to leave. He went back to mainland China in 1962, against the advice of his parents. Months went by. No one ever heard from him. Some of us wrote to the address he had given us before his departure. There was never any reply. He had simply vanished into the bowels of China, swallowed amongst 800 million Chinese.

His 'disappearance' distressed and perplexed us. We knew that something was deeply wrong and suspected that events had not turned out well for him. For me personally, his silence shattered every fantasy of the glorious motherland and I never again seriously considered returning to work in the country of my birth.

Years later, we heard that H. H. had been persecuted and imprisoned during the Cultural Revolution. His gaolers were unable to believe that such an accomplished and highly educated young scientist would renounce his rich family in Hong Kong, his comfortable lifestyle in the West and his promising career in order to serve his country. They insisted that he had an ulterior motive and urged him to confess. H. H. refused and committed suicide in 1967, leaving a note with four Chinese words 一琴一鶴 yi qin yi he (one lute, one crane), meaning that he was incorruptible and upright unto death. He was thirty-eight years old.

Others thrown out of Britain in the purge of leftist Chinese students fared differently. S. T. Sun (Little Sun), a graduate in architecture, was enamoured of Rachel Yu, one of my classmates from Sacred Heart boarding school days. When Little Sun was 'asked to leave', they were dating seriously. He returned to a Hong Kong in the throes of a building boom which went on for over thirty years and continues unabated. He soon started his own architectural firm and became rapidly embroiled in an economic miracle that transformed Hong Kong from a sleepy outpost on the edge of China to the vertical metropolis it is today. All thoughts of motherland faded with the advent of six-figure pay cheques. Away from London and Rachel, he went back to his childhood sweetheart. Later his whole family took up Canadian citizenship and now commute between Hong Kong and Vancouver.

The years went by. I attended many weddings, feeling increasingly empty and forlorn. Those of my friends who were not already married seemed poised on the brink whilst I floundered in a relationship leading nowhere. Though I had been successful in keeping my emotional bondage to Karl secret, I had lost out in the larger sense because I was unable to form a simultaneous attachment to anyone else. The basic neurosis of our affair fed upon itself. While believing that our mutual feelings were irreplaceable, Karl was also convinced that it would be disastrous for us to marry. He persisted in encouraging me to go out with Chinese boys my age. Sometimes he even came along to vet my escorts. One evening, when I was sitting between a would-be suitor and Karl in a dark cinema, he suddenly reached over and caressed my hand.

After my graduation and internship I spent two years working and studying for post-graduate degrees in Edinburgh, perhaps in an attempt to escape from Karl. I passed my boards in internal medicine, becoming MRCP (Member of the Royal College of Physicians) London and MRCP Edinburgh. In that gloomy, wet, cold and windy city, I finally accepted that I had to leave England. So many times I had tried to break free from this impossible entanglement. None of the conflicts would ever be resolved. Towards the end, on a rare day when Karl had been particularly loving, he told me he was so happy he wanted to die. Then he added sadly, 'We are all wrong for each other. It is easier to die for you than to live with you.'

The parting, when it came, was wrenchingly hard. In a way, I never got over it. Karl was my teacher, my mentor, my first love, my larger-than-life surrogate father. But, no matter how I rationalized it, he had rejected me and the relationship had failed. In a moment of shattering anguish, I destroyed all his letters.

Soon afterwards, in 1963, I left England for Hong Kong.

My Grand Aunt was also known as *Gong Gong* ("Grand Uncle") because of the respect granted her as president of the Shanghai Women's Bank, which she founded in 1924. As a child of three, she refused to have her feet bound. She attended a missionary school founded by American Methodists and was fluent in English. Her bank at 480 Nanjing Lu in Shanghai is still in operation.

My brothers and sisters. Back row, from left: Gregory, James, Edgar. Front row, from left: Lydia with baby half-sister Susan, and Adeline. This picture was taken in Tianjin in 1942 before the death of our grandmother. We were all fashionably dressed in Western clothes and had stylish haircuts.

The boom days of Tianjin provided economic opportunities for Ye Ye, my grandfather, on right; his son, my father, at left; and K. C. Li, at the center. K. C. was one of the first Chinese graduates of the London School of Economics and the founder of Hwa Chong Hong, a highly successful import/export firm. Both my grandfather and my father worked for him.

My brothers and sisters a few years later. Back row, from left: James, Edgar, Gregory, Lydia. Front row, from left: Susan, Franklin, Adeline, and the dog, Jackie. This picture was taken in 1946, about the time we were given a little duckling as a pet.

My stepmother, Niang ("Mother"), and my father with Ye Ye (middle) in the 1940s. Ye Ye was a devout Buddhist. He always shaved his head, wore a skullcap in winter, and dressed in Chinese robes.

Niang, Franklin, and my father in the early 1940s. My half-brother, Franklin, was their favorite child. Niang bought his clothes at the best children's boutiques on Avenue Joffre. She had his hair cut in the latest styles at the most fashionable children's hair stylists.

Ye Ye and my baby half-sister, Susan. The picture was taken soon after their arrival in Shanghai from Tianjin in October 1943.

Jeanne Prosperi was seventeen when she met my recently widowed father. We called our stepmother *Niang* ("Mother") after she married my father. She had a French father and a Chinese mother and was a strikingly beautiful woman. Though she was fluent in English, French, Mandarin, and the Shanghai dialect, she never learned to read and write Chinese or to speak Cantonese.

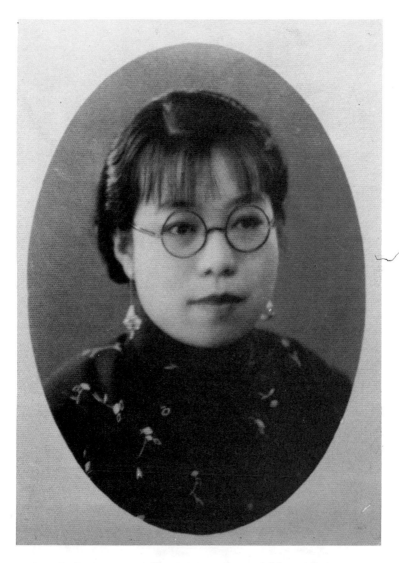

Aunt Ba Ba never ceased to nurture me as a child, praising my accomplishments in school, checking my homework, and sharing her pedicabs with me. She never married and was financially dependent on my father and stepmother all her life. She was gentle, patient, and wise. I loved her very much.

My two half-siblings, Franklin and Susan, with their tutor/
nanny, Miss Chien. Ours was a family with two systems:
We stepchildren were the lower-class citizens; Franklin and
Susan received preferential treatment from birth.

Franklin stands next to Jackie, my father's precious pet.
Father employed a German dog trainer who taught
Jackie to be obedient only to Father, Niang, and Franklin.
I was very much afraid of Jackie, who used to bark at me.

Niang and my father enjoying their comfortable lifestyle. They were a glamorous and handsome couple in the 1940s and 1950s and socially prominent in Shanghai and Hong Kong.

CHAPTER 15

釜中游魚

Fu Zhong You Yu
Fish Swimming in a Cauldron

A few weeks before I left London, I wrote to Professor McFadden, Lo Mac, at Hong Kong University medical school. He welcomed my application as assistant lecturer in his department, commended me for my advanced degrees, quoted the salary and added that housing would be available. It was, therefore, with confidence and regret that I flew to Hong Kong in November 1963.

Gregory and James met me at Kai Tak airport in Father's chauffeured Mercedes. They had both been working for Father for a year. James returned first, after finishing his studies at Cambridge. His salary was so low that he could only afford to live at the YMCA. Life became easier when Gregory returned from Montreal, where he had obtained a master's degree from McGill University. Father paid them each a monthly salary of 2000 Hong Kong dollars, equivalent to 250 US dollars. Together, they were able to rent a tiny studio apartment above a nightclub on Nathan Road in Kowloon.

Hong Kong was no longer the sleepy city I had left behind eleven years ago. The narrow, cramped, neon-lit streets were teeming with pedestrians and traffic even though it was after nine p.m. There were a great number of new buildings, some of them half completed and covered with bamboo scaffolding. Colourful electrical signs blinked out their advertisements. The vitality was almost tangible.

'This is not the Hong Kong I left behind,' I gasped to my brothers. 'This is Shanghai reincarnated!'

'Except bigger, better and more modern,' James replied. 'Kowloon and Hong Kong are like one long Nanking Road.'

'I'm glad you've come back,' Gregory said warmly. 'This is the right place and the right time. The city is going to explode. Our clever Old Man is making an absolute killing.'

'Is Father still in the import–export business?'

'Import–export!' Gregory snorted, incredulous at my ignorance. 'Haven't you heard of the Korean War? Didn't you know that the Allies put an economic blockade on China when Mao Zedong supported North Korea? Father's markets were closed to him overnight. The setback prompted him to diversify into manufacturing and light industry. He started three factories making plastic flowers, leather gloves and enamelware and now calls himself an industrialist.'

They told me that Father's enamelware factory was especially profitable, turning out brightly coloured cooking utensils, camping implements and an assortment of unbreakable tableware. Father had recently been approached by the Nigerian government to build a branch factory in Port Harcourt. The terms were extremely favourable, with the Nigerian side providing subsidies, tax incentives and cheap land. My two brothers were involved in the project.

We had reached the Yaumati vehicular ferry, at that time the only means of transport between Kowloon and Hong Kong. After boarding, the three of us got out of the car and stood by the railing for the crossing. In front of us lay Hong Kong Island, glistening like a jewel, with thousands of lights twinkling in the night. Both my brothers were dressed in dark suits with white shirts and conservative ties. The two of them looked as if they were going to attend a business meeting.

Glancing disdainfully at my old-fashioned Marks and Spencer dress which was a shade too large for me, Gregory commented, 'If you decide to settle down and practise medicine in Hong Kong, you really ought to pay more attention to your clothes. Hong Kong people are very fashion-conscious. What you're wearing just isn't good enough.'

'I've never been a beauty,' I stammered, feeling defensive. 'Besides, I just got off the plane.'

'She looks all right to me,' James said gallantly with a warm smile, while putting his arm around my shoulder. 'I don't know anyone who can look like a fashion plate after being cooped up in a plane for hours and hours.'

'What's their present apartment like?' I asked, steering the conversation away from myself. After Franklin died in 1953, Father became convinced that the *feng shui* (wind and water, or geomancy) of the villa on Stubbs Road was nefarious. He then recalled that Ye Ye had passed away in 1952 while living in the same house. They terminated their lease and rented an apartment on the Peak.

'It's a nice, luxury two-bedroom unit,' Gregory replied. 'They've lived there for ten years now.'

'At 115 Plunkett Road, the Peak,' I said. 'Nowadays, is there any discrimination against Chinese living on the Peak?'

'During the nineteenth century, Chinese weren't allowed to live there. I think that ended in 1904.' Gregory went on to explain that these days cash was king and we Chinese could live anywhere provided we had money. However, there was still a disproportionately larger number of whites living in the Peak area. He added that Father had recently bought a new flat at Mid-levels called Magnolia Mansions, overlooking the harbour. It had four bedrooms and Father had mentioned there would be plenty of room for me to stay.

'How nice of them!' I exclaimed, glowing with happiness.

'Don't celebrate too soon!' James said darkly. 'The Old Lady objected. She kept saying the flat is just not big enough. I think the Old Man's idea has been shelved for the time being.'

Meanwhile, our car was climbing up steeply winding roads to the top of Hong Kong Island, where the view was spectacular and the air fresh and smog-free. My ears ached from the altitude and my stomach felt queasy from fatigue and the serpentine bends. As we waited for the lift inside the lobby paved with marble and granite, I was filled with the same sense of trepidation which overwhelmed me whenever I was about to face my parents. Though I had been in England for eleven years and was now a physician, at that moment I felt no different from the schoolgirl who left in 1952.

I was greeted formally with smiles and handshakes. Father looked much the same but Niang's lissome figure had thickened and her features had coarsened. Their flat was elegantly but impersonally furnished with stiff, wooden, antique Chinese chairs, western-style sofas sprouting antimacassars and a Tianjin carpet. Below was a panoramic view of Hong Kong city and Victoria Harbour.

We sat rather tensely around a rosewood dining-table eating noodles brought in by a maid I did not recognize. For some reason, conversation was in English. They never spoke to me in Chinese again after my return from London. It enhanced my feeling of exclusion, as if I was an employee justifying my salary. I told them that Professor McFadden had offered me a position as assistant lecturer in his Department of Internal Medicine.

'I've been thinking about this,' Father started, slowly and deliberately as if he had rehearsed the speech. 'That's not a good move. You should consider obstetrics and gynaecology instead. Remember Dr Mary Ting who delivered all of you? She is one of the greatest doctors I know. Internal medicine is not a good field for a woman. Male doctors won't refer patients to you.'

I had completely forgotten that Father had already sketched out my career eleven years ago before my departure for England. I could not speak. This was a serious decision involving my future but, as far as Father was concerned, that decision was his, not mine. He added that Professor Daphne Chun, a friend of his in the Department of Obstetrics and Gynaecology at Hong Kong University, was willing to give me a position as a special intern. The salary he quoted was insultingly low.

The job was offered only because I was his daughter. Professor Chun had given him 'a lot of face'.

I knew it was a *fait accompli*. Father would lose face if I failed to accept this 'favour'. Even so, I tried to protest, reminding him that I had already completed an internship in London two years ago. Professor McFadden's offer of an assistant lectureship meant that I would have an unusually senior position for a young doctor of twenty-six. Father totally ignored my explanations.

'Why don't you try the job offered by Professor Chun? If you don't like it you can always switch later. You'll not regret it. Besides, you haven't made a commitment to Professor McFadden, have you? So you're under no obligation there.

'I have your welfare at heart,' he continued. 'Would your father lead you wrong? Remember, you're still very young, fresh out of university. Take the wrong turn now and you will regret it ten years later. By then it will be too late.' He reminded me of Lydia and Samuel thirteen years ago, insisting on going back to Tianjin against his well-meaning advice. 'Look what a mess they're in now. It is entirely their own doing. They will rot there for the rest of their lives!' He said this with relish, sounding almost glad that his prophecies of doom had been fulfilled with a vengeance.

As I listened, my former resolutions disintegrated. All I knew was that I wished above all else to please my father. Oh, so very much! To gain his acceptance. To be loved. To have him say to me, just once in my life, 'Well done, Adeline! We're proud of you!'

It obviously meant a lot to him to have me working under his friend. To turn down Professor McFadden's offer of an assistant lectureship (with housing) for Dr Chun's promise of an internship, I was giving Father an enormous dose of face. Surely, that would give me some brownie points in his eyes?

Once again I betrayed myself and went along with Father's wishes. By the time we retired I was practically thanking them for all the trouble they had undertaken on my behalf.

On the fourth day of my return to Hong Kong, Niang told me to pack my bags. Father was away that day playing golf with a business associate.

It was a brilliantly sunny Sunday afternoon when Ah Mo, the chauffeur, drove Niang and me to Dr Chun's Tsan Yuk Hospital. The place seemed deserted. We stood awkwardly in the entrance hall talking to the busy hospital operator who was manning the switchboard and acting as receptionist. She eventually understood that I was the new extra intern from London University hired by Professor Chun to start work on Monday. She told us that since neither Professor Chun nor any of the attending physicians were there to show us around, we were to return on Monday morning.

But Niang was not to be thwarted. She ordered that the intern on call be paged. When a young woman doctor arrived, Niang demanded, in English, that I be shown my sleeping quarters. Though I was now a grown woman and a physician, Niang ignored me as if I was still a child. She was told there was no accommodation for interns.

'Where do *you* sleep then?' Niang asked imperiously while I cringed with embarrassment.

'I sleep in the on-call room,' the woman intern, Dr Chow, replied, glancing briefly at me and quickly looking away as she sensed my uneasiness.

'How many beds are there and how many are occupied?' Niang persisted.

'There are four beds and two are occupied today. One by me and one by the pediatric intern on duty.'

'I see,' Niang said, her mind turning. 'So there are two unoccupied beds in that room.'

'Yes, but they are only unoccupied until tomorrow when the new on-call weekly rotation schedule is posted.'

'That will be fine,' Niang said, with her most charming smile. 'Will you please take us to the on-call room?'

Her tone was authoritative and her presence commanding. When Dr Chow hesitated at this unusual request, Niang twisted the six-carat diamond ring on her finger. The gaudy jewel caught the sunlight, sending a message of money and power. Then Niang added, 'Professor Chun is a very good friend of mine.'

By now thoroughly intimidated, Dr Chow dutifully led the way, followed by Niang, me and Ah Mo carrying my two suitcases containing all my possessions. We entered a large bare room with four cots, one in each corner. There were no wardrobes. The only furniture was a small night table by each berth, on which perched a telephone. The street clothes of the on-call doctors were hung on wall-hooks next to their stations.

Niang walked over to the curtainless window, the panes of which were grimy with dirt. She looked out and there, below us, was Victoria Harbour in all her splendour. The sun was shining, the air was clear, the sea was a sparkling blue and the boats were colourful. She ordered Ah Mo to place my suitcases by one of the unoccupied beds. She turned to me and smiled. 'Oh, Adeline!' she exclaimed, 'What a wonderful view you have from your bedroom! How lucky you are!' As I stared at her, dumb with dismay and embarrassment, she added, 'Unfortunately, Father and I will be busy all next week. But maybe we could have dinner together next Sunday. Phone me on Thursday to confirm, why don't you?' With that she turned to Ah Mo. 'Take me to Mrs Nin's now!' she commanded. 'I am late for her tea party.'

Ah Mo hurried after her, followed by Dr Chow muttering something about having to see a patient. I was left alone.

I stood by the dirty window looking out at the 'wonderful view' for a long time. My whole being was suffused with loneliness and that familiar feeling of total rejection. I wondered why I had bothered to return home.

Hong Kong in the early 1960s was an extraordinary place. Poised on the cusp of a glittering destiny, it had replaced Shanghai as the gateway to the West. Everything was in flux. Life revolved around passports and money. People were moving in or getting out.

Ninety-nine per cent of the population were Chinese. Most of them were from the neighbouring province of Guangdong (Canton). After 1949, large numbers poured in from Shanghai and other parts of China. As time went on, it became increasingly hazardous to reach Hong Kong across the stretch of water separating it from the mainland. Later, the British army erected a twenty-four-mile steel wire fence along the Chinese border, patrolled by platoons of Gurkhas (mercenary Nepalese soldiers) and dogs, to keep out those who wished to enter illegally into the overcrowded colony. Those who made it were filled with a fierce determination to make a better life for themselves and their children.

I encountered citizens in all walks of life working fourteen to sixteen hours a day for meagre wages: taxi-drivers, hairdressers, waitresses, nurses, telephone operators. Compared to London, everything was cheap except for housing. This was the period when Hong Kong developed its reputation as the bargain basement and shopping mecca of the world. Talent and opportunism were the keystones of the economy. Hong Kong became a brave new world to the downtrodden of China.

Stories abounded about ordinary wage earners, some even illiterate, who, by persistent hard work and saving every penny, were able to buy a small flat and even send their children abroad to study. Maids and chauffeurs began to invest in property and speculate on the Hong Kong stock market.

My work at Tsan Yuk was physically demanding but not intellectually challenging. No medical research of any kind was performed while I was there. Sexual discrimination was rampant and blatant. Male doctors earned 25 per cent more than female doctors of the same rank, although we did identical work and took equal numbers of night calls.

I was not at all popular. My fellow interns were piqued that I was permanently installed in the on-call room. Eventually, I was assigned a private room at the hospital for which I paid a very high rent. The hospital administrator congratulated me on my good luck in getting the room. She had been told by Professor Chun that my family was enormously rich and I was independently wealthy.

There was nowhere for me to go in the evenings and weekends. I ate most of my meals at the hospital. I spent most of my meagre salary on rent, food, books and (in a misguided effort to gain their affection) expensive presents for my parents such as silver boxes and cashmere sweaters.

My colleagues resented me because I was not Cantonese, and my degree was from London, not Hong Kong. My two advanced diplomas in internal medicine did not belong in the Department of Obstetrics and Gynaecology. The way I spoke English was considered un-Chinese, different, unintelligible, and irritating. They nicknamed me Loy Lu Foh, 'imported merchandise'.

When I eventually contacted Professor McFadden, he confirmed the offer of a position as assistant lecturer in the Department of Internal Medicine, with free housing. I was sorely tempted to accept, but I simply could not let Father lose face. Later on, I found out that interdepartmental rivalry was rife, and it was a minor feather in Professor Chun's cap for me to have chosen her offer of an internship over Professor McFadden's promise of an assistant lectureship, especially when I already possessed my MRCP from London and Edinburgh. There was another reason for not accepting: by then I already knew that I had to get away from Hong Kong and make my life somewhere else. The position with Professor McFadden would have been permanent. He had been more than generous towards me because he had left the job offer open for one year.

Every Sunday night, we were expected to dine at Father's and Niang's newly purchased flat at Mid-levels. Those dinners were ordeals. We had to be on guard the whole time. Niang seemed to know everything, especially those matters we did not want her to know: Gregory's chronically overdrawn bank account and abundant parking tickets all over Kowloon and

Hong Kong ('worthy of *The Guinness Book of Records*,' according to Father); James's consumption of whisky; my attempts to rent a larger flat for my two brothers and me so that we could have some semblance of a home life; Susan's correspondence with a male American friend.

I came to loathe their views expressed at those Sunday night dinners where I invariably remained silent, like a 釜中游魚 *fu zhong you yu* (fish swimming in a cauldron) and seething with frustrated discontent.

My parents regularly decried and condemned the Hong Kong Cantonese for their avarice, blatant materialism and ostentatious vulgarity. Yet I could not help but notice their own obsession with money. Their prejudices were broad and catholic. Besides the Cantonese, they criticized the Jews, the Indians and the Japanese. As for their potential Nigerian business partners, Niang considered them subhuman and beneath contempt.

By 1963 a whole generation of bilingual young Chinese were part of Hong Kong's work force. Already some of the very rich in Hong Kong were wealthy beyond belief. Their sons and daughters returned from the best universities in England and America, impeccably turned out in dark designer suits tailored in London and Paris, even in the height of summer. They spoke flawless English. The sons sometimes had *fan gui nui* (foreign female devils) on their arms. The best and most élite clubs in Hong Kong no longer excluded Chinese members. The new divider was not race, but money. In this new Hong Kong of the 1960s, there were many Cantonese millionaires far richer than Father and Niang. Since my parents were convinced of their innate superiority over the Cantonese, this state of affairs was difficult for them to digest. Their only defence was to dismiss all Cantonese as uncouth, though inwardly they were envious of those who were making their way even faster in this new society. With exquisite irony Niang occasionally deplored inter-racial marriages, predicting that their offspring would be 'neither fish nor fowl'.

CHAPTER 16

匹馬單鎗

Pi Ma Dan Qiang
One Horse, Single Spear

Seven months into my internship, a twenty-five-year-old Chinese-American medical student arrived. Martin Ching was an exchange scholar from New York University medical school for the month of July. He was the only son of working-class parents who had emigrated from Guangdong to America in the 1930s. His industrious laundry worker father and waitress mother placed all their hopes in Martin, saving every cent to send him to medical school and buying a house in Queens so that Martin could live away from New York's Chinatown ghetto when he entered college. They continued to reside above their shop while Martin rented out rooms to other students to help pay the mortgage. He was a good boy, studious and responsible.

A couple of times in the evenings after work, Martin and I sat around talking. We were both at loose ends and had nowhere to go. He could barely speak Cantonese. The doctors and nurses found it inconvenient to translate everything into English when he was around. Besides, Martin was 'only' a medical student.

'I have never met such discrimination as that which I'm encountering in Hong Kong,' Martin told me. 'The people here keep their distance. They are wary and regard me with contempt because I look Chinese but cannot speak or write Chinese fluently. They think I'm dumb.'

That summer of 1964, the weather was unbelievably bad. It seemed as if the rains would never end. And then one day, typhoon warnings were posted by the weather bureau. All employees except those on emergency call were told to stay at home. Elective clinics were cancelled. Martin and I remained at the hospital because we had nowhere else to go.

Outside, the rain cascaded down in sheets, whipped by a ferocious wind swirling the blue ocean waters into choppy, angry, white waves. Services were suspended at the Star Ferry: no more harbour crossings between Hong Kong and Kowloon until further notice. Traffic disappeared from the roads. We were stranded inside Tsan Yuk Hospital, surrounded by thunder, lightning, torrential rains and gusts of typhoon. Protective wooden shutters were put up in front of plate-glass windows. For those less affluent, long strips of paper tape were stuck across the panes against the wind. Hong Kong was a city under siege from the elemental forces of nature.

Martin and I sat at one end of a long rectangular conference table in the library and watched the fury of the storm outside. The violence of the deluge created an enclave of comfort and safety within.

'You're wasting your time and talents here,' Martin told me. 'You can do the work here with your eyes closed, but you still have to put in the hours and get up at night. Why don't you go to Professor McFadden and accept the job he offered you?'

'I can't go to Lo Mac!' I replied. 'I've got to get out of Hong Kong.'

'Go back to London then! You can easily get an academic post with two MRCPs.'

'No, no. London is out! I'm not going back there!' I thought about Karl, and felt a spasm of pain. I could never return to *that* again. 'Besides, I'll get nowhere. The cards are stacked against me. Chinese. Female. Racism and sexism are very much in evidence in England.'

'So what else is new?' Martin asked rhetorically. 'Racism and sexism are everywhere, even in America.'

'What was it really like, growing up in America?'

'You mean what was it really like, growing up in white America with an Asian face?'

He told me about going to school in Chinatown in New York and identifying only with white America. He hated Chinese school because he did not wish to be different from his white classmates. Gradually he realized that although he thought of himself as American he would always be a foreigner, a Chinese, to his white peers. Martin felt himself caught between two worlds. He became convinced that prejudice was inherent in human nature and was present in every society, including his own home. His parents objected strongly when he once dated a West Indian girl, calling her a *see yu gui nui* (soya-sauce female foreign devil). He finally concluded that compared to every other place, America was still the most tolerant and enlightened. He considered himself lucky to have been born in the USA.

Martin was a history major at Columbia University before entering medical school. He divided Chinese emigration into three separate waves. Before the Opium War, the egress consisted of artisans, craftsmen and merchants who moved from southern coastal provinces into neighbouring countries such as Thailand, Vietnam, Malaya and the Philippines. For about seventy years after the Opium War, uneducated peasants (the destitute and the poor) poured into America hoping for a better life, until exclusionary laws curtailed their numbers. After the Second World War, affluent Chinese businessmen in Taiwan and Hong Kong started sending their offspring for university education abroad, especially to America. Recent immigration reforms in America facilitated this new wave of 'intellectual immigration'. Often, these students ended up staying in America and never returning home.

'I've got two guys from Taiwan renting rooms from me right now,' Martin continued. 'Neither of them plans to go back.

One is a pathology resident, the other is an engineer. Since you're not happy in Hong Kong, why don't you come to America? A medical degree from London University is well thought of in New York. Come to think of it, a couple of profs on the faculty at NYU are English medical graduates.'

A new vista suddenly opened before me. America! 美國 *Mei Guo* (Beautiful Country)! I stood by the window and looked at the stormy devastation outside, half expecting to see a rainbow over the horizon. 'Thank you for your generosity. You've cheered me up more than you'll ever realize. Your words have filled me with optimism. Why, everything is possible!'

'Listen, I'll be going back to New York next week. I'll help you find a job. Don't look so anxious. You'll have no problems at all.'

When Martin left Tsan Yuk, it was already the end of July. My contract with Professor Chun was to end in three months. Desperate to leave Hong Kong, I applied to every hospital suggested by Martin. Most of the replies suggested a starting date of 1 July the following year. However, the Presbyterian Hospital in Philadelphia accepted me to begin a residency in obstetrics immediately. I later learned that they were anxious to have me because their residency positions had not been filled and they ran the risk of having their entire training programme cancelled. At that time in America, there was a doctor shortage.

I immediately accepted the job offered. Pay was 450 US dollars per month besides board and lodging. There was just one problem. I did not have enough money to buy the airline ticket from Hong Kong to Philadelphia. I wondered if Father and Niang would consider making me a loan.

During Sunday dinner, I summoned up enough courage to announce that I had decided to emigrate to America. This was greeted by absolute silence. Father knew that I was unhappy at Tsan Yuk. He was also aware of Professor McFadden's standing offer to me at the Department of Internal Medicine. My American plan was new to them.

I hinted at my lack of resources and wondered aloud whether banks would give me a loan to buy the airline ticket. Niang said, 'Well, Adeline, you'll never know until you apply, will you? And if the bank refuses, I suppose that's just too bad, isn't it?' With that sort of response, I understood that my chances of getting a loan from them was zero.

That night, I left early because I had an early surgery scheduled the next morning. Around midnight, Gregory telephoned. 'They talked about you after you left.'

My heart sank. 'What did they say?'

'They said that they had tried their best to help you in Hong Kong. Since this isn't good enough, you're henceforth entirely on your own. They don't care where you go from this point. London, New York, Tokyo, Philadelphia; it's all the same to them. But don't think you're going to get a free ticket from them, because you're not.'

We were both silent for awhile. 'Well, thanks, Gregory,' I finally said. 'I'll think of a way.'

After Gregory's call, I could not sleep. I started to cry and thought how mean they were to begrudge me the price of a plane ticket to Philadelphia when it was nothing to them. Not to express any regrets at my leaving Hong Kong. Not to say a few kind words such as 'We'll miss you' or 'Write to us often, will you?' My imminent departure was of no concern except for the possible burden of an airline ticket.

I got up from my bed, put on my scrub clothes and went to the hospital library. It was deserted. I told myself, 'Feeling sorry for yourself and crying isn't going to get you an airline ticket.'

I sat down and wrote a long letter to the secretary of the Medical Education Department at the Presbyterian Hospital in Philadelphia.

I confessed to this stranger my sad story. I was single, female and Chinese. All my life I had dreamt of starting a practice in Hong Kong close to my father. When I finally returned home after eleven years, I found nothing but disenchantment. I had decided to emigrate to America and had accepted a job offer from the Presbyterian Hospital.

I then told her that I did not have any money for the airline ticket and wondered if I could borrow the sum against my future earnings. 'I don't know your origin or background,' I wrote, 'but perhaps someone once reached out a hand to help you achieve your American dream. I'm humbly asking you to do this for me now.'

The Presbyterian Hospital did not fail me. Within two weeks, I had a reply. Apparently my request was not unusual. They had a policy at the hospital of advancing travel expenses to medical doctors from overseas who had passed the ECFMG, a special examination for foreign medical graduates. The cost of the airline ticket plus interest was deducted in monthly instalments from their pay. A standardized form was enclosed for my signature.

There was also a handwritten note from the secretary of the Medical Education Department. 'I was touched by your letter. I just want you to know that our home will always be open to you should you need help when you come to Philadelphia.'

This was my introduction to an American stranger. She was kinder to me than my parents.

I left Hong Kong soon afterwards. Gregory and James came to the airport to see me off. Niang went to her usual bridge game. While Gregory was parking the car, James quietly slipped a crisp, twenty dollar bill into my handbag. His gesture moved me to tears because I knew it was a sum he could not afford.

Half an hour before departure, Father rushed in to say goodbye. We gathered at the gate for take-off and all shook hands when the time came to board. I wanted to tell Father that I had tried my best to please him but the words would not come. After a painful pause, Father finally said, 'Well, you're truly on your own now. 匹馬單鎗 Pi ma dan qiang (One horse, single spear: meaning that I was engaged in single handed combat against life). Let's see what you can achieve.'

CHAPTER 17

嫁鷄隨鷄

Jia Ji Shui Ji
Marry a Chicken, Follow a Chicken

Martin came to meet me at the airport. In order to save money, I had purchased the cheapest available ticket, which bought me a journey that took almost forty-eight hours. On the plane I had been too nervous to sleep and now longed for nothing else as Martin drove from La Guardia to Queens against the headlights of on-rushing traffic. My eyelids drooped as he spoke animatedly about introducing me to his friends, going bowling or even dancing. Soon I was fast asleep.

He had to shake me awake when we arrived at his three-storeyed terraced house in a quiet, suburban neighbourhood. Inside the dimly lit living-room I noted drowsily that the vinyl sofas and plastic coffee table were neat and tidy. A light shone from the adjacent kitchen where someone was shuffling pots and pans.

Martin ruffled my hair after carrying my two suitcases into the house. 'Welcome to America, sleepy head!' he exclaimed cheerfully. 'This is where I hang out. What do you think of it?'

Someone coughed behind us. I turned and saw a tall, graceful young man with a crew cut. Tired as I was, I registered that he was startlingly handsome. He came striding forward, his right hand outstretched. 'Hi, I'm Byron Bai-lun Soon. I live here Martin's house.' He spoke with a heavy northern Chinese accent.

Martin draped his arm possessively around my shoulder as he introduced me. Instinctively, I moved away and sat down wearily on the couch.

'Now that you're safely here,' Martin said, 'let's all three have a beer before I take you out to dinner.'

'Not me,' Byron answered, 'Chinese girls don't drink beer. What she needs is nice cup boiling water on cold night like this. Then big bowl noodles with lots of peppery meat sauce. I fix right this minute.'

'Hot water!' Martin exclaimed, wrinkling his nose. 'She's not an old lady from Chinatown like my mother! What she needs is an ice-cold beer. She doesn't want any noodles. I just told you we're going out to dinner.'

Soon I had a cup of hot water and a cold beer placed in front of me, alternately sipping both.

Martin took me to a local Japanese restaurant, even though the idea of Byron's noodles and then a soft pillow were more appealing. I went through the motions of eating a few tempura shrimp while Martin enthused about New York. By then I was practically sleepwalking. Finally he took the hint and we returned to his house where he showed me my room. Like a zombie I agreed to be ready at nine in the morning so that I could visit his medical school where he had Saturday grand rounds.

Next morning, I slept through the ringing of my alarm clock and Martin's hammering on my door. Bright sunlight streamed through the curtains when I woke with a start at one. I knew that I had let Martin down. Hurriedly I dressed and stumbled downstairs. In the living-room, I found Byron by himself, quietly reading an engineering textbook.

'I was wondering when you would come down,' Byron said, smiling. He was dressed in a new white shirt and royal blue pullover. In the light of day, he looked even more dazzling. Now that we were alone, he spoke to me in fluent Mandarin, obviously more comfortable in his native tongue. Sheepishly he handed me a note that Martin had left on the coffee table. In a faintly accusatory tone, Martin had scribbled, 'Tried to wake you without success. Almost broke my hand but to no avail. You must be really bushed! I'll be home around five thirty. See you then. Let's go bowling tonight!'

'I'm glad you overslept,' Byron announced. 'Now I have you all to myself for a few hours. Shall we have lunch? It's all ready.' We sat at the kitchen table and ate the noodles with peppery meat sauce that Byron had prepared. He was born in 1938 in Hunan Province where his father was a general in the Kuomintang army. After the Communist takeover, his parents separated. His mother remained in China with a younger sister, while his father escaped to Hong Kong with Byron and Arnold, his older brother. The two boys completed middle school in Hong Kong before attending Taiwan University. After graduation they both travelled to America for post-graduate study. Arnold married his college sweetheart and was studying for a Ph.D. in mathematics at the University of Pennsylvania. Byron had an evening job at an engineering firm and was working towards a master's degree at Brooklyn Polytechnic Institute. He already had a green card and wished to become an American citizen. He had been renting a room from Martin for nine months.

'I thought about you all last night,' Byron confessed. 'When I read Martin's note, I decided to cut my classes. This is going to be my lucky day! My day in the sun with you. Alone!' His eyes glistened with tears. He took my hand. 'I never felt this way about anyone before. Tell me, do I stand a chance?'

I was astonished. I blinked my eyes and he was still there: the handsome hero of all the Kung Fu novels pledging his devotion. I did not withdraw my hand and, as the afternoon wore on, became increasingly captivated by him. Finally he stood up to go. Gently caressing my hair, he said, 'This is the happiest day of my life. I have a prediction to make. Before 1964 is over, you are going to be my wife.'

That night I found on my pillow a letter from Byron, written in Chinese. It was short but beautifully phrased, peppered with quotations from the T'ang poetry I had told him I loved. I scribbled the time of my planned departure on the back of the envelope and slipped it under his door as instructed.

In the morning the three of us took a taxi together to Pennsylvania station with Martin and Byron openly competing for my favours. Martin became increasingly exasperated. I was flattered but it was an awkward situation and I felt relieved when at last my train left for Philadelphia.

I married Byron in City Hall, New York City, just six weeks after my arrival in America, and before the end of 1964 as he had predicted. Martin asked Byron to move out immediately because his parents forbade him to rent to married couples. Neither of us ever spoke to or saw Martin again. In a rare reflective moment shortly after the ceremony, I calculated that the time Byron and I had spent alone together was less than ten hours.

To Father and Niang, I sent a telegram informing them of my marriage. A month later, I received a letter of congratulation from them, enclosing a 600-dollar cheque as their wedding present.

I rationalized my marriage by telling myself that most arranged marriages in China would have started out the same way. After all, every marriage is a gamble and living together with anybody must involve daily compromises.

My contract with Presbyterian was for seven months until June 1965. In order to commute to see Byron at weekends, I went further into debt and bought a second-hand Volkswagen.

Two weeks after the wedding, while doing his laundry, I found, in one of his trouser pockets, a letter from Chase Manhattan Bank cancelling his account because it was overdrawn.

When I telephoned him at the engineering firm where he claimed he worked, I was informed that he only came in occasionally on a part-time basis. A call later came from someone speaking with a rough-hewn Cantonese accent. It became clear from the caller's message that Byron's main occupation was that of a waiter in a Chinese restaurant.

Somewhat alarmed, I decided to confront him. We had gone to see the movie *My Fair Lady* in Queens. While we waited for the film to begin I spoke of my hurt at discovering that he had not been entirely truthful.

'There is nothing to discuss,' he scowled. 'Besides, I married you, didn't I? What else do you want?'

'I want to understand you, just as I hope you'll try and understand me.'

'I don't feel like talking right now. I want to watch the movie and have a good time.'

'Can we talk after the movie?'

'No! I want you to understand that when I say no I mean no. There's nothing further to discuss.'

'What's this, a dictatorship? Are we husband and wife or master and slave? Why can't we talk things over in a calm and logical way?'

'嫁雞隨雞、嫁狗隨狗 *Jia ji shui ji, jia gou shui gou* (Marry a chicken, follow a chicken; marry a dog, follow a dog).'

'What rubbish!' I exclaimed, adding sarcastically, 'Is this what you have absorbed from your extensive perusal of the great Chinese classics? Has your passion for T'ang poetry been distilled down to this profound bit of wisdom?'

In the dim light I sensed his rising fury. Without a word, he rose and walked out.

In his haste, he had left his winter coat and gloves on the seat. I started to worry about him wandering the freezing streets of New York dressed only in a pullover and thin polyester trousers. I blamed myself for those cutting remarks. I was disappointed to discover that my husband's reading was confined to newspapers and engineering textbooks. But his pretended love of T'ang poetry was no more than a desire to impress the girl he loved.

The movie flickered on and on. I dared not leave for fear he might return and not find me. When it ended I filed out with everyone else, half expecting to find him waiting in the lobby.

He was not there. Snow lay in drifts around the unfamiliar streets. I hailed a cab back to his apartment for which I had no key. It was after eleven. Byron was not yet home. I huddled in the doorway like a homeless bag lady, terrified that some drunk would spot me and pounce in the darkness.

'Marry a chicken, follow a chicken. Marry a dog, follow a dog.' Perhaps I should humour him and play the submissive Chinese wife. The alternative would be a complete break, a divorce. I brushed that aside. I could never admit my failure to Father and Niang. I made up my mind to save my marriage, whatever the cost.

Byron finally returned at around two in the morning, surly and glum. He had gone to the Chinese restaurant where he normally worked, ordered a big meal, then helped out until closing. He headed straight for the bathroom without a word while I prepared some noodles in the kitchen. When the food was ready I placed it in two bowls and called him. He was fast asleep, looking angelic. I ate both bowls by myself.

Next morning Byron behaved as if nothing had happened. Elated, he showed me a letter from his immigration lawyer stating that his chances of getting a green card were 'highly probable', forgetting that at our first meeting he had told me he already possessed a green card. I bit my tongue and said nothing. We sat around drinking coffee, eating doughnuts and reading the Sunday edition of the *New York Times*. He was looking for a permanent engineering position with a big company in the sunbelt. On the back page of the paper we came across a full-page announcement: 'Engineers! Come to glorious Southern California where the sun shines everyday! Come and work for Douglas Aircraft in Long Beach! We need you.'

Somewhere in the back of my mind, I recalled that marvellous photograph of Clark Gable, autographed and sent from Hollywood to one of my Shanghai schoolmates years ago. How we had coveted it! These were the reasons we eventually ended up in southern California: through an ad in the *New York Times* and the magic of Clark Gable.

Douglas Aircraft hired him at 800 dollars per month. In order to obtain a California medical licence, I had to take a special exam and do an internship at a recognized Californian hospital. So began my third internship on 1 July 1965, at St Mary's Hospital in Long Beach.

Pay was only 300 dollars per month but I was given the use of a separate bungalow adjoining the hospital. Despite Byron's good looks and fine physique, I continued to feel towards him a profound indifference. Emotionally, he remained a stranger. Whenever he touched me, I seemed to turn into stone.

Simultaneously, I was guilt-ridden by my unresponsiveness. I had married him for the most practical reasons: companionship, children, emotional security and social acceptance. Naively, I believed that if I tried hard enough, love would follow. It never did.

Byron and I kept our distance. This was how he wanted the marriage to be. Heart-to-heart conversations made him acutely uncomfortable. He often quoted the Chinese proverb 夫妻相敬如賓 *fu qi xiang jing ru bin* (husband and wife should respect each other like honoured guests). By this he meant that I was to refrain from any criticisms, negative remarks or intimate *tête-à-têtes*. I avoided any controversial subjects and tried to be cheerful. There was no conversation and therefore no intimacy.

The television was his constant companion. He turned it on the minute he came home and sat in front of it hour after hour, compulsively switching channels every few minutes. He would leave it reluctantly when I called him for dinner and rush back to it while I washed up. We ate our meals in silence. Byron read the *Los Angeles Times* and I read my books. At night, we lay next to each other like two squatters compelled to share the same bed.

By October 1965, though, I was pregnant. Byron seemed pleased at the prospect of becoming a father. With a baby on the way, I narrowed my career choice down to anaesthesiology, a hospital-based speciality. The practice of anaesthesia has been described as hours of boredom interrupted by moments of panic. Responsibility was onerous. Patients were routinely rendered unconscious and suspended between life and death. Fees earned were proportionately steep. I applied and was accepted for an anaesthesia residency at Orange County General Hospital, University of California, Irvine.

The baby was due at the beginning of June. Byron and I pooled our income, paid off our loans and prepared to move out of the bungalow. We put a down payment on a new house in Fountain Valley, ten miles away.

We were both overjoyed by the purchase of the house. It satisfied our yearning to put down roots in America. That evening when the contract was signed, I cooked a celebratory meal. Relaxed by the food, we began to discuss the status of our visas. Byron had received his green card and was already a permanent resident, but mine was still that of an 'exchange visiting scholar'.

'You should consult an immigration lawyer, and get your status changed as soon as possible,' Byron told me. 'If you had started the process when we first met, you would already have your green card.'

'When we first met, you were still on a student visa yourself,' I said unthinkingly.

His face darkened. 'Are you calling me a liar? If I hadn't married you, you'd never have been able to get a green card.'

'First things first. You know very well you didn't have a green card when we met at Martin Ching's house,' I insisted.

Suddenly he became enraged. He stood up and began to shout, 'If you're secretly hankering after Martin, why don't you go and find him in New York?'

To my relief at that moment the telephone rang. The hospital operator was unable to locate the intern on call. Could I come in immediately to assist two patients just admitted after a car accident? Muttering something about being needed for an emergency, I rushed out of the house.

Four hours later I returned. By then I was exhausted. My

large, pregnant belly hung like a sack of stones below what had once been my waist. My ankles were so swollen that I had difficulty kicking off my shoes before turning on the light. What greeted my eyes was an unbelievable scene of chaos. In his anger Byron had ripped out all the drawers from their rails and strewn their contents on the floor in the middle of the living-room. Scattered haphazardly here and there were clothes, sheets, kitchen utensils, books, toiletry and food. In the kitchen, dirty dishes were strewn across the table and in the sink. Byron was nowhere to be seen.

After I cleared the kitchen, I made myself a cup of tea. Then I started tackling the mess in the living-room, mechanically putting everything back in its proper place. 'In the face of utter disaster,' I told myself, 'everyone feels better with positive action. It could have been worse. At least he didn't burn the place down.'

Towards six in the morning, when the cleaning was half finished, a key turned in the lock and Byron entered. I was on my hands and knees. Something in my abject posture must have touched a chord because he did not disturb me. He strode into the bedroom, packed a small bag and hurried out again without a word.

He was gone for five days. I believed my marriage to be over. The baby was due in two weeks. My work routine became my refuge, creating an illusion of order and normality. It was comforting to feel needed by my patients even though my own world was crumbling.

Then suddenly he came back. I returned home from the hospital at around six one evening to find him watching television and switching channels as if he had never been away. I cooked dinner and we ate in silence while he scanned the *Los Angeles Times*.

Labour pains started at seven in the morning of 8 June 1966. Byron was solicitous. He walked me to the hospital, took the day off, and sat at my bedside in the labour room. Our son, Roger, was born that evening, beautiful and healthy.

Towards our adorable baby, I lavished all my tenderness. I would rush home from work to bathe and feed him. I felt incredibly lucky to be able to give him all the love I had been deprived of during my own childhood.

Though the marriage was a complete sham, outwardly we gave the appearance of a nice, wholesome Chinese-American family.

CHAPTER 18

種瓜得瓜

Zhong Gua De Gua

You Plant Melons, You Reap Melons

South Coast Plaza, an ultra-modern, regional shopping centre, had just opened its doors in Costa Mesa about fifteen miles away. Byron and I were both eager to see it. We set off together bright and early on New Year's Day, 1967, to buy a new suit for Byron. Traditionally in China, new clothes are worn on 1 January to symbolize a new beginning. That same evening, Byron had invited four of his college friends from the University of Taiwan to come for dinner with their wives.

It was a gorgeous morning, sunny, breezy and smogless. As we drove south on the newly extended stretch of the San Diego Freeway, we could see the snow-capped mountains etched against a cloudless sky. The air smelled clean and fresh. A jaunty tune came over the radio. We were both in excellent spirits when Byron drove into the enormous parking lot, locked the car and handed me the keys to carry in my handbag. He looked dashing in a thick woollen pullover over his shirt. We walked into the men's shop at Sears Roebuck. While he was selecting his suit, I sauntered to the baby's department to choose a toy. On my return, I saw a salesman helping Byron put on a jacket.

'You really should take that bulky sweater off before trying on these jackets,' the salesman was saying. 'This is the fourth one you've tried. It's not going to fit because it's not your size.

The sleeves are too long because the garment is simply too big.'

Byron was gazing into the mirror and adjusting the lengthy sleeves. Ignoring the salesman, he turned towards me. 'How do you like the colour? What do you think?'

The salesman now appealed to me. 'You see, ma'am, over here, the collar even hangs wrong. This is a size 44. He's really a 40. At most a 42.'

Without thinking, I said to Byron, 'I think he has a valid point. Why don't you take your sweater off as he suggested and try on a 40?'

He glared at me. Then, without a word, he took off the jacket, turned abruptly and walked out of the room.

I hung about looking foolish, then went to the car and waited for two hours. I phoned Mrs Hsu, Roger's nanny, but she told me he had not returned. It was almost one. I drove home.

Mrs Hsu helped me decorate the house and prepare a few dishes. Three o'clock rolled around and there was no sign of Byron. I began to worry about him not showing up at all. I hardly knew the names of his Taiwan friends, let alone their wives. What would I do when they all arrived and there was no Byron? Finally, I could stand it no longer. I phoned his guests one by one, told them that Byron had come down with food poisoning and cancelled the dinner party.

I must have dozed off in the living-room when I heard Byron's key in the front door. He had walked home from the shopping plaza. It had taken him three and a half hours.

'Where are my guests?' he asked, taking a sideway glance at the food we had prepared and laid out on the kitchen table. I looked at my watch. It was after six.

'Since I didn't know whether you were coming home,' I replied groggily, rubbing the sleep from my eyes, 'I cancelled the party.'

'Who gave you permission to do that? They are *my* guests! That was *my* party!' he exploded.

I didn't answer, for fear of provoking him further. I rose from the couch and walked into the bathroom.

The next minute I heard the loud bang of a bedroom door being forcibly thrown open, the breaking of furniture and the terrifying wail of my baby. I ran into the nursery and saw Byron standing arms akimbo over the screaming six-months-old infant in his collapsed crib. I was seized with murderous fury. I picked up my crying son, marched into our bedroom and locked the door.

Next I heard a tremendous crash from the kitchen. Then the front door banged shut and Byron was gone. My baby would not stop crying. I examined him carefully, noting with relief that there was no serious injury. In the kitchen, I saw an alarmed Mrs Hsu surveying the broken crockery and spilt food splattered everywhere. Byron had simply lifted the edge of the table laden with dishes and thrown the whole lot overboard.

Mrs Hsu was an educated widow originally from Beijing, then in her seventies. I had grown very fond of her and was deeply ashamed that she should have witnessed such an ugly scene.

We cleaned up the mess in silence. Then we ate the longlife noodles we had prepared to bring in the New Year.

'There are lots of men like your husband in China,' Mrs Hsu said. 'In the old days, men routinely mistreated their wives. Now he's doing the same to you. The more you put up with it, the more savage he will be. If you have no other rice to eat, then you must swallow this bitterness. But, in your case, you have your profession.'

Byron stayed away for a week. On his return, he placed his salary cheque on the table after dinner as a peace offering. I was touched but could not shake off the loathing I felt.

Unwilling to face him, I wrote him a note: 'For the time being, please sleep in the guest room upstairs. I'm leaving your cheque on the table. I shall understand perfectly if you prefer to spend your money separately.'

When Byron understood that this time I would not attempt

a reconciliation he became more aggressive. To my shame, he often expressed his frustration by physical violence towards me and our baby. I suffered guilt and humiliation whenever I lied about my black eyes and bruised face to my colleagues, unwilling to air my domestic problems in public. I endured his blows because I could not bear the shame of divorce and the subsequent dishonour it would bring on my family.

I worked harder than ever, taking a shift in the emergency room whenever the opportunity arose. Byron and I ceased to have any social life together. At weekends, he dined with fellow-engineers from Taiwan University and colleagues from work while I took my baby and Mrs Hsu to amusement parks and Chinese restaurants. After Mrs Hsu's retirement I was enormously lucky to find a Caucasian widow in her fifties, Ginger Morris, to be Roger's new nanny. Ginger came to us in 1968 and stayed with me for eleven years.

My residency was completed at the end of June 1968, by which time I had my green card. Jobs were plentiful. By doing locums and volunteering to take extra night and weekend calls, I soon built up a thriving practice. My income for July alone equalled my salary for a whole year as a resident. Byron and I led our separate lives but kept a joint account. A substantial balance was being built up.

Towards the end of 1968 Byron decided to buy a Chinese restaurant in Costa Mesa. He came home early one evening and presented me with some papers for my signature. Byron was at his most charming. 'You probably don't know this,' he told me, 'but I used to work like a slave in various Chinese restaurants in New York. Now that I can afford to buy one, I want to run it the way it should be run.' I shrugged and signed the papers.

After his restaurant opened, I noticed that our joint account was being quickly depleted to support the new venture. He engaged a young man, Lee Ming, as manager. Every day after work, he drove directly to his restaurant, eating all his meals there and coming home after eleven. Weekends were particularly busy and he was away from ten in the morning until midnight.

My own work schedule was getting more and more loaded. This was the heyday of private medical practice in America. Medicare legislation had recently been implemented. In spite of general misgiving among my colleagues, it turned out to be an open conduit to a seemingly endless supply of government funds for the treatment of America's elderly during the next fifteen years.

Running a restaurant proved more difficult than Byron had imagined. Soon he was embroiled in numerous unpleasant confrontations with his staff. One Friday evening the restaurant ran out of eggs. Byron rushed out to the local market and bought ten cartons. During his absence Lee Ming took charge. A rush of customers came in. Lee Ming seated the majority and asked the rest to wait. Byron came back to a packed dining room and half-a-dozen waiting couples. He began aggressively going from table to table, urging those who were lingering over their coffee and dessert to hurry. Overriding Lee's protestations, he went to the storage area and carried out some spare tables and chairs and seated everyone. The two men had a tremendous row. Lee knew that the restaurant would collapse without him so he offered to buy the restaurant from Byron. Most of the staff had followed Lee from his previous place of employment and were loyal to him personally. They now launched a deliberate campaign to sabotage Byron. The chef claimed sick leave at critical times when the restaurant was full. Dishes were spiked with salt or hot sauce and rendered almost inedible. Key deliveries were not made at crucial moments. Tables were left uncleared with plates and glassware unwashed in the sink.

One day in June 1969, Byron left a note on my pillow. He was planning to sell the restaurant to a man whom he had met the previous night at a party. What did I think? I wrote 'yes' at the foot of his message and placed it on his bed upstairs, reflecting sadly that our communication had dwindled to notes scrawled on the backs of tattered envelopes. To my astonishment Byron's buyer was serious and the business was actually sold for cash soon afterwards. According to Byron we recovered most of our investment because of tax write-offs. Lee and his team agreed to stay on and I heard later that the restaurant prospered and was resold at a great price a few years later.

We now had 20,000 dollars in our joint account. For the first time I had more money than I knew what to do with. One August afternoon after giving seven anaesthetics, I drove to a car dealer and bought a brand-new white Mercedes, registering the vehicle in both our names.

Returning home I placed the registration papers on Byron's bed for his signature. He signed without comment but from then on no longer contributed any part of his salary towards our household expenses.

At the end of 1969, he suddenly departed for a position in Hong Kong, leaving a farewell note on my pillow, telling me that he would return within the year. I read his message with relief, content that I could now channel all my energy into my son and my career.

While in Hong Kong, Byron went with his father to pay a social call on my parents on Chinese New Year, traditionally a time for family reunion. Their visit was not a success. They brought a large basket of fruit and arrived fifteen minutes early. Niang complained that 'being early was as impolite as being late. In both cases the guests were inconveniencing the hosts.' Niang insisted on speaking English and later commented on their 'poor grasp of the language and atrocious accents'. When my parents unwrapped the colourful cellophane paper enveloping the fruit basket, they found that many of the fruits were rotten, from which Niang assumed that the basket was well past its sell-by date and had been purchased cheaply.

Byron returned from Hong Kong after an absence of seven

months. He took up his job at Douglas Aircraft again and we resumed our separate lives under the same roof.

In October of that year, 1970, Father and Niang were on a world trip and decided to pay us a visit. Throughout the last six years, I had hidden from them the truth about my dismal marriage. My letters were limited to milestones, achievements and glowing reports of the Californian weather. On their arrival, Byron and I took Roger to meet them at the airport. Niang insisted on staying in Universal City, fifty miles from our home, at a hotel owned by their rich American friends, the Jules Steins. Between them they had brought six suitcases. During the long drive from the airport to their hotel, I was desperately keeping an awkward conversation going. Niang was wearing her usual perfume, familiar to me since childhood. I knew that Byron was unacquainted with the complicated maze of freeways in that area. While trying to decipher the road map in the dim car light, I was terrified of giving the wrong directions and causing Byron to throw a temper tantrum. When we finally arrived, I rushed to the bathroom and vomited.

Two days later, I took time off from work to drive them home for a weekend visit. In the lobby of their hotel, Father and Niang had an argument. Father had directed the concierge to pack their clothes and place their baggage in storage during their absence. Apparently he had not previously consulted Niang.

She countermanded his orders. 'There's no need for that. Our clothes should hang in a wardrobe, not wrinkled up in a suitcase. Leave them where they are! We'll pay for the room while away.'

Father said nothing. There was no doubt as to who was in charge. During the silent fifty-mile drive home, Father fell asleep, looking crestfallen and browbeaten. I glanced at him in the rear-view mirror. His sloping shoulders, drooping head and folded hands were reminiscent of another time, another place. Suddenly I remembered. Yes! Father had begun to re-semble Ye Ye in his last years.

I took them to the hospital where I worked, introduced them to my colleagues and visited an apartment complex which I had made an offer to purchase. I was investing in my first income-producing property and, to my delight, perceived that Father wished to participate. Niang was far from pleased and manoeuvred it so that Father and I were never alone.

During their stay, I vacated my bedroom for them. Byron remained upstairs while I slept on the living-room couch. They must have sensed that our marriage was in trouble. Byron, meanwhile, was on his best behaviour. He arranged a big dinner in their honour at a fancy restaurant called Delaney's and introduced my parents to all his colleagues, forgetting that I had never met his co-workers either.

Father, Niang and I were by ourselves when I drove them back to their hotel. Part of me longed to pour out the sorry tale of my disastrous marriage. Another part wished to maintain the façade of a daughter who was successful in every way: career, home life, health, money, adorable son, handsome husband. I despised myself for keeping up this pretence.

We chatted on and on about inconsequential matters for quite some time when Father asked unexpectedly, 'Tell me, Adeline, who paid for the dinner at Delaney's last night?'

His simple question, coming out of nowhere, took me by surprise. Did Byron pay out of our joint account or his separate, personal account? I had no idea.

Meanwhile, Father was waiting for an answer. Somewhat defensively, I said, 'I really don't know,' adding with a forced laugh, 'Does it matter?'

'Sometimes,' he advised, 'it is wise to pay attention to money matters. At present your career is just starting to take off. You're young and healthy. The whole world is at your feet. If you're careful, you have the opportunity to build up a large fortune. But it won't always be like that. One day you will become old and feeble. Be sure you are prepared when that day arrives. You must arrange things so that you have control over your own money. Trust no one. People change and their feelings change also.'

Niang nodded in agreement. 'This husband of yours,' she suddenly asked, 'is he all right? I mean, is he perhaps a little cracked in the head?'

I was astonished. I had often wondered myself about Byron's sanity. Not wishing to reveal too much, I answered with a question, 'Aren't we all a little crazy? He probably thinks I am the unbalanced one in the family.'

'The block of apartments you showed us two days ago,' Father said, 'the one you are thinking of buying. Whose name will be on the deed as the legal owner?'

'I have put both our names down as the buyers, Father,' I answered truthfully. 'This is the way it's done in America. When we bought our house, it was also purchased in our joint names.'

'What you are doing is unwise and will lead to complications.' Father admonished. '種瓜得瓜 *Zhong gua de gua* (You plant melons, you reap melons). When Byron was in Hong Kong, he and his father told us they had bought a property in Kowloon. Is your name on the deed there?'

I faltered, shocked. 'I don't think so, Father. Byron never asked me to sign any papers.' The conversation was veering painfully close to a discussion about the state of my marriage.

'Then why are you putting his name on your apartments when he has not contributed one cent towards their purchase? Don't be naive, Adeline! Don't think you are above these money matters, because you are not. Consult a good lawyer and make sure the property is in your name and your name alone. Do you hear?'

A lump appeared in my throat and my eyes were damp with tears. They had seen through my pretences. Father's stern directives were his expressions of care and concern. He was trying to protect his daughter. I nodded my head and swallowed hard.

As we approached their hotel, Niang added, 'There is something not quite right about that husband of yours. Remember, no matter what happens, your parents will always be your parents. Listen to your father and do what he says.' Those were the kindest words she ever said to me.

I mulled over their advice during the long drive back. Though they did not come out and say so, indirectly they were signalling that I should get a divorce. I decided to act and consult a lawyer immediately. They had given me permission to do so.

A few days later, armed with a legal document prepared by a divorce lawyer, I waited for Byron to come home. After we had eaten dinner and Roger had been put to bed, I went into the living-room and sat next to Byron on the couch. Together we watched a televised boxing match. Eventually I plucked up enough courage to hand him the document and explain its contents, informing him that his signature was needed.

Byron glanced glumly at the paper and went back to the boxing while I held my breath. Finally he enquired whether I was asking him for a divorce and was there someone else? Something in the bleakness of his voice touched my heart. I started to cry, 'No, there is no one. I sincerely believe this is best for all three of us.' For the first time I saw anguish in his eyes. Wishing to lessen the hurt, I added, 'I'm truly sorry. We both took a gamble and we both lost.'

A few weeks later Byron did sign as requested. Afterwards he locked himself upstairs, coming down only for his meals, which he took up to eat alone. Having made up my mind, I was strangely at peace and hoped for an amicable parting. That Christmas, I bought him a gold watch, wrapped it in pretty paper and placed it on his pillow. Ginger signalled to me the next day to follow her to the back of the house. There I saw my gaily wrapped gift discarded in the garbage can, unopened and still beribboned.

The day after Christmas Byron was transferred to work in Oceanside. My lawyer served him with divorce papers before he left for Hong Kong again some time in 1971. He offered not to contest the suit if I signed over my half-share of the Fountain Valley house and if I desisted from making demands for alimony or child support. I acquiesced immediately and moved into another house. After the divorce, Byron neither wrote to nor saw his son again.

CHAPTER 19

心如死灰

Xin Ru Si Hui

Hearts Reduced to Ashes

In 1965 while the Vietnam War was raging, Father moved his enamelware factory from Hong Kong to Port Harcourt in Nigeria, with the help of a generous subsidy from the Nigerian government. He went into partnership with his foreman, Mr Fong. It was a major undertaking, including the transport of numerous pieces of machinery and hundreds of skilled Hong Kong workers. Living quarters for the Chinese staff were built in Port Harcourt alongside new factory buildings and administrative offices.

That same year Gregory married Matilda, a Chinese girl whose parents were part of the wave of talent that flooded south from Shanghai in 1949. They appeared overjoyed when their daughter married into our family. At that time, Father was considered one of Hong Kong's moneyed élite and Gregory, the oldest son, his heir apparent.

Father made Gregory manager of the Nigerian factory. Soon after their wedding, the newlyweds moved into a bungalow next to the plant in Port Harcourt. Away from family and friends, deprived of social and cultural outlets, or even a decent grocery store, Gregory and Matilda found life in Africa harsh and lonely. James continued to work for Father in Hong Kong.

In October that year the Star Ferry Company applied for a

rise in the fare for the seven-minute ferry ride across Victoria Harbour, at that time the only means of transport between Hong Kong and Kowloon. Though the fare was modest, and had not risen since 1946, there were sit-in protests, demonstrations and rioting which resulted in one dead and many injured.

A collective shudder shook the colony. Suddenly every Hong Kong resident was asking himself, what if the Communists should march into Hong Kong? Where would he go without a valid foreign passport? Who would accept him?

In our family, Father had become a naturalized British citizen in 1955. Niang was a French citizen from birth. Lydia was in Tianjin and, in Father's view, 'lost to the Communists by her own choice'. Susan and I, being under twenty-one, had the right to British citizenship when Father was naturalized. My three brothers, however, remained Chinese citizens and this worried them.

In Port Harcourt, Matilda was now pregnant and Gregory wrote to Father suggesting that they should return to Canada where they had both been students and try to obtain Canadian citizenship. Moreover, it would be better for their baby to be born there. During his absence, Gregory suggested that James could take over temporarily in Nigeria.

A few days later, Gregory had second thoughts. Oscillating between his loathing for the Nigerian lifestyle, his fear of statelessness and his concern that James might usurp him, he wrote a follow-up letter asking to remain in Nigeria after all. It was too late. Father wrote to say that he had decided to replace him with James.

His letter continued, 'The Fongs have brought to my attention that you have been squandering the Company's money.' Gregory and Matilda were accused of spending extra money on food and drink, besides taking a nap once after lunch to escape the relentless heat of a West African afternoon. Father ended his letter by demanding a satisfactory explanation for such wasteful extravagance.

No word of thanks for all that Gregory had accomplished, only a trial without jury, dismissal and banishment from Father's enterprises. Gregory did as he was told but the injustice rankled, and it was hapless James who became the target of his frustrations.

In April 1966, an industrial dispute in Hong Kong led to a clash between strikers and strike breakers. Those were the months immediately preceding the Cultural Revolution which was shortly to convulse China. The chaos on the mainland eventually spilled over into Hong Kong and Portuguese Macau. Left-wing circles mounted full-scale riots against the police. Anti-colonial slogans were plastered everywhere. Loudspeakers blared forth pro-Communist propaganda. Bombs were found in the streets. Stones and insults were hurled at foreigners. In Macau, Portuguese troops opened fire and killed eight people.

Hong Kong residents became panic-stricken when reports reached them about the activities of the Red Guards and their reign of terror on the mainland. Most people were convinced that China was about to take over Hong Kong and drive out the British. Everyone wanted to sell. No one was buying. Properties were being dumped for a song. There was a run on the stock market and prices plunged.

Along with thousands of Hong Kong's most affluent residents, my parents fled. They went to Monte Carlo, where they bought a flat overlooking the Mediterranean. Father adopted a wait-and-see attitude, transferring most of his liquid assets to Swiss banks, but holding on to his Hong Kong properties. They returned in early 1967, after the Portuguese governor's startling offer to surrender Macau was dramatically refused by China. This gesture made it clear that both Hong Kong and Macau were to remain western-administered colonies for the time being. Prices remained depressed and did not begin to recover until the end of 1968.

Towards the tail-end of my stay in Hong Kong in 1964, James was seriously dating Louise Lam. Because of his good looks, family background and Cambridge education, James was an eligible bachelor, much fêted by mothers with marriageable daughters. From the beginning I suspected that Louise was special to James because, in her case, Niang was the matchmaker.

Louise's mother, Beverly, was a friend of Niang's. It was an unequal friendship, with Niang dominating her friend. Beverly was beautiful and presentable yet self-effacing. Burdened with five daughters and a difficult husband, she found it hard to cope. As soon as Louise was old enough, Beverly relegated her responsibilities to her eldest daughter. While Beverly played with her girlfriends, Louise organized her younger sisters' daily lives, packed their lunches, arbitrated quarrels and supervised their studies.

Niang encouraged the romance because it suited her to have James take a wife from a family which was neither so poor that the Yens would lose face nor so rich as to undermine Niang's power and control.

James took Louise out regularly once a week, neither more nor less. He was always gallant and courteous but never intimate. Once Gregory reported, somewhat gleefully, that he had spied Louise dancing with a handsome escort at a well-known night club the previous evening. James merely shrugged. Gregory accused him of feigning indifference but I felt that he was cautiously suspending commitment while awaiting instruction from above. I was certain that if our parents had raised any objections, Louise would have been dismissed at a moment's notice.

James and Louise were directed by Niang to have a simple wedding in America in 1966, far away from Father's many friends and business associates who were almost bankrupting themselves on similar occasions. 'Much more private and romantic', according to Niang. They married in Maryland at the home of Louise's uncle. James was ordered not to inform or invite any of his siblings.

Before their wedding, Father instructed James to buy one

of his newly constructed flats in Happy Valley, at full price, without regard to the shaky political situation or the deeply depressed state of the property market. For over two years, ever since being told to marry Louise, James had carefully saved up his miserable salary, dollar by dollar, in order to have a small nest egg when he settled down. Now he was commanded to exchange all his savings for one of Father's speculative units which no one wanted at the time. Resentfully, James complied. When Louise protested that Red Guard sympathizers were practically at their door and his total net worth might be confiscated in one swoop, James threw up his hands and said, '*Suan le!*' (Let it be). Of the twenty-four flats Father built that year, none of the others were sold.

After Gregory and Matilda left for Canada, James became Father's right-hand man. For the first ten years of his marriage he worked in Port Harcourt in Nigeria. Louise stayed in Hong Kong with their three children. James was allowed to come home to his family only twice a year: for six weeks from Christmas to Chinese New Year, and for eight weeks in the summer, to replace Father when he and Niang escaped the humid heat of Hong Kong for Monte Carlo.

Almost immediately after James's and Louise's marriage, Beverly and Niang had a falling-out. With her daughter safely settled, Beverly became more assertive and made it clear that she was no longer content to be Niang's handmaiden. Their friendship quickly deteriorated from casual nods at social functions to mutual non-recognition.

After Gregory's dismissal, James was appointed general manager of the Nigerian branch. Gregory was given 60,000 US dollars as severance pay to establish himself in Canada. He and Matilda bought a house in Vancouver and had two children. Matilda trained as a pharmacist and Gregory gained steady employment as an environmental engineer for the Canadian government. However, he still dreamed of returning to the fold, erroneously believing that Father would recall him back to Hong Kong.

From time to time, he would complain of 'usurpation' by James or 'sabotage' by Niang. His requests for business loans were invariably turned down. Though Father had a soft spot for his eldest son and looked forward eagerly to Gregory's letters and visits, he was convinced that Gregory was feckless and incapable. Niang called him *hu tu* (muddle-headed), lazy and extravagant. As the years passed, Gregory's dreams of building his own business empire faded. He became increasingly frugal, placing all his hopes in his two children and limiting his ambitions to waiting for his share of the inheritance.

After medical school, Edgar and I had no contact for many years. Edgar specialized in general surgery. Consultantships were hard to come by for Asians in Britain. Edgar initially moved to Canada in 1969 after receiving his FRCS. Well-paid jobs were scarce and opportunities limited. He decided to join me in California.

In October 1970, while Father and Niang were staying with me in Fountain Valley, a surprisingly civil letter suddenly arrived from Edgar. He expected me to help him get a job in the California hospital where I was working.

My initial reaction was one of pleasure and gratification. I had such hunger for affection from my family that even this sort of olive branch was welcome. I showed Edgar's letter to Father.

'Let me ask you this,' he said. 'Are you happy where you are? Do you get along with your colleagues and is there a bright future?'

'Yes. I love my job and can see myself staying there for the rest of my life.'

'In that case, Adeline,' Father continued, 'I strongly advise you not to answer this letter. We all know how Edgar feels towards you. I predict that nothing good will come of it. The more successful you are, the more jealous he will be. You have carved out an excellent career for yourself. Go ahead and pursue it. America is a big country. There is no need for Edgar to come over to your little corner. He has the rest of America in which to create a niche for himself.'

I looked over at Niang. She nodded. 'Always listen to your father, Adeline,' she said. 'He knows all of you like the back of his hand.'

I took Father's advice and did not answer Edgar's letter. I certainly wasn't going to disobey my father just to please Edgar. My silence was interpreted as a deliberate insult and he never forgave me.

He underwent further training in St Louis, Missouri, where he married an American girl of German descent who was twenty years younger. He moved from city to city in California searching for an ideal location to establish his practice. For a while, they settled in a small town in the San Joaquin Valley. Most of the population were born and bred in the immediate vicinity. They found life there unbearable. After a few years Edgar sold his practice and moved to Hong Kong while his wife attended college in America. They had no children and the marriage was an unhappy one.

In Hong Kong, Edgar worked at a private, missionary hospital. Though he was hard-working and conscientious, he had neither the talent nor the panache to join the ranks of the 'society surgeons'. He also didn't speak Cantonese. His fluency in both Mandarin and English proved to be no asset in Hong Kong. Behind his back the nurses whispered that Edgar was really a 大陸医生 *dai luk yee san* (doctor from mainland China). It was also difficult to break into the tightly knit circle of local physicians, most of whom had graduated from Hong Kong University with referral patterns entrenched since medical school. Outside doctors were seen as unwanted competition.

After two years he returned to the US and bought a practice in another small town in the San Joaquin Valley. His young wife graduated from college and they divorced. In 1986 Edgar married his office nurse, a white divorcée with two sons. They had three daughters and appeared to be well suited.

In 1964 Susan graduated from college in America and returned to Hong Kong. She worked as a schoolteacher at Maryknoll Convent School and lived at home with our parents. Pressure was soon brought upon her to marry. Susan was very beautiful and had a string of admirers. Niang questioned her every move, every letter, every phone call. There was a dentist whom Susan had been seeing for three months. Niang kept asking if he had proposed. Susan resented her interference and would say nothing. This infuriated Niang. She decided to find out for herself.

The next time the dentist telephoned, Niang intercepted the call. After reminding him that he had now been taking Susan out for three months, Niang curtly asked what his intentions were. When told he was not sure, Niang haughtily replied that Susan had many suitors and could not 'waste any more time' seeing him while he sat on the fence. In short, he should not call again until his mind clarified. With that, she hung up. Faced with such a formidable potential mother-in-law, the dentist never called again.

Susan, who had overheard the conversation, was livid. Mother and daughter had a horrendous argument. Susan packed her bags and threatened to move out. Niang took to her bed, while Father scurried from one to the other, attempting to placate them both. One night two weeks later, the sound of Father sleeplessly pacing the living-room awoke Susan. Next morning, the sight of Father's anxiety-ridden features finally broke Susan's resistance and she apologized to Niang.

The rapprochement was temporary. Both knew that it was only a matter of time before a new conflict erupted. Soon afterwards, Susan was introduced by Gregory to Tony Liang, graduate of Massachussetts Institute of Technology and son of a prominent Shanghai businessman who had prospered in Hong Kong. They decided to get married.

At Niang's insistence, the wedding was held in Honolulu and was small and private. Neither Father nor Niang attended and the rest of us weren't even informed. Susan received no dowry. She became Mrs Tony Liang and brought to her marriage precisely two suitcases of old clothes. Nor was she given any jewellery. Tony's mother, a kindly, old-fashioned woman, was astonished when she saw Susan's scant belongings. Placing her arms around Susan, Mrs Liang asked sympathetically, 'Are you sure you are Mrs Joseph Yen's real daughter and not her stepdaughter?' With that, old Mrs Liang took off her rings, bracelets and necklace and gave them to Susan.

Tony inherited his father's businesses and business acumen. The young Liangs rose to prominence among Hong Kong's high society. Susan's name and photograph were often in the *South China Morning Post* and *Hong Kong Standard*. In public, Niang was being constantly upstaged by her daughter.

She became very critical of Susan. Her jewellery was too gaudy, her gowns too revealing, her make-up vulgar, her taste atrocious. Susan was a selfish show-off and lacked filial piety. For Mother's Day, Susan bought her a box of chocolates. The box was too small and the chocolates too cheap.

Susan began to dread seeing Niang. She had a happy marriage and her in-laws were proud of her. Her home visits became more and more infrequent, reduced eventually to the obligatory Sunday night dinners. With Edgar and me in America, Gregory in Canada and James in Nigeria, Susan had become Niang's sole scapegoat.

Shirley Gam, a close childhood friend of Susan's, came to Hong Kong from New York for a whirlwind visit. The only convenient time for the two to get together was Sunday. Susan called Niang to excuse herself from Sunday night dinner. The conversation did not go well. Susan changed her plans and gave a Sunday luncheon instead for Shirley and their classmates. That evening, promptly at seven, she appeared as usual at Magnolia Mansions.

Niang was cold and abusive all through dinner, calling Susan ungrateful, unfilial and untrustworthy, and bringing up a litany of Susan's every transgression since early childhood. She accused Susan of conceit and shallowness. She started to cry over Franklin's death and said she wished it had been Susan instead. This was more than Susan could endure. She exploded, 'Franklin was a sadistic monster and I'm glad he's dead! Even though you're my mother, I think you are vicious and vindictive. You love no one but yourself. You certainly don't care for me, and you never have.'

Niang was completely taken aback. White with anger, she slapped Susan across her face. 'How *dare* you speak to me this way! I've spent so much money on you, sending you to the best schools and even to the United States! You are nothing, Susan! Nothing except for me! And to think you dare say such awful things when you owe me everything!' She slapped Susan again, this time with all her strength.

Susan calmly picked up her purse and took out her chequebook. 'How much do I owe you?' she asked. 'Whatever you think the sum is, let me write you a cheque for it. Remember, I am now a married woman, with a daughter of my own. Treat me as an adult, not your slave who owes you everything.'

Niang screamed, 'Get out! Get out now! Don't ever come back! As far as I am concerned, you are dead! Dead!'

Father rushed out of the front door after Susan. He looked shrunken and tired. As they waited for the lift in the hall he said sadly, 'You didn't have to make such a scene, Susan. Your mother was just offended that you didn't invite her to Shirley's luncheon. Why didn't you include her? She felt left out.'

Tears ran down Susan's swollen face. 'Daddy, you don't understand. You're too good for her.' As the lift door was closing, she added, 'Daddy, I'll phone you for lunch next week.'

They met for lunch at the main dining-room of the elegant Hong Kong Club, a short walk from Father's office at Swire House (then called Union House). They were given a quiet corner table, away from a musical group playing Beatles' tunes.

They sat in low armchairs across from each other and ordered drinks.

Father looked terrible. His features sagged as he gazed vacantly past Susan. One side of his face drooped slightly from an old bout with Bell's palsy, always more noticeable when he was under stress. When he blinked, only the eye on the healthy side would close, giving the appearance of a roguish wink.

'Has it been bad, Daddy?' Susan asked. 'Has Niang taken to her bed again?'

It was as if he had not heard. Robot-like, he reached into his inside pocket and took out a thin sheet of paper. Susan could see Niang's distinctive handwriting, almost identical to her own, through the transparent, pink, airmail stationery. Father put on his glasses and read off a list of rules and conditions to which Susan had to adhere if she wished to remain a member of the Yen family. Slowly, she shook her head.

Father removed his glasses. In a hollow voice quaking with emotion, he asked whether she was choosing never to see her parents again and to be disowned by them.

'What choice do I have, Daddy? Have a heart!'

Father placed some money on the table and stood up to leave.

'Daddy! You haven't touched your juice or eaten anything. Won't you be hungry?'

Staring vacantly ahead, he said, 'I shall give your mother your message.' He blinked nervously, his own spastic, winking blink which pierced Susan's heart. As he hurried down the stairs, past the lunch crowd waiting for tables, the white-uniformed bellboys and the captain in his peaked cap punctiliously opening the sparkling glass door, the musical group struck up a familiar Beatles' song, 'Let it be'.

That is how my half-sister Susan was disowned in 1973.

The four of us who were living abroad at this time received the following curt announcement by registered airmail.

Dear Gregory, Edgar, James and Adeline,

We wish to inform all four of you that Susan is no longer part of the Yen family. You are not to speak, write or associate with her ever again. Should you disobey our instructions, you too will be disinherited.

Affectionately yours.

Father and Mother

The letter did not include Lydia because she had already been disowned since 1951. James commented that it seemed to have been written by parents with 心如死灰 *xin ru si hui* (hearts reduced to ashes), completely devoid of human feelings.

None of us replied. We dealt with the matter in our separate ways. Gregory and I continued to see Susan on our visits to Hong Kong. Edgar ignored her from then on.

When James came home from Nigeria for his annual summer leave, Susan turned to him and Louise for solace. The two women were approximately the same age and held many interests in common. James found himself in an unenviable position. He could not afford a total break with our parents. He thought Susan had been treated unjustly but confessed that he and Louise were compelled to show at least token compliance with Niang's demands. She had categorically forbidden him and Louise to associate with Susan. Soon, all contact ceased. Even when Niang was away in Monte Carlo, Susan's invitations were refused, her phone calls unreturned, her letters unanswered. When the couples met by chance at social functions, James and Louise practised 'selectavision' and 'non-visualization', a common practice in Hong Kong's high society. The only time they communicated with Susan was when their youngest daughter was applying for admission to Maryknoll nine years later. A recommendation was needed from Susan as trustee of the renowned convent school.

Gregory kept his meetings with Susan a secret from James. Once James spotted Gregory riding in Susan's chauffeur-driven Mercedes on Queen's Road Central. Later when he met Gregory, he asked after Susan. But Gregory denied he had been with her, no doubt fearing that James might report back to Niang.

'This hurt my feelings very much,' James indignantly complained to me. 'Gregory doesn't trust me at all! What do *I* care if he sees or doesn't see Susan? That's his own business entirely. But does he really think I'd stoop so low as to tell tales behind his back to curry favour with Niang? Is Gregory's opinion of me really that deplorable?'

It was true that Gregory no longer trusted James. From time to time, Gregory would say to me, 'Susan and I both feel that James has changed. He is now entirely Niang's creature.'

Instinctively, I would leap to the defence of my 三哥 *San ge* (Third Elder Brother). 'I don't think so, Gregory. He has such a good heart. He is just like a reincarnated Ye Ye.'

'Don't trust him so much. Don't trust *anyone* so much. You'll get hurt.'

I would shake my head and laugh. 'One day, when Niang is gone,' I told Gregory, 'you'll see the real James emerge, 一塵不染 *yi chun bu ran* (not contaminated by a single particle of dust). Pure as the lily's innermost petal.'

Many of James's contemporaries from universities in England had returned to Hong Kong. Civil engineers and architects were especially in demand as skyscrapers mushroomed across every inch of available land. Residents of older highrises on slopes above the harbour were dismayed to find their peerless view of the bay blocked by newer and taller structures lower down the hillside. Towering office complexes were constructed on land newly reclaimed from the sea. Jobs were plentiful, especially for bilingual male graduates from prestigious western universities. Hong Kong gradually burgeoned into one of the world's major trade centres with the highest population density in the history of mankind: a whopping 165,000 people per square kilometre. Many of our fellow students in England founded companies employing hundreds, even thousands, of workers. It was exhilarating to see the rapid expansion of their enterprises. Manufactured goods stamped 'Made in Hong Kong' were exported to every corner of the world. While all this was happening it seemed incredible that James, the brilliant Cambridge-trained civil engineer, could remain a puppet blindly carrying out his parents' orders.

Niang interfered in every facet of their lives. She objected to the children's piano lessons, ordered Louise to quit painting and take up cooking, criticized her clothing and even scolded her for spending too much time visiting her own mother. Since Louise dared not stand up to Niang, all she could do was to practise little deceptions, sometimes with the connivance of her children.

Niang was often annoyed at Louise and would ignore her for months on end. At Sunday evening dinners, she would belittle her to James, who remained seemingly unperturbed while his wife was being systematically insulted. Father usually kept quiet, offering no opinion except on financial matters.

James never refused food proffered by Niang, no matter how much he had already eaten or how little he liked the dish. It became a symbol of his subservience. He was the garbage can, accepting all that Niang discarded. All she had to do was glance at the leftovers on his children's plates, and James would lean over and plop them in his mouth.

The children, normally vivacious and high-spirited, were cowed into timid silence. Niang hated noisy children. They loathed going to 'Grandma's' where they were not allowed to be themselves.

When Father first became ill in 1976, James, then forty-two years old, was finally permitted by Niang to leave Nigeria and make Hong Kong his year-round residence. However, every major decision had to be approved by Niang, who took credit for every success and blamed James for each failure.

On my frequent visits back to Hong Kong, James and Louise filled me with tales of their unhappy lives. Louise confided that she found Niang's insults and constant meddling insufferable.

Meanwhile, Niang complained bitterly about Louise, ending invariably with the lament that, regrettably, she was the one responsible for their union.

Repeatedly over the years, I advised James to take his family to the US and make their own way there. It was clear to me that their only chance of happiness was to escape from Niang's clutches. 'Come to Huntington Beach and live with us,' I would urge. 'You are so smart, James. Probably the smartest member of our entire family. You can do anything. We could all go into business together and have some fun. Share and share alike. It's not so bad out there. Nothing is as bad as life under Niang's thumb. Surely you know that, James!'

'We're like prisoners over here,' Louise would lament. 'I feel as if I am in a straitjacket! I can't breathe! Let's get away from her, James. I am willing to do anything, live anywhere. I don't need very much.'

'I know,' James would reply, hanging his head and pouring himself another generous helping of whisky, 'but not yet.'

CHAPTER 20

腹中鱗甲

Fu Zhong Lin Jia
Scales and Shells in the Belly

In Shanghai, Aunt Baba continued working at the Women's Bank. She stayed on in the Avenue Joffre house with Miss Chien and two maids. Miss Chien, Franklin's nanny, was fearful of dismissal and did everything to please my aunt. She rose at dawn to wax the parquet floors and brush the carpets. She persuaded my aunt to dispense with one of the maids and undertook the most unpleasant tasks such as scouring the toilets and scrubbing the stove. She washed and ironed all of my aunt's clothes and laundered the drapes. Every evening, my aunt came home to a sparkling house and a tasty meal, prepared personally by Miss Chien. As winter approached, she knitted thick and colourful cardigans for my aunt.

After Father sold his Buick in 1948, the garage was converted into a storage room. Because times were uncertain, my aunt kept a supply of basic commodities on hand: sacks of rice, jars of oil, dried vegetables, salted fish, soya sauce. Besides food, the garage contained many cartons of silk cotton and Australian wool. Decades ago, Ye Ye had purchased some shares in a Shanghai silk factory. Over the years, this well-run firm prospered, exporting silk cotton and importing Australian wool. Instead of paying dividends in cash, they paid their shareholders surplus bolts of silk cotton and skeins of wool. The cotton was of the finest quality, very light and fluffy, and was used as padding in quilts, comforters, gowns and jackets. However, towards the end of 1951, the factory owner was targeted during the 三反五反 *San fan - wu fan* (Three Antis - Five Antis) campaigns. His factory was undergoing reorganization and no more dividends were issued. Silk cotton became scarce and valuable.

三反五反 *San fan - wu fan* (Three Antis - Five Antis) were two overlapping sister movements launched by the Communist government in 1951. The three antis were against waste, corruption and bureaucracy carried out by Communist Party members. The five antis were aimed at their counterparts outside the party who had profited through bribery, fraud, theft, tax evasion and inside information. The two groups were frequently linked.

About this time, my aunt was transferred to work at a branch near the Cathay Cinema, two tram stops away from home. Many customers were locals known personally to her and one of them was a tailor named Yeh. Tailor Yeh owned a small shop next to the bank and often dropped in for a chat when business was slow. One day he asked Aunt Baba to deliver a padded jacket he had just finished for someone living in the same lane. His customer was Miss Chien.

The moment my aunt saw the jacket, she knew that Miss Chien was dishonest and had 腹中鱗甲 *fu zhong lin jia* (scales and shells in her belly). As was customary, Tailor Yeh had placed all the unused cotton with other leftover material in a paper bag with the jacket. Silk cotton of such superior quality was unavailable anywhere in Shanghai. Miss Chien had been stealing from the garage.

That evening, Aunt Baba asked her to return the household keys and discovered that the former nanny had been pilfering food and wool as well. She reported the theft to Father and asked him to dismiss her, adding that she could no longer share the house with someone so untrustworthy.

Father's reply made her cringe. His orders were that Miss Chien was not to be dismissed, not ever. She was to go on living in the house with my aunt and continue drawing her salary as well as a bonus at Chinese New Year. My aunt need not be concerned with the 'missing' items. The Yen family could well afford to absorb the loss. Clearly Father had his own secret agenda.

Aunt Baba and Miss Chien stopped speaking to each other. Miss Chien continued to knit with the wool she had squirrelled away, shamelessly selling the sweaters and even taking orders. Her abundant supply of imported wool was the envy of the neighbourhood. During endless evening meetings held to discuss the Three Antis – Five Antis campaigns, many eyes in their *hu kou* (residence unit) were focused on the busy knitting needles of Miss Chien while party hopefuls babbled away about corruption and bribery.

She no longer addressed my aunt as Miss Yen, but referred to her as that 'upstairs character'. She started entertaining her own family members in the parlour downstairs, conferring with the maid, Ah Song, about the menu. She gossiped with the neighbours and whispered that her Hong Kong employers had instructed her to 'guard and write reports on' my aunt, intimating mental imbalance, amoral dalliance or worse.

The atmosphere at home became intolerable to Aunt Baba. Ah Song began to adopt shades of Miss Chien's airy attitude. One morning, when Ah Song was being particularly impertinent, Aunt Baba fired her on the spot in a fit of anger. The maid went crying to Miss Chien but there was nothing they could do.

Aunt Baba engaged a new maid, Ah Yee, who worked only for her. She installed cooking facilities in the spare room on the second floor, eating her meals there privately. The dismissal of Ah Song seemed to deflate Miss Chien's arrogance somewhat. An unspoken semi-truce followed. Miss Chien's previous overt hostility was replaced by an icy politeness. She continued to file her weekly 'secret progress reports' to Father.

In the winter of 1951, during a routine audit of Grand Aunt's Women's Bank, an inventory was taken of all the commodities stored at the bank's giant depository. In the process, Aunt Baba received a letter from the Bank Auditing Authority addressed to Wang Jie-xiang, my grandmother, who had died in Tianjin in 1943.

For various reasons in the 1940s, Father often purchased commodities and property in the maiden name of his deceased mother, Wang Jie-xiang. Initially, it may have suited his purpose to use her name because the Japanese were after him. Father soon discovered that there were advantages in having a 'ghost' as the registered owner of tangible assets. It was impossible to sue, contact, threaten, blackmail or kidnap a ghost. This was common practice during the lawless days of the 1940s.

Third Uncle, the third and youngest brother of my own dead mother, had been apprenticed to my father as a teenager. Father gave him the English name Frederick and left him in charge in Shanghai after his own departure for Hong Kong.

At first, it was business as usual after the Communist takeover. Some time in 1949, probably under orders from Father, who was anticipating a price rise in certain commodities, Uncle Frederick purchased a few hundred cases of white beeswax in the name of Wang Jie-xiang and stored it in the depository of Grand Aunt's bank. The price of beeswax continued to fall. Reluctant to sell on the downward spiral, he decided to wait. Two years later, as the political climate worsened, my uncle accompanied my brother James to Hong Kong with the beeswax still unsold.

Two months after receiving the notice from the Bank Auditing Authority, Aunt Baba was summoned by the administrator of her *dan wei* (work unit). Registration in a *dan wei* was mandatory. The vast majority of workers remained in one *dan wei* for life as it was extremely difficult to transfer from one *dan wei* to another. At the meeting. she was surprised that the head of her *hu kou* (residence unit) was also present. *Hu kous* were set up initially in the spirit of neighbourhood committees, homeowners' associations where meetings were held and grievances aired. By 1951, they had become powerful tools of government control. Eventually, registration at a *hu kou* became compulsory and when food rationing was instituted, only registered dwellers were issued food coupons. Between the *dan wei* and the *hu kou*, every inhabitant in urban Shanghai was accounted for. The two committees intruded into every aspect of a citizen's private life. Nothing was too trivial.

My aunt was asked who Wang Jie-xiang was. Where could she be reached? Why was she not registered? Although the committee were cordial, my aunt could see from the thick dossier in front of them that they meant business. She reported truthfully the bare facts as she knew them and was told to return in a week with more details. Hastily, she consulted Grand Aunt, who was in the throes of a struggle herself. My aunt was referred to Mr Nee, a fellow employee, whose full-time job was to deal with government agencies. Tall, suave and personable, he and his wife became friends with my aunt, on whose behalf Mr Nee underwent many interrogations. They met frequently to discuss developments as the case progressed. Mr Nee's arrival and departure times were openly recorded by Miss Chien and duly reported to my parents. After twenty-eight months of painstaking investigation, Mr Nee was finally successful in winding up the beeswax affair. Everything was blamed on my conveniently absent Uncle Frederick. The beeswax was confiscated and my aunt reprimanded but not punished. This was no mean feat. Nobody wanted to take responsibility and Mr Nee had been passed from one department to another like a ping-pong ball. On occasions, he felt completely misunderstood, 'rather like a chicken talking to a duck'.

Aunt Baba's favourite pastime, playing mah-jong, was declared decadent. One of her friends had a basement at home and, at first, Aunt Baba's mah-jong group gathered there in secret to play 'soundless' mah-jong at night behind locked doors. To muffle the noise, they covered each tablet with cushioned slipovers. To avoid detection, they placed a lookout at the door. However, the risks were great and their courage limited. They soon gave up and switched to bridge because card-games remained acceptable.

As campaign followed campaign, the situation at the Women's Bank began to worsen. The Thought Reform Movement was aimed at professors and the Land Reform Movement was against landowners in the countryside. Then came the Three Antis (against party members) and Five Antis (against capitalists such as merchants and bankers).

In 1952, struggle meetings were started against my Grand Aunt to 'assist her in interpreting her past waywardness' and 'give her the opportunity to correct her mistakes'. Many of her former employees denounced her. Some went along to save their own skins. Her guilty verdict was a foregone conclusion. My Grand Aunt was fined a large sum of money in 1953 and forced to resign from all her duties at the Women's Bank but allowed to continue living in her sixth-floor penthouse apartment. Her privileges were stripped away one by one. They took away her chauffeur, car, cook and even the use of the lift to her penthouse. She now began living like a hermit under house arrest. Walking up and down the five flights of stairs caused her acute chest pains. Even so, almost every day, she was required to climb those stairs to attend all the meetings organized by her *hu kou* and former *dan wei*.

Over the years there followed many other campaigns. All of them adopted the same pattern. First there were tremendous propaganda drives in the newspapers, on radio broadcasts and on wall posters to explain which group was being targeted. Then came processions with drums and gongs, military music and uplifting speeches from loudspeakers. Endless compulsory meetings followed, during which relatives, friends, workmates and neighbours were encouraged to spy and inform on each other, sometimes anonymously by dropping names into suggestion boxes.

Aunt Baba had always avoided the limelight and disliked 出鋒頭 *chu feng tou* (emerging at the head of the vanguard).

During these meetings, she sat in an unobtrusive corner: a meek, harmless, quiet, middle-aged spinster who went along with the majority and voiced no opinions of her own. When Grand Aunt was being struggled against, Aunt Baba never uttered a word in her defence. She knew this was the only way to survive.

In 1955 there came the Rural Co-operative Movement, when rich peasants were denounced. Soon afterwards, there was the Elimination of Hidden Counter-Revolutionaries campaign. All industries and businesses still in private hands were being nationalized. 'Deserving' owners were given an annual 7 per cent of the net worth of their businesses for ten years as indemnification. The problem was deciding who 'deserved' and who did not.

In 1956, the campaign known as Let 100 Flowers Blossom urged everyone to voice their criticism of the government. This movement was referred to as 'freedom of speech'. A year later, during the Anti-Rightist campaign, those who had spoken the loudest against the regime during the previous year received their punishment for 'daring to release their stinking farts'. The victims were mostly teachers, artists and scientists.

1958 was the 'Great Leap Forward' when Mao Zedong decided to increase China's steel production and turn the country into a world-class industrial power overnight. The campaign was a failure and led to economic collapse and widespread famine. Rice, oil, tofu and meat were all rationed; so were cloth, knitting wool, sewing thread, cotton padding and quilts. Government control tightened. My aunt was suddenly informed that all Father's rental properties in Shanghai were being confiscated. She had long been expecting this and was almost grateful when the authorities relieved her of the responsibility.

Aunt Baba was often assigned to work at banks far from home. This was one method of cross-checking to prevent embezzlement. Getting to work entailed many transfers in crowded buses. She was required to eat her meals alone and attend *dan wei* meetings where she knew no one. Her stomach gave her pains and she started vomiting blood. Through 'back door connections', because 'the front door was always closed', she was seen by a prominent surgeon on his day off. He diagnosed a duodenal ulcer, prescribed some very effective medicines and advised her to retire.

She recovered but was badly shaken. Because of widespread poverty and famine, the government started to encourage the sale of burial plots to overseas Chinese. Aunt Baba wrote to Father about her retirement and asked him to remit to her 400 yuan a month for her support. She also requested that he purchase a plot in a Buddhist cemetery outside Beijing where the *feng shui* (wind and water, or geomancy) was auspicious.

Father agreed and sent Ye Ye's ashes from Hong Kong to be buried next to Grandmother. My aunt travelled to Tianjin to arrange for their reburial. This visit gave her the opportunity to visit my eldest sister Lydia for the first time since liberation.

In 1958, Lydia and her family were still living in Father's house at 40 Shandong Road. Her husband Samuel taught at the University of Tianjin and Lydia looked after their two children at home.

Seventy-two-year-old Aunt Lao Lao also lived with them. The sister of Niang's deceased mother, she was a nice, simple spinster who could neither read nor write. Her feet were unbound and she spoke Mandarin with a thick, almost unintelligible Shandong accent.

It took Aunt Baba only a few days to transfer my grandmother's body to the new burial plot, but she had time to observe that Lydia was a deeply unhappy woman. My eldest sister was resentful that her siblings were all in England attending university while she was mired in a loveless marriage in Communist China. She vented her frustration on Samuel and would hurl insults at him. He never retaliated but would rush out of the house in the midst of a tirade, with Lydia screaming 'turtle egg', 'I hate you', 'get out' and 'drop dead'.

Worse was the treatment they accorded Aunt Lao Lao. She and a maid did most of the housework, hurrying from task to task and hardly daring to say a word. She suffered from arthritis, chest pains and weak eyesight. Lydia bullied her whenever the mood suited her, pounding her hand on the table and shouting abuse at the top of her voice. On several occasions she even hit Aunt Lao Lao. Samuel abetted his wife, making remarks such as 'What is a Prosperi doing in our Yen family home?', forgetting that he was no more a Yen than Aunt Lao Lao.

My aunt tried in vain to reason with Lydia. But she was devoured by envy and bitterness. She begged my aunt to write to Father on her behalf and appeal for his assistance. On her return to Shanghai, my aunt did write such a letter but never received a reply.

The years between 1959 and 1966 were relatively peaceful for Aunt Baba. Food shortages gradually eased and, by the middle of 1963, most items were available. Political meetings became less frequent. In the mornings, she no longer had to rush off to fight for a place in the bus but could luxuriate in bed with the *People's Daily* and hot tea. Many of her friends also retired. A group of them met regularly to play bridge. They even started to pool their ration cards and have dinner parties again.

In the summer of 1966, gangs of local Red Guards roamed the streets of Shanghai looking for trouble. They changed street names: the Bund was renamed Revolution Street; smashed shop windows; looted homes; and assaulted passersby. Aunt Baba no longer dared go out. The usual processions, parades and newspaper propaganda signalled yet another major political purge. The walls in Aunt Baba's lane were plastered with posters denouncing 'enemies of the Cultural Revolution'. *Hu kou* meetings were frenzied and sometimes lasted all day and all night. At first the victims appeared to be school teachers and high-ranking party members.

On 14 September 1966, twenty-five Red Guards banged on

the door of Aunt Baba's house. They were boys and girls in their teens accompanied by a few men in their twenties. Some of the children attended middle schools near by and knew my aunt. They ordered everyone to kneel on the floor. Miss Chien kowtowed and said that she was Aunt Baba's close friend. They slapped her face so hard that two of her teeth were knocked out. Then they shouted at her to admit her true status. When she said 'servant', they sneered and called her a liar but stopped beating her. Instead, they turned on my aunt, the mistress of the house. They broke her dentures, pulled her hair, whipped her with their belts, kicked her until she fell, then punched her injured back.

They built a fire in the garden, burnt all the books, photograph albums and paintings until all that remained was a pile of ashes on the lawn, dampened by a sudden September downpour. They made her remove the key around her neck to open her safe, but were furious to find no money or jewellery, only Ye Ye's letters and my primary school report cards and commendations. Before they left, they smashed the antiques, toppled the furniture, tore up Aunt Baba's treasured letters and my old report cards, broke the utensils, ripped the curtains, slashed the mattresses and cut up the clothes. Miss Chien was ordered to move out within twenty-four hours.

'But where shall I go?' Miss Chien pleaded. 'I've lived here for twenty-two years, before most of you were born. Surely I am entitled to have one of the rooms here until I die?'

'Fuck your mother! Get out of here, you stupid, ignorant old bag! Where do you come from originally?'

'I was born in Hangzhou.'

'Go back to Hangzhou tomorrow! You don't belong in Shanghai and you don't belong in this house!'

Afterwards, for the first time in fifteen years, Miss Chien spoke to Aunt Baba in a civil tone. She expressed her sorrow at the hooliganism, helped bandage my aunt's scalp where it had been pierced by broken glass and asked to borrow some suitcases. My aunt gave her an old valise and they parted amicably.

A week later, Aunt Baba was made to move into a single room at a neighbour's house immediately behind her garden. Meanwhile, many other families moved into her house which was designated off-limits to her. Her bank account was frozen and mail from Father not delivered. She was allotted fifteen yuan per month by the government for living expenses and instructed to wear a piece of black cloth on her chest with the characters 黑六類 *hei liu lei* (six black categories) clearly labelled. She was now a despised 'black'. The blacks were the capitalist, landlord, rightist, rich peasant, counter-revolutionary and criminal element. They were given the most menial jobs and were invariably the last to be served in food lines and other queues, especially when there were shortages. Some were left to suffer and even die while lying on hospital floors waiting for medical attention.

All schools were closed. Buses and trains were crammed with Red Guards who travelled for free all over China. Mail was not delivered and private telephones were disconnected. Buddhist temples and Christian churches were destroyed. Books were burnt. Many city dwellers were sent off to the countryside to 'reform their thoughts through hard labour and learn from the peasants'.

Though labelled a black, my aunt was not sent away. She thought Shanghai was like a city gone mad but put it all down to the Revolution. She believed that Mao Zedong and Zhou Enlai and the rest of the *da ren* (big people) were carrying out a mysterious masterplan for the deliverance of China.

Conditions did not improve until the winter of 1971. Rumours were rife that Lin Biao, defence minister and heir apparent to Mao Zedong, had died that October. Lin was a Communist general whose armies had been instrumental in the liberation of Manchuria, Beijing and Tianjin. He rose to become second in command during the Cultural Revolution when many high-ranking Communist Party members were purged. The official story of his death was that Lin tried to assassinate Mao but failed. He then attempted to flee to Russia with his wife and son in a plane which crashed in Mongolia. After Lin's death, political meetings at Aunt Baba's *hu kou* became significantly less strident. One evening, everyone was told to tear out and destroy the first two pages of Mao's *Little Red Book* which contained Lin Biao's foreword.

After President Nixon's recognition of China, life of the ordinary Chinese improved dramatically; 1972 was a watershed year. Food was more plentiful and political meetings less frequent. Bank accounts were unfrozen and Father's monthly remittance was again allowed into Shanghai.

Aunt Baba wrote begging Father to send Grand Aunt a regular allowance. Like everyone else, she had been driven out of her penthouse home by the Red Guards in 1966. Her bank deposits were permanently frozen and non-transferable. Eking out an existence on the fifteen yuan per month allowed by the government, she was often cold and hungry. After receiving Aunt Baba's letter, Father sent money to Grand Aunt regularly until she died from pneumonia three years later.

In 1974 the Criticize Lin Biao campaign was followed by the Criticize Confucius campaign. Confucius was a nickname for Premier Zhou Enlai, coined by Madame Mao. My aunt's *hu kou* attempted to whip up enthusiasm during meetings. Attendance was supposedly compulsory, but many pleaded illness and were absent. People were simply fed up with these endless campaigns.

On 7 April 1976, there was a mass display of public sentiment in Tiananmen Square to commemorate the dead Zhou Enlai. This was a communal gesture of support for Deng Xiaoping (Zhou Enlai's protégé) and covert criticism of Madame Mao. Police and armed soldiers used batons to disperse the crowds. Thousands of unarmed demonstrators were beaten. A few were injured and some were arrested. This was the First Tiananmen Incident.

In July 1976, a major earthquake registering 8.0 on the Richter Scale shook Tangshan, an industrial city not far from Tianjin. Over one million people died. Everywhere in China, people whispered that the quake was an omen and predicted the end of Mao Zedong. Mao passed away two months later.

On 8 October 1976, a *hu kou* meeting was called after supper in Aunt Baba's lane to announce the arrest of the 'Gang of Four', a term originally coined by Mao Zedong himself to describe Madame Mao and three of her henchmen from Shanghai, Yao Wenyuan, Zhang Chunqiao and Wang Hong-wen, who had grouped themselves together to spearhead the Cultural Revolution. Their power had been absolute because they had had the full support of Mao until his death.

Next day, there was a parade commemorating the downfall of Madame Mao. My aunt pleaded illness and did not attend. Deng Xiaoping was rehabilitated and appointed vice premier in 1977. China's doors started to open to the outside world, and the age of reform began.

CHAPTER 21

天作之合

Tian Zuo Zhi He
Heaven-Made Union

My career continued to flourish after the finalization of my divorce in 1971. Despite the dire predictions of older doctors who warned that within five years at most private practice would be a thing of the past, Medicare legislation went on creating something of an unexpected bonanza for physicians like myself. As an anaesthesiologist, my fees were based on a scale published by the American Society of Anaesthesiology. Three years after I started practice, these standard rates had already risen by 20 per cent. However, most patients were oblivious of this steep increase because they were not out of pocket. Health-related charges were automatically reimbursed by Medicare and other insurance companies. In fact, it was considered somewhat vulgar to discuss fees with the doctor.

In the early 1970s, racial and gender discrimination was still prevalent. The easy camaraderie prevailing in the operating room evaporated at the completion of surgical procedures. There was an unspoken pecking order of seating arrangements at lunch among my fellow physicians. At the top were the white male 'primary producers' in prestigious surgical specialities. They were followed by the internists. Next came the general practitioners. Last on the list were the hospital-based physicians: the radiologists, pathologists and anaesthesiologists – especially non-white, female ones like me. Apart from colour, we were shunned because we did not bring in patients ourselves but, like vultures, lived off the patients generated by other doctors. We were also resented because being hospital-based and not having to rent office space or hire nursing staff, we had low overheads. Since a physician's number of admissions to the hospital and referral pattern determined the degree of attention and regard accorded by his colleagues, it was safe for our peers to ignore us and target those in a position to send over income-producing referrals. This attitude was mirrored from the board of directors all the way down to the orderlies.

Women physicians were still comparatively rare in the late sixties and early seventies. I became friendly with Alcenith Crawford, a divorced ophthalmologist. Thirty years older than I, Alcenith took me under her wing. At a time when it was difficult for even the most privileged of women to qualify as doctors, Alcenith had put herself through medical school by loans and outside jobs. There were only two other women doctors on the staff at West Anaheim Community Hospital where I worked. They used to sit in the doctors' dining-room and complain about their husbands. Actually, all four of us had troubled private lives.

Alcenith explained it this way. 'We women doctors have unhappy marriages because in our minds we are the superstars of our families. Having survived the hardship of medical school, we expect to reap our rewards at home. We had to assert ourselves against all odds and when we finally graduate there are few shrinking violets amongst us. It takes a special man to be able to cope. Men like to feel important and be the undisputed head of the family. A man does not enjoy waiting for his wife while she performs life-saving operations. He expects her and their children to revolve around his needs, not the other way. But we have become accustomed to giving orders in hospitals and having them obeyed. Once home, it's difficult to adjust. Moreover, we often earn more than our husbands. It takes a generous and exceptional man to forgive all that.'

Success in my career could not compensate for the collapse

of my marriage. In my mind, I equated divorce with deep, dark failure. In front of my colleagues, I maintained the façade of the self-sufficient female doctor but inside there was an aching void. My friend Alcenith understood the emptiness of my life when she observed that I was running like a well-oiled machine with a missing part. She decided to supply the absent component and arranged a blind date for me. He was Professor Robert Mah, her son's Chinese-American friend who taught at UCLA. We were to meet in front of the School of Public Health.

It was a typical southern California spring afternoon in 1972: hot, sunny and smoggy. Even though I followed the detailed directions that Professor Mah had given over the telephone, I got lost. When I asked the attendant at the filling station how I could get to UCLA, I was told that the best way was to study hard!

When I arrived, thirty minutes late, I saw him standing on the steps, scanning the road. I was thrilled to note that he was rather handsome and quite tall, with thick, glossy, black hair and a boyish air. He smiled and said, 'Yes, you've come to the right place. I'm Bob.'

Bob was born in California and had never set foot in China. Originally from Toishan village in Guangdong Province, his parents emigrated to San Francisco in 1906. Uneducated and without special skills, they eked out a living in the restaurant trade in Fresno, then a small farming community of about 30,000 people in the San Joaquin Valley. Converted to Catholicism, they had eight children (six boys and two girls) of whom Bob was the youngest. When he was three, his father died of a heart attack, leaving his widow with very little money and many offspring, the oldest of whom was only seventeen. With so many mouths to feed, Bob's mother had no alternative but to go on welfare.

When Pearl Harbor was attacked, nine-year-old Bob was told to wear a little badge in class declaring 'I am Chinese' to distinguish him from his Japanese schoolfriends and avoid being branded as the 'enemy'. Even at that age he was baffled and angered to see Japanese children taunted and interned. His own family had to combat racial prejudice as well as poverty. The children developed a fierce loyalty to each other and to their widowed mother. She encouraged them to participate in the war effort and be good Americans. Two of Bob's older brothers enlisted. Nineteen-year-old Ed, who had dropped out of Stanford University to serve his country, was sent to fight in Germany. Stranded in a shack with nine wounded soldiers, he single-handedly held off a murderous German counter-attack. He was awarded the Bronze Star for bravery and heroic achievement.

Another brother, Earl, was rejected by the army because of a deformity of his hand. He put himself through engineering school at Fresno State College while working full-time as a sheet metal worker at Rohr Industries. As soon as it became economically feasible, their mother directed Earl to write to the Welfare Department and relinquish their benefits. To supplement their meagre income, she planted Chinese vegetables in the garden of their West Fresno home, donating part of the proceeds towards the war effort. Her health was frail and she suffered a massive stroke soon after the war ended, leaving her crippled and aphasic.

The older children now jointly took on the responsibility of looking after their mother and the two youngest brothers. Bob's eldest sister stayed at home to give constant care to their mother. His other sister, only a high school sophomore, volunteered to do the domestic and cooking chores. Besides attending college and working at his demanding job as an engineer, Bob's brother Earl found time to care for Bob, correct his homework, pack his lunches and wake him so that he would catch the school bus. The others pooled their paycheques towards the household expenses and Bob's college education. With their assistance, Bob graduated with a Ph.D. in microbiology and became a professor. I could not help but compare their love and mutual support to the strife and jealousy in my own family. While his family had helped Bob fulfil his ambition, I felt that whatever I had accomplished was achieved in spite of mine. Whereas he had had an abundance of love, I was starved of it.

When Bob invited me to dinner at his home I found that he had been preparing for two days in advance. He chopped and cleaned the fresh vegetables; and had trimmed off every bit of fat from the pork and chicken marinating in separate bowls. Much thought went into the choice of wines to accompany the different dishes. As we shared this meal prepared with so much love I dared to hope that we were destined for each other. Were the gods smiling on me at last? Was this the 天作之合 *tian zuo zhi he* (heaven-made union) celebrated by the T'ang poets?

That evening I told him about my childhood. A floodgate opened and I could not stop. As he sat holding my hand, I poured out my pain and yearning. I was the ostracized outsider longing for acceptance; the ugly duckling hankering to return as the beautiful swan; the despised and unwanted Chinese daughter obsessed with my quest to make my parents proud of me on some level. Surely some day, if I tried hard enough to help them in dire need, they would love me.

Since I was working as hard as possible and taking emergency calls three out of four nights, I didn't have time to see Bob except on my rare evenings off. Not infrequently, my pager would go off at the most inopportune moments, summoning me to the operating room as if I was being pulled on a leash. Operations often lasted well into the night. But, no matter what time I returned home, I would find dinner cooked and Bob waiting for me. In my whole life, I had never encountered anyone so caring or felt so cherished. He was good not only to me, but also to my son, taking him to basketball games and attending his school functions even when I was away on emergencies. Most of all, he provided the stability I had always yearned for. Bob was the only man I knew who professed his love, not by words, but by his every action. Towards the end of that year, for his birthday, I sent him a card. 'The day you were born was the luckiest day in my life. Your love shields me from life's worst blows. With you, I feel completely safe. Thank you for always being there for me.'

With trepidation I wrote to my parents, asking their permission to marry Bob. I received a short note enclosed with their annual Christmas card. 'I am glad you found a moment to write to us before your wedding,' Father wrote, reminding me of my negligence the first time around. 'Bob sounds like a nice man employed in a suitable profession. However, why is he still single at this advanced age? Does he have any homosexual tendencies? Be sure to retain all your properties in your own name.'

We were married soon afterwards. Our daughter, Ann, was born two years later. I felt that I had come home at last. It took me a long time to accept that no one was going to rob me of my happiness.

We moved into a new home in Huntington Beach. The house sat on a small waterfront plot. Its front door led into an arching stairway suspended over an atrium filled with bamboo, palm, philodendrone, bromeliads and a tall schefflera tree. It was a large house with space and light and we fell in love with it at first sight.

CHAPTER 22

四面楚歌

Si Mian Chu Ge
Besieged by Hostile Forces on All Sides

Through the sixties and early seventies Father's businesses,
remained enormously profitable. He developed several blocks
of apartment complexes and some large residential houses in
Hong Kong that he successfully sold. His industrial building in
Cha Wan, erected on land purchased at fire sale prices during
the Hong Kong riots in 1966, was fully leased out. He owned
two tons of gold safely stored away in Swiss bank vaults.

That summer of 1976, Father and Niang flew to Monte
Carlo as usual to escape the heat. During his regular private
French lessons, Father participated less and less in spite of his
tutor's exhortations, refusing to repeat French phrases after
her. The sessions deteriorated into long, expensive daily tête-à-
têtes between Niang and the French tutor, with Father staring
vacantly at his *Beginner's French, Part 1*.

On social occasions, he became more and more withdrawn.
During the annual Red Cross Ball hosted by Princess Grace, he
refused to dance with anyone. At home, he sat for hours reading, or pretending to read, the *Wall Street Journal* and the
International Herald Tribune. More often than not he dozed
off.

Once, when driving along the winding roads of Monaco, he
scraped the side of his Mercedes. When Niang questioned him
about the dents he claimed that the mountainside had never

been there before. As she ranted and raved about his *hu tu* (confusion), she was surprised to see that he had nodded off in the midst of her spirited harangue.

On his return to Hong Kong he stopped dyeing his hair. He had difficulty signing his name and practised for hours behind closed doors, trying to keep a steady hand. After his death, I found a stack of notebooks hidden underneath some towels. Every page was diligently filled with his signature. As I read his name over and over, I sensed his bewilderment and shame.

In the mornings he got up earlier and earlier. On golfing days he would summon his chauffeur at four to drive him to the club at Stanley. They would arrive in pitch darkness and snooze in the car, waiting for the gates to open at six.

In early 1977 I received a letter from Niang. A prominent Hong Kong physician had advised Father to go to Stanford University for medical consultation. I invited them to stay with us in our new home. Though I was deeply concerned about Father, I was thrilled that they had turned to me for assistance.

It was thus with a combination of dread and anticipation that Bob and I, both having taken the day off work, drove to the airport to meet them. I wept when I saw my Father, looking so frail and feeble, his hair completely white. There was a vacant, scared look in his eyes. We greeted each other formally with a handshake.

Bob had met my parents for the first time on a two-day visit to Monte Carlo three years earlier and was shocked at so drastic a change in their appearance. Though immaculately dressed in a mauve cashmere coat and wearing pearls and diamonds, Niang looked much older than her fifty-six years. Our housekeeper Ginger opened the front door when we arrived. Framed against the backdrop of tall bamboos in the airy atrium were our two children, Roger and Ann, running eagerly towards us to greet their grandparents.

Father crossed the threshold, stopped and gave a small gasp of pleasure at the glorious view of the harbour from our doorway through the soaring, bright, plant-laden foyer.

Father's look of pride was apparently too much for Niang. 'Go in and sit down, Joseph,' she said irritably. 'What are you staring at? It's *only* Adeline's house.'

Bob and I flew up to San Francisco with them. We rented a car and checked into the local Holiday Inn before driving to the medical centre where Father was admitted. Various tests were performed, including a CAT scan. The four of us were then ushered into Professor Hanbury's office where Father was to have a face-to-face evaluation. Father was able to answer all the routine questions until Professor Hanbury asked him to subtract seven from one hundred.

There was a short pause.

Finally, to my relief, Father replied, 'Ninety-three.'

'Please continue. What is seven from ninety-three?'

Father thought and thought. He started to sweat. His face turned red. He could not think of the answer. In desperation, he finally blurted out, 'Why is everything so difficult for me? These problems used to be so easy to solve. They are impossible now. Why, doctor? Why?'

I felt his fear and wished with all my heart that there was something I could do to reassure him. I glanced at Niang standing glumly next to me and tried to put a comforting arm around her but she moved away with a slight frown.

'I am afraid it is part of the process of growing old,' Professor Hanbury replied. 'Leaving maths aside, Mr Yen, how many children do you have?'

Again Father hesitated. Twice he tried to answer but held back each time. Tears rolled down my cheeks. I could not bear it.

Bob took my hand and led me outside. He dried my tears with a tissue. 'Don't cry. That's a loaded question, the one about the number of children. Your poor father probably doesn't know what the party line is just now. Do you count the disowned daughters or don't you? Besides, the ones that were dispossessed yesterday may be in favour tomorrow.'

Father had further tests and stayed at the centre for a few

days. Professor Hanbury was to inform us of his final diagnosis by post. We queued up at the business office for Father's discharge papers. Because Father was a British citizen from Hong Kong and had no valid American medical insurance, we were told to settle his accounts immediately. When Niang was handed the statement, I could see she was startled by the amount. She was unaccustomed to American medical fees. Gently, I took the bills from her and wrote a personal cheque for the whole sum, promising her that Bob and I would meet all Father's medical expenses in America.

At San Francisco airport, sitting with a snack in a coffee shop while we waited for our flight to Los Angeles, Niang wandered off looking for postcards. Father was relieved, almost cheerful, at the completion of his examination. To take his mind away from his illness, I asked him about his past. When was the happiest time of his life?

He thought for a while. 'When I was a young man in Tianjin,' he replied, 'and you were all very small. I had started my own company and it was doing well. I began to export walnuts and drove from field to field inspecting the quality of the kernels. I used to start off at dawn and, before I knew it, it was dark again and time to hurry home for supper. I would be famished and suddenly realize I had eaten nothing all day. That was a very happy time for me.'

'Tell me about Adeline,' Bob said. 'What was she like as a little girl?'

'She was a bookworm who excelled in her studies,' Father answered with a smile. 'I got so used to her being top of the class that when she came in second, I would reproach her.' His chest swelled with pride as my eyes filled with tears. 'I remember once she even won a writing competition open to all the English-speaking schools in the world . . .'

His voice trailed off. An expression of uneasiness crossed his face as he stared past us. Bob and I looked around to see Niang standing directly behind me. We had been so engrossed that no one had heard her approaching.

215

'Well!' she said sharply. 'What are you talking about?'

None of us knew what to say. We did not wish to displease her. 'Joseph!' she exclaimed irritably. 'Has the cat got your tongue?'

Father remained mute but suddenly looked deflated. As we filed into the plane, I thought that over the years, his silence had become his armour.

Back at home in Huntington Beach, Father's spirits revived sufficiently for us to suggest that James should join us for a short holiday.

Shortly after James's arrival, the letter from Professor Hanbury finally arrived. Niang had been forewarned by the physician in Hong Kong, and the confirmation of her fears came almost as an anticlimax. Father was suffering from generalized brain atrophy due to Alzheimer's disease. CAT scans revealed that his brain had already shrunk to two thirds of its normal size. His was a hopeless diagnosis, forecasting the steady, irreversible deterioration of his mental faculty into that of a human vegetable. Otherwise he was healthy and would not suffer any physical pain. There was no known treatment except for general supportive measures.

My mouth felt dry as I read the letter over James's shoulder. I glanced at Niang sitting next to James, and wondered if she understood the tragic connotation of such an affliction. She suddenly stood up and went to her room, murmuring that she was at the end of her tether and needed a rest. James and I were left alone.

We talked of many things that afternoon, as the implication of Father's growing senility and Niang's eventual control of his business empire dawned on us. I advised him, once again, to make his own way in life. 'I can't leave them now,' he said, 'not while they are being 四面楚歌 *si mian chu ge* (besieged by hostile forces on all sides). There is no one else.' I reluctantly nodded my agreement. 'Besides,' he confessed, 'the Old Lady is mellowing. Yesterday, she said something rather curious. 'Your father had so many children,' she told me, 'yet, when it comes down to it, we can only count on you and Adeline.' There is a lot of truth in that statement, don't you think?'

'Only you can put up with Niang!' I exclaimed admiringly. 'Anyone else would have left a long time ago.'

My personal relationship with Niang improved dramatically after this visit. She even asked me to help them buy a house close to our home where they could come and spend their summers instead of Monte Carlo. The fact that we had shouldered all Father's medical bills, amounting to around 50,000 US dollars, may have touched her. As a doctor, I was only too aware of the strains caused by Father's illness and had genuine sympathy for her.

The result of her *rapprochement* with me was her deliberate exclusion of Edgar. Later that year, she held a gala seventieth birthday celebration party for Father in Hong Kong. Gregory and Matilda flew over from Canada with their two children. Bob and I attended with our Roger and Ann. James, Louise and their brood were also there. Besides our immediate family, she also invited a dozen other guests. Edgar was never informed and only found out much later.

CHAPTER 23

粗茶淡飯

Cu Cha Dan Fan
Coarse Tea and Plain Rice

After the death of Mao Zedong in 1976, Deng Xiaoping became deputy chairman and began a series of liberal reforms, including the opening of China to tourism. In 1979, we were asked by American friends to join them on an organized tour visiting Hong Kong, Guangzhou, Shanghai and Beijing.

In December 1979 we embarked on a journey which would have been unthinkable three years earlier. I was overwhelmed by the thought of seeing my Aunt Baba again when I wrote to her of our impending visit. Our sporadic correspondence, perennially frowned upon by Niang, had been halted by the Chinese government since the beginning of the Cultural Revolution in 1966. My aunt replied immediately. The sight of her handwriting filled me with nostalgia. She had been living in a room at a neighbour's house in the same lane since 1966 and I should look for her there. She was full of joyful expectation at our imminent reunion.

In Hong Kong, our tour group was lodged at the Hilton Hotel (pulled down in 1995), a mere ten-minute taxi ride from Magnolia Mansions. We travelled from the airport in Kowloon to Hong Kong via the newly constructed cross-harbour tunnel instead of the time-consuming vehicular ferry. I had not visited Hong Kong since 1978 and marvelled afresh at the colony's meteoric development as the island's breathtaking skyline exploded into view.

Niang had written that Father could no longer control his bladder functions. We brought from California several large cartons of adult-sized diapers when we visited them. James and Louise were already there when we arrived. Father appeared much worse. After greeting us with a feeble smile, he did not say one word during the meal and seemed incapable of comprehending any of the conversation around him.

After dinner, we retired to the living-room while Father was escorted away by his night nurse. Below us, the lights of Hong Kong and Kowloon beckoned to each other across the harbour. Father used to rhapsodize over the magnificent view from their balcony, lit up each night as if on perpetual electrical parade.

Niang handed a cigar to James and lit a cigarette for herself. This was their nightly ritual whenever James dined with Niang. James had confided to me many times that he loathed those cigars; but it never stopped him from accepting and smoking them.

As she puffed away, she launched into a diatribe against Aunt Baba. Whatever my aunt might have us believe, Niang exhorted, she was keeping up with Aunt Baba's monthly allowance and 'giving her everything she could possibly want'. Then she began to rage against Lydia, warning us that my sister would probably try to enlist our help in getting her children out of China. 'Do nothing of the sort!' she instructed. 'If only your Father could speak for himself, he would tell you that the whole Sung family is poison. I want you to know that Samuel and Lydia blackmailed your Father when they first returned to Tianjin in 1950. To your face they'll flatter you, and behind your back they'll plot against you. Once you start helping one family member, all the others will demand a handout and eventually they will all land on your doorstep. They will turn your life topsy-turvy. No one will be grateful.

'Adeline, take my advice!' she continued. 'Life has been good to you. Why do you need to get embroiled with the likes of Lydia and Samuel? I'm warning you, if you associate with snakes you will be bitten. Tell Lydia that your Father and I

219

forbid you to lift a finger to help them. Let them rot in their misery! They deserve it!' Niang's voice was becoming increasingly shrill.

We left as soon as we decently could. James and Louise drove us back to the Hilton.

'The Old Lady is vindictive,' James commented in the car. 'Aunt Baba must have offended her in the past. Niang hates her and always will.'

'Do *you* think I should help Lydia if she asks me?'

'Have you written to her about your trip to China?'

'No, I haven't. The only person I want to see is Aunt Baba.'

'Then why not leave things as they are? *Suan le!*'

Our tour group of forty people made the train journey from Hong Kong to Guangzhou on Christmas Day 1979. We were shepherded into the thirty-three-storey Baiyun (White Cloud) Hotel. Even though it was only two years old, the rooms and furnishing already seemed frayed and worn. Tips were not allowed and the hotel staff appeared surly. Breakfast was served promptly at seven forty-five. Forty fried eggs appeared on forty plates laid out at four separate round tables, ten to a table. Most of our group were still asleep in their beds while their eggs awaited them, rapidly congealing. Metal teapots were banged on to the tables, together with eighty pieces of toast, twenty per table. At nine sharp, breakfast was over. Eggs, toast and tea were whisked away by put-upon waitresses within five minutes. This was our introduction to life in Communist China.

Two days later, we flew into Shanghai. As our bus drove from Hongqiao airport towards the Jinjiang Hotel, where we were scheduled to stay, I felt tense with excitement. We passed impressive red-brick Tudor mansions built in the British colonial style, complete with walled gardens and lush green lawns. The bus turned a corner and I found myself travelling on familiar Avenue Joffre. I saw once more the wide, straight, tree-lined boulevard stretching on and on. I craned my neck to read the street signs written in the new, abbreviated, Chinese script. Avenue Joffre was now renamed Huai Hai Road. The bus headed east, on and on away from the afternoon sun, dispersing hundreds of bicycles in its wake, like a giant whale surrounded by teeming fish. Now we were on Huai Hai Zhong (Central) Road. Some of the buildings began to be recognizable. It was five o'clock and amidst the tinkling of bicycle bells and swishing of tyres, crowds of workers dressed in identical dark blue Mao jackets were rushing home from work.

Suddenly there they were! As our bus approached the centre of the former French concession, out of the cityscape arose a vision more powerful to me than any other on earth: two modest pillars guarding the entrance to the lane leading to my *lao jia* (old family home). I sighted the concrete grey villas, solid and unchanged as in a painting from the past. Bamboo poles poked out of many windows, heavily laden with underwear, sheets, blankets, Mao jackets and trousers, all flapping in the wind.

Soon our bus was traversing the landmarks of my childhood. I caught a glimpse of Do Yuen Gardens and the Cathay Cinema. The myriad shops between and beyond no longer bore fanciful, bilingual placards. Gone were the neon signs lit up in blue, red, yellow, green, purple and white. Gone were the hair salons, boutiques, booksellers, coffee shops and French bakeries.

Now the stores, unpainted and weatherbeaten, carried drab names in the new, simplified characters proclaiming their wares. Nothing frivolous was offered. Thirty years had passed, during which Shanghai had lost its gaiety and sparkle, but at least it was now a city without beggars or newspaper-wrapped female baby corpses.

Our bus turned north a short way east of the Cathay Cinema and pulled up in front of our hotel, only a few hundred yards from my old Sheng Xin primary school. Bob and I dropped our luggage and immediately took a taxi to visit my aunt.

It was a bitterly cold December day. The city horizon was enveloped in a haze of dull yellow pollution. Bob told me to instruct the driver to take a short detour along the Bund, once known as the Wall Street of China. It thrilled me to converse with him in my native Shanghai dialect and to hear it once more all around me after thirty years. Already it seemed as if I had never left the city. Fifteen minutes later we were driving along the wide loop of the Huangpu River, whizzing past the well-remembered Huangpu Park (once infamous for prohibiting entry to dogs and Chinese) and the majestic office towers erected by the British in the 1930s. None of the exterior façades had altered, though some lofty edifices did spout laundry-laden bamboo poles incongruously from their upstairs windows.

Our taxi turned left at the Peace Hotel, with its distinctive triangular tower glowing against a fading sky, on to bustling Nanjing Lu (formerly Nanking Road), awash with pedestrians and bicycles. We drove past the department stores, photography studios, restaurants and provisional markets; past my Grand Aunt's Women's Bank at 480 Nanking Road, still imposing but now called the Bank of Commerce and Industry. It was dark when we arrived at our destination. Aunt Baba was living in No. 21, a once stately dwelling fallen into disrepair, as were all its neighbours. The lane was badly lit and we had to grope our way into the building. Its front door stood half open for the world to enter.

The stench hit us like a physical blow as we stepped into the hallway. We had never smelt anything like it before. The grime and sweat of those who had lived in this house for the past thirty years had penetrated every crevice. It was the stink of rotting food, unwashed bodies, unlaundered clothes and untended plumbing. Although rubbish and dirt covered the stairs and hallway, there were a few polished, oiled and chained bicycles gleaming against the filthy walls.

My chest felt heavy as I slowly climbed the stairs and called out, 'Aunt Baba! Aunt Baba!' All at once she stood there, a tiny figure silhouetted against the light of an open doorway. How small she was! Bob and I both towered over her. I hugged her tightly and felt her bony body inside her bulky padded Mao jacket. She could not have weighed more than eighty pounds.

She led us into her room and made us sit down on her bed. She took a long look at us, her eyes glowing with tender pride.

'Your handwriting hasn't changed much from that of the little girl who left in 1948! It's not the calligraphy of a physician with degrees from England and America. It's still that of a child going to primary school!' she exclaimed, her voice rasping with emotion.

Her room was cold and dingy. The only furniture was a bed, a wooden table and one small, hard-backed chair. All her earthly possessions were kept in one large wooden trunk and some cardboard boxes stacked in rows. Near by was a small kerosene stove on which she was cooking a large pot of soup noodles. She kept a portable enamel urinal under her bed. From the centre of the room dangled some wires, attached to which was a single, naked, electric bulb.

She considered herself incredibly lucky to have been assigned a room of her own for the last thirteen years. Just down the hall, the owner of the house had to share his single room with his wife and two sons. The whole dwelling now gave shelter to nine families.

She served us freshly cooked noodles covered with pickled vegetables. I watched her intently as she bustled about her room, the way I used to when I was little and she was my entire world. Her thinning hair was now greyish white and combed tidily into a neat bun at the nape of her neck. Her large eyes appeared sunken, delineated by eyebrows matching the colour of her hair.

I clasped her small hand while we related the stories of our lives, trying to bridge the thirty-year span that separated us. My aunt's voice dropped to a whisper. Fear of informers and denouncers could not be so soon overcome. 'It seems incredible that we should be sitting across from each other and speaking of absolutely anything and everything. This would have been dangerous during the Cultural Revolution three years ago.'

We talked deep into the night. She recounted the story of our family and begged me to write down these memories before time obliterated all. 'Our entire family suffered when your Niang entered our home. The spell she cast over your Father was like that of the fox-devil of our ancient folklore. Besides her youth and beauty, he was probably in awe of her foreign blood. Remember, he grew up in the French concession during an era which was unique in China. We are all victims of history.'

Before we left that night, Aunt Baba said she had a present for us. She rummaged for quite a while through the contents of her old trunk and finally extracted from the lining of her winter coat a neatly folded envelope. On opening it I saw that it was an old American 100-dollar bill which she must have hoarded for at least thirty years. For a long while we remained silent, afraid that words might shatter the magic of this moment beyond joy and sorrow.

The next day, I took Aunt Baba back to our hotel, where she enjoyed her first bath for many years. Our designated tour guide, a Party member, regarded her with contempt. At that time, an unofficial policy existed in China which divided people into four classes. Each class was treated accordingly.

First class were the white tourists, especially if they were rich North Americans. Second class were the overseas Chinese who could speak Chinese. I belonged to this category. We were dealt with as returning heroes who would provide financial support for a new economic structure in China. Third class were the *hua qiao* (American-born ethnic Chinese) whose parents had emigrated before 1949 and who could not speak Chinese, such as Bob. They were attended to with a mixture of mild contempt and overt honour, the balance being swung by the degree of their prosperity and professional achievements. The general assumption was that anyone from America was probably rich and well connected. Fourth class were the hundreds of millions of native Chinese such as Aunt Baba. Her clothing and demeanour easily earmarked her.

Our tour guide was furious when I invited my aunt to lunch with us at the eleventh-floor dining room of the Jinjiang Hotel. He scolded her for not knowing her place and abusing my hospitality. Bob and I did not hide our anger. With the support of members of our tour group, Aunt Baba was eventually served lunch but refused to set foot in the dining-room again.

On each of the five days we spent in Shanghai I collected my aunt and she would take her hot bath in our hotel room. There wasn't time enough for all we wanted to say to each other.

I offered to buy my aunt an apartment in Shanghai which was being erected at a site close to our hotel. She declined, saying that she had no wish to leave her neighbourhood. 'I have lived in the same lane since 1943,' she told me. 'This is my home. The only place I wish to move to is our old house at No. 15. If you can get it back for me, I shall die happy.' Two years later, Bob and I were able to procure the house on her behalf and she lived there till she died.

I asked her if she regretted staying behind in Shanghai.

Her answer was an unequivocal *no*. 'It has been bad here. All those campaigns and struggle meetings. The savagery of the Cultural Revolution. Poverty, hardship and fear. Quite honestly though, all the miseries put together were more tolerable than living under the same roof as your Niang. I am content with 粗茶淡飯 *cu cha dan fan* (coarse tea and plain rice).

'I often think of life as a deposit of time. We are each allocated so many years, just like a fixed sum in a bank. When twenty-four hours have passed I have spent one more day. I read in the *People's Daily* that the average life expectancy for a Chinese woman is seventy-two. I am already seventy-four years old. I spent all my deposits two years ago and am on bonus time. Every day is already a gift. What is there to complain of?'

Our eyes met. The defiant courage I saw in hers stunned me. Then in a voice whose forcefulness contrasted strangely with the frailty of her body, she declared, 'The way I see it, the nineteenth century was a British century. The twentieth century is an American century. I predict that the twenty-first century will be a Chinese century. The pendulum of history will swing from the *ying* ashes brought by the Cultural Revolution to the *yang* phoenix arising from its wreckage.'

CHAPTER 24

飲水思源

Yin Shui Si Yuan
While Drinking Water, Remember the Source

Our tour group flew into Beijing on New Year's Eve, arriving on a sunny but cold afternoon. On the roof of the new airport terminal, a giant photograph of Chairman Mao beamed down, flanked by two huge scarlet Chinese characters, 北京 Beijing (Northern Capital). Through loudspeakers came the lilting Mandarin of a female announcer, 'Beijing welcomes you!'

As we emerged from an immigration booth, a small, stocky middle-aged Chinese woman rushed towards us. Her black hair was badly dyed and she wore a brown coat with a fake fur collar. '*Wu mei!*' she called, '五妹 *Wu mei* (Fifth Younger Sister)*!* Is that you?'

No one had called me *wu mei* since those forlorn days of my Shanghai childhood. She was now standing in front of me, smiling from ear to ear. Something about her posture, the shoulders a little lopsided and uneven, the roundish flat face tilted, the semi-paralysed left hand held tightly by her right with all ten fingers interlaced, struck a chord from long ago. Involuntarily my tongue twisted into the familiar Chinese language of early childhood. '姊姊 *Jie jie* (Elder Sister),' I answered respectfully. 'It is I.'

Though I was not expecting anyone, my sister Lydia and her entire family had travelled from Tianjin to greet us at the airport. Aunt Baba had telephoned from Shanghai and given her our itinerary. It had been thirty-one years since I had last seen her and her husband. I had never set eyes on their children.

As we stood side by side, I realized that I was now an inch or two taller than Lydia. Excitedly, she gestured towards the rest of her family. Samuel was then already in his sixties, dressed in a Mao suit covered by a shiny, dark blue vinyl overcoat and worker's cap. Behind him stood a tall young man, their 27-year-old son, Tai-way, and their diminutive thirty-year-old daughter, Tai-ling.

Our tour group was booked to stay in the massive Friendship Hotel. Built by the Soviets in the 1950s, it retained a distinctly Russian feel in both its architecture and formal, landscaped gardens, reminding me of photographs I had seen of the tsars' winter palaces. Lydia and her family had made reservations at the same hotel. Their taxi followed our tour bus and we checked in together. I cringed when I saw some bellboys rudely shoving Samuel aside while respectfully ushering a few straggling members of our tour group to the front of the queue.

After dinner, Bob and I went to their suite as arranged. Their daughter Tai-ling was unwell and had already retired for the night. The five of us sat down to begin what was to become a very long evening.

In a tone full of remorse, Lydia confessed, 'It's painful to remember how neglected you were as a child. I was especially at fault because, as the eldest, I should have set an example. This I failed to do. Being the youngest and therefore the most insignificant stepchild, you were not only slighted but often bullied by all of us. My only excuse is that I was only a child myself. Besides, we were not encouraged to be loyal to each other because Niang was afraid that we might unite against her.

'When you were little, our parents made it clear that you were unwanted and expendable. Sometimes, Niang even said out loud that you were abominable.

'When Father and Niang came to Tianjin in 1948, Niang gave orders that I was not to visit you at St Joseph's school or take you out during the holidays. She stressed that she would not tolerate any disobedience and that the nuns had been instructed to send her regular reports. At that time, I was too miserable myself to think about you. I was wrong and I beg your forgiveness.'

Lydia blamed Samuel for his 'stupidity' in bringing the family back to China in 1950 and spoke of their misfortune as if he had been personally responsible. It was *his* fault that the Red Guards had shaved half of her head, locked her in a closet and sent her children away to rural communes. All the while Samuel sat beside Lydia with a frozen half smile on his face. The room was hot and I could see beads of sweat on his bald forehead. There was no change in his expression. Not one muscle twitched.

'Over the years I have repeatedly written to our parents begging for help. They have not even acknowledged my letters. Niang is a sick woman seething with hate. I know her well. What she enjoys most are intrigues. The more we suffer, the happier she is.

'You are the only one in our family who has the courage to do what is right and to defy Niang. Gregory and Edgar are self-centred and stingy. Susan and I are too far apart in age. James is an honest man but he has always been a 'yes' man and he lacks guts.'

Lydia then came to the point. She wanted nothing for herself or Samuel. Tai-ling was as good as settled because she had a very nice boyfriend in Tianjin and had no wish to leave China. Besides, both Samuel and she were getting on in years and needed their daughter around them. But for Tai-way, she made out an impressive case. 'My two children are as diverse as day and night. My daughter is selfish and difficult but my son has a kind and loyal heart. He is also a very talented musician, and has won many piano competitions. He is studying under Liu Shi-kuen, the renowned winner of the Tchaikovsky piano competition in Moscow. I beg of you to give him a chance and sponsor him to go to university in America.'

Lydia now turned to her son. 'Tai-way has a few words to say to you himself.'

Tai-way spoke in Mandarin, 'Fifth Aunt, I don't know you and you don't know me. It's very kind of you to take time out to meet us. From what my mother told me, I understand that you had to struggle hard to arrive at where you are today. Perhaps you could find it in your heart to give me a helping hand.'

He told us how his education had been suspended for ten years because of the upheavals of the Cultural Revolution. He was sent to a commune in Shanxi Province where conditions were primitive and food was scarce. Instead of attending school, he worked on the farm as a common labourer. All this would have been bearable if there had been a glimmer of hope for the future. But that was an impossible dream in China.

'Sometimes, when I think of what my life will be in ten or twenty years, I am filled with despair. I can see myself playing the piano somewhere in a remote village, teaching music to indifferent schoolchildren, or accompanying amateur per-formances put on by peasants. I would be eking out a living trying to keep body and soul together, probably still writing begging letters to your Aunt Baba for food packages.

'My father has rich relatives in Taiwan and my mother's parents live in Hong Kong. But nobody is willing to help me. It is useless and demeaning to write to them any more.

'I have no one else to turn to. You are my only hope. Please help me go to America and I will be grateful to you for as long as I live.'

I was filled with compassion for this young man who hap-pened to be my nephew. I did not have the heart to refuse him. Wiping away a tear with a large, old-fashioned handkerchief, Lydia added, 'What we are asking you to do is a lot: to risk Niang's wrath by sponsoring Tai-way. You could even be dis-owned yourself if they find out you're helping us. Whatever you decide I'm glad we had this evening together for a heart-to-heart talk. No matter what happens, I'll always love you. 飲水思源 *Yin shui si yuan* (While drinking water, remember the source).'

Many thoughts came to my mind. It seemed quite unfair that I should have been given so much while life was dealing her such a disastrous hand. Was this meeting one of those 'crossroads' to test my mettle? If the roles were reversed, and I had been the one left behind in Communist China, I would certainly be grateful for a helping hand from my sister.

I felt that I had no alternative and promised them I would be happy to do what I could for Tai-way. I added that I would ask for contributions from all our siblings, hoping that Tai-way's education in the West might be the catalyst uniting us at last.

On my return to America I was able to enrol Tai-way at the University of Southern California. I signed the affidavit of support and he arrived a few months later. For the next four-teen months we treated him like a second son.

During his second year, he transferred to the University of Indiana where Leonard Bernstein advised him to pursue his musical career in Germany. A year later, he left for Stuttgart and became financially independent after gaining employment as an accompanist at a ballet theatre. We continued to keep in constant touch with him.

In 1983 Professor John Leland, a close friend and colleague of Bob's, was scheduled to spend a sabbatical year at the University of Tianjin. We introduced him to Samuel and Lydia. He and his wife befriended the whole Sung family. We were delighted to hear that he was able to procure a full scholarship at the University of North Carolina for Tai-ling when her romance fizzled. Lydia and Samuel were so grateful that they sent us a rug as a special present.

In 1986, Lydia went to Germany to be with her son Tai-way. I bought her an airline ticket so that she could see her daughter in New York and pay us a visit in California. During the ten days she stayed with us at our home, we spent many hours in intimate conversation about the years we had been apart. I confided that I had been advising James to emigrate from Hong Kong before 1997, which wouldn't go down very well with Niang. I gave her news of Niang's desolate life and showed her photos of our senile Father lying shrunken and mindless in the Hong Kong Sanatorium.

With tears in her eyes, she begged me to intervene on her behalf. Lydia wanted to see Father one last time and be a companion to Niang. I phoned Niang and pleaded with her. Our stepmother finally relented and agreed to receive her. I immediately bought Lydia a ticket to Hong Kong. Lydia and Niang were reunited there and Niang eventually forgave me for helping Lydia's family.

Father had been admitted to Room 525 of the Hong Kong Sanatorium in 1982. He never left the hospital and remained in the same room until he died six years later.

Niang engaged three nurses for him during the day and two at night. A physiotherapist came in for an hour daily. Her two Cantonese maids were instructed to prepare his favourite meals which were delivered by the chauffeur.

Susan was distraught when she heard of Father's hospitalization. She went to see him in his private room. It was too late. Father no longer recognized her. His nurses reported Susan's visit to Niang, who became infuriated. She instructed James to threaten Susan with legal action should our half-sister attempt to visit Father again.

Niang developed her own routine. She spent two hours every morning at Father's Swire House office. James and Mr Lu, Father's loyal chief financial officer, reported to her the winding down and sale of Father's various businesses. Seven afternoons a week, from four to six, she visited Father at the hospital. She spent her evenings at home and no longer socialized. Every Sunday, James, Louise and their three children came reluctantly but promptly to dine with her.

She became a chain-smoker and spent hours sitting on her

imitation Louis XVI couch facing Victoria Harbour, puffing away and filling the whole room with smoke. At night she had difficulty sleeping in spite of large quantities of sleeping pills. She engaged a night nurse to keep her company and chat to her during the early morning hours.

I confessed to James that I found it unbearably painful to see Father reduced to his present state and added that it must be even harder on Niang.

'Don't be taken in by all of that,' James said. 'A lot of it is just for show. Hong Kong society is very small. Both Gregory and Edgar are very unhappy that she has transferred all Father's cash into her own name. If she shows any sign of neglecting him, she'd be opening herself to a major lawsuit. In fact, our two elder brothers have already questioned the legitimacy of her financial dealings. Haven't they mentioned their uneasiness to you?'

'Yes. Gregory phoned to ask if I would join him and Edgar in legal proceedings against Niang. He is afraid that Niang might remarry. I told him to forget it. I think at this moment Niang needs our moral support.'

Whenever the subject of 1997 was broached, Niang vacillated between remaining or leaving Hong Kong. 'Nothing is going to happen. Hong Kong is much too valuable to the Chinese Communists,' she argued. 'It would be financial suicide for the whole country. It's more likely that the economic miracle of Hong Kong will take over China after 1997.'

At one point she said to me, 'Your father and I are really citizens of the world. If the situation looks bad, we can fly to any country at a moment's notice. I would like you to find a house for us in Huntington Beach within walking distance of your home, in case we have to leave Hong Kong.'

In 1984, a joint declaration was signed after years of dialogue between Britain and China. The whole of Hong Kong was to be handed back to China on 1 July 1997, including Hong Kong Island, Kowloon Peninsula and the New Territories.

However, Hong Kong citizens were assured that they would enjoy the same legal rights and freedoms for another fifty years afterwards. During the interval between 1997 and 2047, Hong Kong and China would belong to one country, but with two different systems of government administration.

Property values in Hong Kong took a steep dive after this announcement. James was pessimistic about the colony's future. His affluent friends were all planning to emigrate. Many had already established citizenship in America, England, Australia or Canada. In most cases, the emigrant stayed in his adopted country for the minimum required period to obtain a passport, then returned to Hong Kong. Sometimes, only the wife and children remained abroad while the husband turned into a *tai hong ren* (astronaut–commuter) between the two countries.

CHAPTER 25

一刀倆斷

Yi Dao Liang Duan
Sever This Kinship with One Whack of the Knife

In May 1988, James phoned to say that Father had taken a turn for the worse and was not expected to live for more than twenty-four hours. I called Lydia in Tianjin, assuming that no one else would have thought of notifying her. 'Nobody ever remembers me,' she whined over the phone. 'I'm of no significance. I'll probably get nothing from Father's will.' On hearing this, I remembered that Father had disowned Lydia when she and her husband blackmailed him. So her fears were not groundless. 'Don't worry Lydia,' I said, 'I'll share what I get with you.' Father died a few hours later.

In Hong Kong, James met my plane and drove me to a small hotel near his flat, the New Asia, where Niang had arranged for us all to stay. I came alone because Bob was unable to get away. We were all surprised to learn that Lydia had already arrived from Tianjin and had been invited by Niang to stay with her at Magnolia Mansions.

James drove us to the funeral parlour at North Point where we met Niang, Lydia and Louise. In a large, bare, chilly, over-air-conditioned room covered with tiny white tiles and reeking of disinfectant, Father's body lay on a black divan under a white silk sheet emblazoned by a large, yellow cross. He looked shrunken, small and withered. Alzheimer's had taken its toll, brain cell by brain cell over twelve long years, until he was no longer a person.

A Catholic priest came and said a few words: 'Ashes to ashes and dust to dust.' Besides the finality of Father's absence, we 'children' were suddenly the older generation.

We filed past numerous rooms where other families mourned their deceased. Buddhist monks with shaven heads and flowing robes stood shoulder to shoulder in the lift with Catholic priests in black habits. Banks of floral arrangements stood everywhere and the chill of death hung in the air.

Besides the family there were only the nurses, the amahs and Mr Lu, Father's trusted employee for the last thirty years. Though Gregory and I had both informed Susan of Father's demise, Niang had not invited her and deliberately left out her name in the newspaper obituaries. No friends came. We followed the hearse to the Catholic cemetery. Father's coffin was carried by professional pallbearers up the steep steps to the grave site carved out from the face of a hill.

For those few days, time took on a different dimension as past and present fused. We found ourselves gathered at Johnson, Stokes & Masters for the reading of Father's will. The last time we were all together was forty years ago in Shanghai. I sat bolt upright in my chair with my black skirt pulled primly over my knees, half expecting some maids to appear bearing a few dishes for dinner. At the head of the table, Niang and the young solicitor conferred gravely in hushed tones.

Lydia sat glumly on my left with her healthy right arm draped affectionately around me. Gregory's eyes were still swollen and red. There was a film of perspiration beading James's brow as he nervously clasped and unclasped his hands, while his wife Louise looked elegant in her simple black dress. Edgar's features were set in their familiar scowl, magnified by grief.

When the young solicitor read out the first page of Father's will and then announced that there was no money in Father's estate, a collective gasp was audible. We sucked in our breath and looked up at Niang. She calmly glared back at us one by one. Her expression was a combination of triumph and disdain as in a cold but distinctive voice, she announced that Father's will was meaningless because he had died penniless.

Although we knew that she had transferred all of Father's cash to her own private account, we were staggered to learn that she had taken everything else as well: two tons of gold bullion in Switzerland, stocks and shares, condominiums in Monte Carlo and Hong Kong, industrial buildings in Cha Wan, the leased office at Swire House, land in Florida . . . Father had died penniless and may have been penniless for some time.

Years ago, in 1950, Father had taken Gregory to visit a renowned fortune-teller in Hong Kong, nicknamed Iron Abacus because of the accuracy of his predictions. Foremost in Father's mind was the all-important question: 'Is Gregory, my eldest son, going to be a wealthy man?'

Mr Iron Abacus was noncommittal. 'Wealth is so relative,' he told Father. 'To the rickshaw coolie, one hundred Hong Kong dollars is a very large sum. To you it is nothing. Your eldest son will lead a very comfortable life.'

That wasn't good enough for Father. 'What I want to know is, will my son be richer than I?'

Mr Iron Abacus did some more calculations, then exclaimed, 'Yes! Yes, Mr Yen! Your son will be many, many times richer than you. Of that I am absolutely certain.'

Father was very satisfied. As the years passed and Gregory's career failed to blossom, Father would shake his head and mumble that Mr Iron Abacus enjoyed a false reputation. 兔角龜毛、有名無實 *Tu jiao gui mao, you ming wu shi* (Like rabbits' horns and turtles' hair, the fortune teller had the renown but not the substance).

As we filed out of the granite lobby of Johnson, Stokes & Masters, I nudged Gregory and muttered, 'Mr Iron Abacus has scored another bull's eye!'

And Gregory whispered, 'I always told the Old Man to give me time.'

*

That night Niang wished to go to bed early. Lydia telephoned and said that Niang's chauffeur would drop her off
at our hotel. She wished to spend the night with me.

After dinner, Lydia and I returned to my hotel room. We
changed into our nightdresses and got into our respective twin
beds, side by side.

By the night-lamp on the small table separating our beds I
could see her expression, a sort of dogged determination, a
fury of concentration. The bitterness of her life came pouring
out in a torrent of words.

She began by blaming me for not helping her daughter, Tai-
ling. I was miserly and should have given Tai-ling the same
amount of money that I had given to Tai-way. 'Besides,' she
added coldly, 'you only helped Tai-way because he's young and
handsome.'

'And what do you mean by that?' I demanded angrily.

'Draw your own conclusions!'

I was utterly bewildered by her outrageous accusations,
totally unexpected and contrasting so dramatically from her
previous outpourings of love and gratitude. Soon we were embroiled in a battle of words. I was plunged into a vortex by this
strange, unhappy woman. My every response brought on fresh
venomous onslaughts.

'What's happening between us? What's the grievance you
have against me?' I asked pathetically.

'These days you behave like a queen and treat me like a
maid.' So she went on, relentlessly.

Eventually, I had had enough. It was after three in the morning and I was exhausted.

'If this is how you truly feel about me, then let's put a stop to
it. I've done my best to help you, your son and your daughter.
But for reasons best known to yourself, you seem to bear a
grudge against me. The solution is simple. 一刀倆斷! *Yi dao
liang duan!* (Let's sever this kinship with one whack of the
knife!)'

Lydia abruptly turned her back, pulled the bedclothes

around her and started to cry. I watched her heaving shoulders and, as her tears soon turned to snores, I realized that the reason she came tonight was for the sole purpose of making a break with me.

Two days later, I flew home to Los Angeles absolutely drained and full of premonition.

CHAPTER 26

無風起浪

Wu Feng Qi Lang
Create Waves Without Wind

Despite my quarrel with Lydia, Tai-way stayed in constant touch, with us. In March 1989, we received an invitation to Tai-ling's wedding in St Paul, Minnesota. Bob advised me not to go. 'Not after all those nasty things Lydia said to you in Hong Kong.'

Then Tai-way phoned from Stuttgart. He pleaded with me to attend. 'My parents have come all the way from Tianjin for the occasion. Won't you join us and make it a real family reunion?'

He would be staying in the US for a month after the wedding and was planning to visit us in California. We were delighted. 'Mother is worried that you might still be angry at her. But I told her you're not the type to go on sulking. Will you please come to the wedding as a special favour to me? I know it will also mean a lot to Tai-ling and my father. Besides, I'm sure it can all be cleared up when you see Mother face to face.'

We flew to St Paul the night before the wedding. At church the next morning Lydia, Samuel and Tai-way greeted us very warmly. It was as if our quarrel had never happened. I was the only member of our family to have made the trip, Lydia said, and had given her a lot of face. She would never forget this kindness.

It was the first time we had seen Tai-ling since our brief

meeting at Beijing airport nine years ago and we barely recognized her. When we presented her with a large cheque as a wedding present, she handed it carelessly to her Caucasian bridegroom, Alan, and told him to 'put it somewhere'. Her hostile tone was puzzling.

After the ceremony, we drove Lydia and Samuel to the reception in our rented car. The subject of our quarrel in Hong Kong came up. 'Both of you are our guests for dinner tonight,' Lydia said. 'I shall explain it all to you then.' I asked whether Tai-ling was angry at us. 'If you really want to know,' she answered after a long pause, 'she's not happy with you because she felt you should have given her the same help as you gave Tai-way.' I reminded her that Bob's friend, Professor Leland, had procured a full scholarship for Tai-ling and she wasn't in want of anything. 'That's not the same thing at all,' Lydia replied with asperity. 'Tai-ling believes that it is your duty as an aunt to give her the same amount of money as you gave Tai-way. She felt discriminated against.' At this point we arrived.

Tai-way approached us with a wide smile and glasses of champagne. He enthused over his work as an accompanist at an opera house in Munich. He thanked us both for giving him and his whole family 'that essential ingredient for happiness . . . known as hope'. He went on to confirm arrangements for dinner later that evening 'when Mother will explain everything about Hong Kong'.

'You know we'd never have come if you hadn't insisted,' I told him. 'Tell me, truly, is your mother really pleased that we made the trip?'

'Of course she is!' Tai-way exclaimed. 'Let me tell you something in confidence. Niang ordered Mother not to invite you to Tai-ling's wedding but Mother disobeyed her.'

When I heard his words, a warning sounded. It wasn't so long ago that I had been severely rebuked by Niang for helping Tai-way leave China. There had been nothing but animosity between the two women for over thirty years. Now that they were reconciled, why would Niang be counselling Lydia not to invite me to Tai-ling's wedding?

A gong announced that luncheon was served. Bob and I were placed at Samuel's and Lydia's table. There were speeches, toasts and a piano recital by Tai-way. I couldn't concentrate. Tai-way's words echoed in my brain. I pushed my food back and forth across my plate. There was a lull in the speeches. I leaned across Bob towards Lydia and whispered, 'Tell me, is it true that Niang advised you not to invite me to Tai-ling's wedding?'

Lydia was silent for so long that I wondered if she had heard. My question seemed to freeze her. At last she said in a hoarse little voice, 'Yes. Tai-way must have told you. I'll explain everything at dinner tonight.'

After lunch a reception was held at the home of Alan's mother, who lived alone near by. We helped her set out refreshments and were chatting merrily when Lydia interrupted our conversation and took us aside. Samuel was feeling unwell and she asked us to drive them back to Alan's house where they were staying. We were to meet later for dinner. She had made reservations at the 'best Chinese restaurant in St Paul's' and would call to give us directions at six thirty.

The phone rang at six thirty in our hotel room. Bob answered. It was Tai-way. Bob appeared perplexed. 'But why?' he asked. Next I heard him say, 'You'd better tell your aunt yourself.' He put the phone on hold and turned to me. 'Tai-way says the dinner is cancelled. He couldn't give me any reason.'

I sat down on the bed and picked up the extension. I was prepared for a long conversation, but it was not to be.

I heard the stilted voice of my nephew curtly repeating the message. I pressed him for a reason. After a long pause, he replied in Mandarin, 'It has something to do with your childhoods. This is all too complicated for me to understand. In any case, the dinner is cancelled.'

'May I speak to your mother?' I asked.

Again there was silence. Finally he said, 'She cannot come to the phone. She doesn't want to speak to you.'

'What about your father?'

'My father!' He sounded incredulous, as if his father was the last person I should wish to consult. 'He doesn't know anything! He can do nothing about it. Besides,' he added, 'my father doesn't want to speak to you either.'

'And you,' I asked, 'do you also have nothing to say?'

'I've no right to say anything to you.' His voice became even more guarded. 'I do have to tell you that I will not be visiting you in California.'

'I suppose this is goodbye,' I told Tai-way, feeling baffled and hurt. My nephew said nothing and gently I hung up the phone.

This was how Bob and I left St Paul's after Tai-ling's wedding. Afterwards, there was neither a letter nor a phone call from any of the Sungs to clarify matters. However, our bank statement that month revealed that the wedding cheque we gave Tai-ling had been cashed on the Monday following her Saturday wedding.

When I conferred by phone with James, he told me emphatically not to confront Niang on the matter of Tai-ling's wedding invitations. 'Don't 無風起浪 *wu feng qi lang* (create waves without wind). How do the English say it? Let sleeping dogs lie.'

CHAPTER 27

近朱者赤, 近墨者黑

Jin Zhu Zhe Chi; Jin Mo Zhe Hei
Near Vermilion, One Gets Stained Red; Near Ink, One Gets Stained Black

There is a Cantonese saying, 'When China sneezes, Hong Kong catches pneumonia.' Momentous events were taking place on the mainland. Tai-ling's wedding in April 1989 coincided with the beginning of student demonstrations in Beijing, calling for human rights, justice, democracy and the elimination of corruption and nepotism. Encouraged by the western press, 50,000 students marched through Tiananmen square on 4 May. The rest is history.

Hong Kong residents awoke to the fact that 1997 was now only eight years away. In sympathy with Beijing's students, 40,000 people went on the first march in Hong Kong on 20 May despite torrential rains and howling winds brought on by typhoon Brenda. Next day, 500,000 people took to the streets. Eventually, on 28 May, over a million inhabitants crowded into the downtown area known as Central clamouring for democracy. On the night of 3 June, President Yang Shang-kung's 27th Group army opened fire in Tiananmen Square and arrested the student leaders. In Hong Kong the stock market fell by 581 points in one day. A sympathy strike was called on 7 June. People marched in black and white, mourning the dead in western and eastern colours. Riots broke out on Nathan Road while police dispersed the demonstrators with tear gas. Fearful of Communist China, Hong

Kong residents demanded right of abode in Britain after 1997. James and Louise still had no foreign passports. They knew that Niang wanted them to stay on with her in Hong Kong after 1997. She, of course, with her French passport and Monte Carlo condominium, was free to go whenever she chose. If James should decide to emigrate, he knew that Niang would wish to join them in their new country. To broach the subject without inviting her would risk her displeasure and threaten his inheritance. Secretly, James started arranging for his family's emigration to Canada where income tax concessions were advantageous. He engaged lawyers for the essential paperwork and bought a house in Toronto in the early summer of 1989.

When I called Niang in July it was her amah, Ah Fong, who answered. She said that Niang was in the Hong Kong Sanatorium and remarked how sad it was that no sooner had Father passed away than Niang was struck by illness.

I dialled her room at the Sanatorium. 'Oh, hello, Adeline!' She sounded cool and polite. 'How nice of you to call! How did you get my number?'

Eight thousand miles away, I sat bolt upright in my chair and straightened my skirt. 'Ah Fong gave it to me when I tried to call you at home. How are you feeling? What happened? Would you like me to fly over?'

In a rather frosty voice she said she had noticed blood in her stools and had undergone a colon biopsy. Then she added, 'I'm feeling fine and can go home in a few days. There is no need for you to come. I can look after myself perfectly well.'

'Is James with you?'

'No. James and Louise are on vacation in Toronto.'

Her symptoms didn't sound good. I thought of Niang alone, about to face probable bad news in a hospital room not far from the one where Father had languished for seven years. The picture saddened me. I pleaded with her to let me come to look after her. She remained adamant: she was perfectly fine. Besides, she had no time to 'entertain' me.

'Entertain me?! Nothing is further from my mind! I just want to be of some help.'

'I don't need your help. Why are you pestering me? I've repeatedly said that I would phone if I need you. If you don't mind, I'm going to hang up now. I need my rest.'

I reasoned that James must be ignorant of Niang's illness or he wouldn't have gone to Canada.

James seemed surprised when I called him. 'How did you know I was in Canada?' His voice was tense and nervous. 'Who gave you my phone number?'

'I don't remember,' I teased. 'Now, was it the CIA, FBI or the Canadian Mounted Police?'

'Come on! Who was it?' he pressed me irritably.

'Calm down! Actually it was Niang who told me you were in Canada and Ah Fong gave me your number.'

He was audibly relieved. I told him that Niang was in the Hong Kong Sanatorium and her symptoms pointed to cancer of the colon. It was obvious he did not know. 'I offered to fly back to look after her, but she didn't want me. I can't understand why Niang has been acting so cold towards me. Have I offended her inadvertently?'

'It's probably her illness,' James replied. 'I don't think it's anything against you personally. I'd better go back myself and see that everything is taken care of. If she told you not to fly to Hong Kong you'd better not go against her wishes. Anyway, I'll phone you as soon as the biopsy results are known.'

But James did not call. I waited for about a week before phoning him in Hong Kong. My diagnosis had been correct. Niang had cancer of the colon and needed surgery. James gave her the option of having the operation in California but she declined.

'In that case, I'll fly over to be with her during the operation.'

James hesitated. Then he said quietly but with finality, 'She doesn't want you to come just now.'

246

For a moment I was unable to speak. At the other end I could hear James yelling, 'Hello! Hello!' then in Cantonese the equivalent, '*Wei? Wei?* Are you still there?'

I gritted my teeth. 'Why?' I asked.

He fielded the question. 'I thought we'd been cut off,' he yelled, as if shouting would reassure me. 'I think we should hang up now. The connection is very bad. Niang has decided on Dr Lim to perform the operation. He was trained at Harvard medical school. She has instructed me to send you a copy of the biopsy report and Dr Lim's office phone number in Hong Kong. Niang would like you to phone him and check him out.'

'What's going on, James?'

'The poor Old Lady's sick,' James replied. 'Just do as she says.'

'Right. But what's going on, James? Why doesn't she want me to be with her?'

'You'll be hearing from me by fax,' he said, leaving my question unanswered. We hung up.

In a few days I received the biopsy report. The news was terrible. Her surgeon excised the lesions from her bowel, but found two large cancerous growths in her liver. Niang refused to have these operated on or undergo chemotherapy. Her sister, Aunt Reine, had died a few years earlier from cancer of the liver despite massive doses of drugs and radiation which had caused tremendous suffering. I tried in vain to persuade Niang to come to America for a second opinion. Whenever I phoned, the nurse told me that she was resting and could not be disturbed. James even called once to warn me not to 'disturb her rest'.

However, a few days after her major operation, Niang phoned to invite my whole family to Hong Kong for a Christmas visit. She sounded friendly and apologized for not writing or calling while in hospital, saying that she wished to forget her illness and get on with her life.

Bob and I took our two children and spent a happy

Christmas with Niang in Hong Kong. She showed no sign of illness and joined in all the celebrations, exchanging presents and signing her cards 'Affectionately, Mother'. We parted amicably.

During the next eight months she called me quite often to discuss her plans of emigrating to America before 1997. Edgar had helped her get a green card and she had recently purchased a condominium in San Francisco's Nob Hill. I yearned to have a heart-to-heart conversation with her and fantasized about a soul-baring *rapprochement* at her sickbed where everything would be explained and she would die peacefully, surrounded by my loving family. I pleaded with her to come and spend some time with us in Huntington Beach but she always declined.

One day in late August when I phoned, Ah Fong informed me that she was back in hospital. Dressed and ready to go for a check-up, Niang suddenly felt weak and was unable to walk. She was admitted to the Baptist Hospital in Kowloon. When I rang her, she confessed to feeling dreadful and then, to my utter amazement, added, 'I wish you would come here and take me to America.'

I could not believe my ears! I had offered so many times to fly over to Hong Kong to help her. And here she was, from hospital, entreating me to take her to America. Gathering my wits, I asked if Dr Lim considered her fit enough to travel. She said that she did not care what the doctors advised: all she wanted was for me to scoop her up and take her to be made well in the United States. Did James know of her hospitalization? No, he didn't. She became insistent. Was I coming to her rescue or not? I promised I would and hoped that she could rest in the meantime. Her reply was bitter. What was the point of lying there and getting rest and more rest when she could not sleep? And sleep would not come ever since Father died. I asked if her doctor could prescribe some sleeping pills. She answered in an exasperated voice, 'Oh Adeline! I'm very tired. Just do as

I say. Make the arrangements. Come over here and take me with you to your home in America.'

I phoned her doctor at the Baptist Hospital who revealed that Niang had fluid in her abdomen. He doubted if she would last another month, let alone walk again. As for going to America, she might survive the journey, but only on a stretcher. Regarding her insomnia he had this to say: 'She has taken so many potent sleeping pills for so many years that nothing works on her any more. Quite honestly, the doses are alarming. But maybe I can give her some morphine to make her more comfortable.'

I telephoned James, who was in Boston enrolling his daughter at Tufts College. I repeated Niang's unexpected request. Should I comply or obey Dr Lim who said she was dying? James advised me to wait until he flew back to Hong Kong and consulted Niang himself. He planned to leave the very next day.

Two days later, James arrived back in Hong Kong. In a subdued voice thick with fatigue, he phoned to say that Niang no longer recognized him. I asked if there was any point in my flying over and taking her to California. 'Look! She is on her deathbed and in no condition to go anywhere. Dr Lim says she will die in a few days. You might as well prepare yourself to fly over here for the funeral and the reading of the will. I'm making the arrangements now.'

Niang, although unconscious and dying, was about to deal her last and most triumphant card. Of her own two children, one was dead and one was disowned; but she was left with five stepchildren with whom to play her final game. She had had us believe that she held in her vaults one of the great fortunes of the world. At one time, perhaps in the early 1970s when Father was still competent, the Yen family was considered one of the richest in Hong Kong. By the end of the 1980s, Father's fortune had dwindled. Only James had access to documents and had revealed to us that its real worth was about thirty million dollars.

For me, the yearning was not for the money as such. After all, both Bob and I had secure, well-paying jobs with good pensions. It arose instead from a basic need: a longing for acceptance, a craving for my rightful place in the family, a primal cry to be included – all of which had been denied in my youth. It was a deep-seated desire for all of us to be treated with justice and equality. I could not bear the idea of me, or anyone of us, being singled out for neglect and discrimination. Although I knew that Niang was neither kind nor good, I hungered for her approval just as I had hankered after Father's blessing. In this respect, Father and Niang represented a single unit.

Niang played upon our traditional Confucian concept of filial piety to permeate her pervasive influence. Her continued domination transcended all logic. The extension of the family unit has been held to be the motivating force binding all Chinese to their roots. Except for Susan, who through sheer strength of will had made herself independent, all of us were emotionally shackled to Niang throughout our lives.

I phoned Gregory in Vancouver and we discussed Niang's imminent demise. He sounded concerned that he would not inherit much, if anything, because Niang had always disliked him.

'Do you think she loved any of us?' I asked.

'Of course not! But I think she was most wary of me, because as eldest son, I threatened her position in the family hierarchy.' Then Gregory really startled me. 'Will you help me, Adeline, if James gets it all and no one else gets anything? I am counting on this inheritance.'

I answered as truthfully as I could. 'You know it will be difficult for me to fight James. But I don't think she will be so unfair. Besides, I think James deserves a larger share. After all, he has given Niang thirty years of his life.'

Gregory was unimpressed. 'No one twisted his arm. Obviously, he felt his chances of making it were better by throwing in his lot with Niang than going out on his own. Don't be so sure of anyone's behaviour where money's involved. 近朱者赤、近墨者黑 *Jing zhu zhi chi; jing mo zhi hei* (Near vermilion, one gets stained pink; near ink, one gets stained black). James has changed a lot over the years.'

Another week went by. On Sunday, 9 September, James left a message on our answering machine. 'The Old Lady passed away an hour and a half ago, at four o'clock on Sunday morning.'

CHAPTER 28

酒肉朋友

Jiu Rou Peng You

Wine and Meat Friends

Niang's funeral was set for 17 September 1990. Before Bob and I left for Hong Kong, James and I discussed arrangements for Niang's interment. During the course of our phone conversation, I related Gregory's misgivings.

Niang had taken such excessive quantities of sleeping pills for so many years that Gregory and his pharmacist wife Matilda feared for her sanity. They were concerned that she might have altered Father's original will under the influence of drugs. Could she have singled out Gregory or anyone else besides Susan for exclusion in her will?

James said that he had never been consulted and consequently had not the faintest idea what was in Niang's will. He suddenly asked if I remembered Franklin's old tutor-nanny, Miss Chien. The Red Guards banished her from Father's house in 1966, after which, for twelve years, she lived in abject poverty with her brother's family in Hangzhou as the despised spinster-aunt. Fortune did not smile upon her and she developed skin cancer which spread to her bones and liver. One day in 1978, James received an unexpected letter from Miss Chien addressed to Father, who was already senile. Miss Chien was obviously dying. Her body was racked by pain and she had no money for food or medicines. She pleaded for a small sum to ease her last days. James was preparing to send her a bank draft when Niang walked into the office. 'Do nothing!' she commanded. 'Miss Chien has outlived her usefulness.'

'I felt the hairs stand up on the back of my neck when I heard her orders,' James confided. 'No one should expect fairness or justice from Niang. I tell you she was ruthless! Anyone of us could have been disinherited at any time without cause.'

The wake was held at the same mortuary in North Point where Father's funeral had taken place two years before. Niang lay on a narrow bed in an inner sanctum. Her face appeared mottled, despite the mortician's heavy make-up. She was dressed in an elaborate black dress with her arms lying stiffly by her side. Her dyed ebony hair was severely pulled back, revealing the prominently protruding forehead she took such pains to hide while she was alive.

Niang's Cantonese amahs Ah Fong and Ah Gum came, dressed in their white tunics and loose black trousers. They had served Father and Niang faithfully for over thirty years. Her chauffeur made a brief appearance. Two nurses arrived; both had been employed by Niang to keep her company at night.

Susan and her husband, Tony, were the last to make their entrance. Our youngest sister looked stunning in a glamorous black suit, her mane of shining hair stylishly waved. She told us that she had arranged a mass to be said for Niang that evening in a Catholic chapel.

We sat on metal chairs in that chilly, antiseptic room waiting for guests to arrive. I had seen photographs and heard numerous accounts of lavish lunches, dinners, dances and receptions. 'The only bad thing about living in Hong Kong,' Niang once told me, 'is the constant round of parties and more parties.' I kept expecting a group of her friends to come marching through the door. But no one came to pay her their respects or say a last farewell.

I thought back upon my miserable childhood and the abuse Niang had dispensed to those around her. I recalled my elation when I finally escaped from her reign of terror and oppression.

And yet it continued to matter to me whether or not she loved me.

I came out of my reverie and saw Mr Lu, Father's faithful chief financial officer, get up from his seat and move himself next to Bob. He was whispering, 'I don't think anyone else is coming. She had no true friends, only 酒肉朋友 *jiu rou peng you* (wine and meat friends). As you both know, she was an unusual person. She wasn't fond of many people. Look how she cut Susan out of her life and her will. Susan was her only daughter, her own *gu rou* (bones and flesh).'

My right eyelid began to twitch involuntarily as I stared at Mr Lu, trying to read meaning into his words. 'What are you trying to tell us, Mr Lu?' I asked candidly. 'Why don't you come right out and say it instead of hinting around?'

Mr Lu addressed Bob, though his words were meant for me. 'Nobody seems to tell her anything,' he lamented. 'Her Niang didn't want her to know this, but she may get nothing when the will is read tomorrow.'

'I don't believe you!' I cried. 'Just three weeks ago, she was begging me to take her to my home in America! Surely, she must have had *some* feeling for me to wish to die in my home?'

Mr Lu shook his head, while steadfastly avoiding my gaze. 'Her request may have arisen from ulterior motives designed to turn all your siblings against you. She had a green card and was a permanent resident of the United States. The *US* government would have imposed death duties on her estate if she had died in America. You would have been blamed for taking her to your home to die.'

I began to shiver and found it hard to breathe. I was six years old and it was Chinese New Year. Dressed in bright new clothes, we children gathered at lunch eating traditional, glutinous, sweet rice cakes while festive sounds of firecrackers banged and crackled from the lanes. One by one, my siblings were handed their *ya sui chien*, a traditional red paper package with gold characters announcing 'Happy and Prosperous New Year' and containing money. Everyone except me. I was the only child left out – punished for speaking out against Niang's beating of baby Susan.

'Just a minute,' Bob intercepted firmly, 'are you sure of your facts? Have you read Niang's will? Has James read it?'

'No, neither of us has actually sat down and read the will,' Mr Lu explained, 'but we are absolutely certain of the major items. Believe me, I wouldn't have mentioned anything, except that I don't see the point of Adeline going to the will reading tomorrow afternoon and being hurt unnecessarily.'

The rest of that afternoon and evening passed in a daze. We all attended the Catholic mass which Susan had arranged. I couldn't wait to go back to the hotel and get the whole truth from James. I telephoned him as soon as we returned. His maid informed me that Louise had gone to bed, but James was with his brothers at the New Asia Hotel. Bob and I took the lift down to Gregory's room.

The sounds of merriment hit us as we approached his door. Inside we found my three brothers, my sister Lydia and Mr Lu. They were still wearing their black mourning clothes. On the coffee-table stood a half-empty bottle of whisky and some glasses. A party was in progress. Niang's stepchildren were in the highest spirits, celebrating their windfall. Obviously, Niang's will had been known to them for some time.

An unnatural silence fell upon the room when we entered. I looked across at James, who was flushed from whisky and still grinning from the memory of their last shared joke. 'Excuse me for interrupting your party,' I said directly to him, 'but may I speak to you in private for a few minutes?'

The smile faded from James's lips. 'Actually,' he replied, 'I was just about to take Mr Lu home in my car. It's getting late.'

'Bob and I will ride with you, if we may?'

'Come along then,' James muttered. 'Let's go now.'

During the ride through the cross-harbour tunnel to Mr Lu's flat in Kowloon, Bob held my hand in the back seat and we said nothing. It was almost eleven and traffic was light. Against the background of Mr Lu's constant, nervous chatter, my mind returned to a long-forgotten incident.

It was a blistering summer day during the height of a Shanghai heatwave. I had just completed my homework and was lying on my bed, blissfully re-reading my latest report card. Father and Niang had gone away for a few days. The entire household was feeling lazy, relaxed and carefree. We were luxuriating in their absence.

The maid came in and said that my brothers wanted me to join them in the dining-room. They had a special treat for me. I sprang to my feet when she reassured me that James was there too. To be beckoned by all three of my big brothers was mysterious and exciting. I ran downstairs. On the dining-room table was a large jug of orange juice surrounded by four glasses. Three were empty. One was full.

Edgar spoke first, grinning from ear to ear. 'Seeing it's such a hot day, and the fact that you have received so many honours in your report card, we thought you should be rewarded with a glass of orange juice because Father is not here to praise you himself.'

'Why?' I asked suspiciously. 'You've never been kind to me before.'

'Drink it!' Edgar ordered, giving me a shove.

'I don't want it. Why must I drink it? Why don't you drink it yourself?'

'It even has ice in it, see?' Edgar held up the glass and the ice cubes tinkled temptingly. 'It will cool you down at once.'

I eyed the juice longingly before turning to Gregory. 'Is it all right to drink it, 大哥 Da ge (Big Brother)?'

'Of course it is. We made it ourselves, from this bottle of orange concentrate here, see? We made this glass of juice especially for you to celebrate your star performance at school.' They laughed hysterically.

The room was hot and muggy. The ice floated enticingly in the orange coloured liquid.

I lifted the glass and appealed to James, knowing that he

would never deceive me. 'Is this all right to drink, 三哥 *San ge* (Third Elder Brother)?'

'Yes,' James replied. 'This is your prize for doing well in school.'

Satisfied, I took a big gulp. Immediately I spat it out. My three older brothers had mixed their urine with the orange concentrate and duped me into drinking it. As I burst into tears, what troubled me was not Edgar's malice or Gregory's treachery, but James's betrayal.

Now when Mr Lu was dropped off, I moved into the front seat as James started on the return trip back to the hotel. I could tell that he was under great strain. Despite his repeated denials, how could he possibly not have known what Mr Lu had just told me? Worse, he must have been in collusion with Niang to deliberately keep me in the dark.

James paid the ten-dollar-toll charge, rushed through the tunnel and emerged on Hong Kong island. I was grateful for the darkness as he drove at breakneck speed.

It started to rain. James turned on his windscreen wipers. 'Mr Lu informed me,' I began quietly, 'that I had been cut out of Niang's will. He said that I would get nothing.'

James made no reply as he turned a corner and manoeuvred the car on to Wong Nai Chong Gap Road. For once, he voiced no denial. All pretences were dropped for the moment. With another turn we were parked in front of the hotel. We had arrived and still he would not speak.

'Say something!' I pleaded. 'Is Mr Lu telling the truth?'

Without turning the engine off, James looked straight in front of him, mesmerized by the whoosh-whoosh of the windscreen wipers swinging to and fro before his eyes. 'Yes,' he said.

'And Father, what about Father? Was I cut out of his will also?' Tears ran down my cheeks. I thought of my white-haired Father, lying mute and motionless year after year in Room 525 of the Hong Kong Sanatorium. Had he also rejected me?

'I've already told you that I haven't read Father's will,' James snapped irritably. 'How am *I* to know what Father wanted?

Besides, Father's will is irrelevant. It's useless. All his assets were in Niang's name.'

'But why did Niang cut me out? How did I offend her?'

'Look,' James replied, quite harshly, 'I don't have all the answers either. Niang formed a very bad impression of you when you stayed with her in 1987. She claimed that you wished to put Father in an apartment in Kowloon. Also that you weren't grateful for the medical education she gave you in England.'

'Put Father in an apartment in Kowloon? That's so ludicrous that it's laughable! Why would I want Niang to do that? And you believe that's the reason?'

'I don't know who or what to believe. I'm merely repeating what Niang told me. I loathe confrontations. Though I hate to admit it, I'm getting on and life doesn't go on for ever. I don't want a fight that goes on and on in the law courts. It's important to me to enjoy in peace whatever years I have left. Remember,' he added, 'I'll be the executor of the will. If you decide to file a lawsuit you'll be fighting me. If you should go to court I'll be your adversary.'

As he spoke, I felt a chill that penetrated into the marrow. I was listening to a cautiously prepared speech. This was not the spontaneous outburst of a concerned brother.

Bob, who had been sitting silently in the back seat, leant forward and put his hand on my shoulder. 'Don't you see that this is breaking her heart? At this moment she feels deserted, cheated and violated.'

'Don't give me all those fancy words!' James burst forth violently. 'It's money you're after, isn't it? Money I can help you with. Tell me, how much money do you want?'

I glanced at my brother slumped behind the wheel, tense and unhappy. His face was flushed and swollen with embarrassment. 'You and I, James, we have gone through so much together. Has it come down to this? Surely you, of all people, should know that it's not about money. It's about family and fair play and our common journey in search of a mother.'

Neither James nor Bob said anything. 'I still can't understand why Niang disinherited me while playing me for a fool. Tomorrow,' I continued, 'I shall go to the funeral in the morning. But the will reading at four o'clock . . . that will be unbearable. I shall wait for you in my hotel room. Will you come and tell me when it's all over? And please bring me a copy of her will.'

The will was read at four o'clock and at six thirty James arrived with my copy. There was drink on his breath and he was in a tremendous hurry to get away. They had gone directly from the solicitor's office to the Mandarin Hotel's Clipper Lounge to celebrate. A dinner was planned later that evening at the Shanghai Club. Susan, I and our spouses were not invited.

'I am a man of my word,' James announced. 'This is your copy of Niang's will, but I can't stay very long. They're all expecting me for dinner. I'm the host.'

'What does it say?'

'Gregory and Edgar each get 20 per cent. I get 50 per cent. Lydia gets 10 per cent. Susan gets nothing. You get nothing.'

I flipped through the papers, scanning the pages rapidly until I found my name. 'Adeline Yen Mah,' I read aloud to Bob. 'In no event is my daughter, Adeline Yen Mah, to receive any portion of my estate.' My voice cracked. 'Why, James, why? Why did she loathe me so? "In no event", it says here. "*In no event*"!'

James, who had remained standing all the time, suddenly walked over to our mini-bar and poured himself a large whisky. He drank it in one gulp.

'Don't take it so much to heart,' he began. 'Look, let me give you something. What about Niang's flat? Why don't you take that? Remember, if you go to court, only the solicitors will win. Besides,' he added, 'you've got enough money already – 10 or 20 per cent more isn't going to alter your lifestyle. Look, I've got to go. Dinner is at seven thirty and I still have to come back here and pick up Lydia. She wanted to telephone her children and tell them her good news.'

'Isn't it incredible that Lydia, whom Niang hated and didn't even want to see four years ago, receives 10 per cent, whereas I, who bought the airline ticket for Lydia in 1986 so that the two of them could be reconciled, should be left out in the cold?'

'That's how the Old Lady wanted it in the end,' James said. 'Who knows why? In any case, tomorrow morning everyone is invited to go up to her flat and divide up her furniture, antiques and jewellery. Give me a call if you're coming. I really have to go now. See you tomorrow.'

CHAPTER 29

無頭公案

Wu Tou Gong An
Headless and Clueless Case

Susan saw the matter more clearly than I did. 'What!' she exclaimed. 'Lydia gets 10 per cent and you get nothing? What sort of justice is this?'

'You inherited nothing either, 小妹 *Xiao mei* (Little Sister).' I was moved by her outrage on my behalf when she had suffered the same fate.

'She has disowned me since 1973. I expected nothing and didn't want anything from her! But you, what did *you* do to deserve this? How devious she was! Why should she punish you like this?'

I thought how sad it must be for Susan to have to admit that such a person was her *gu rou* (bones and flesh). Then I remembered her fortitude in daring to walk away from Niang seventeen years ago, something the rest of us were never able to do.

'James said it's because I wanted to put Father in an apartment in Kowloon and wasn't grateful for my medical education.'

'What absolute rubbish! So they must have discussed the will between them . . . and if that's the case, why didn't James defend you?'

My little sister had placed her finger on the exact aching spot. 'I don't know the answers but before I leave Hong Kong, I must find out what was in Father's will. James did offer to give me Niang's flat. He has also invited all of us, and you too, to go up to Magnolia Mansions tomorrow to divide up the contents.'

'He's got to be joking!' Susan laughed. 'No way am I going up there. Niang's personal effects would give me the creeps and bring me bad luck. The last thing I want is to be reminded of her! As for her flat, don't be taken in by that! Prices have fallen drastically and are still depressed because of Tiananmen. James is trying to buy you off as cheaply as possible. He's probably scared that you'll challenge the will, which you have a perfect right to do.'

That night my sleep was agitated. At four o'clock in the morning I was wide awake, tossing and turning. Bob held me for a long time. Unable to go back to sleep, we went for a long walk around the racecourse in Happy Valley, ending up like homing pigeons at James's and Louise's flat. It was eight and they were having breakfast.

Soon, Gregory and Edgar arrived; the latter left the instant he saw me. Gregory settled down comfortably next to me and accepted a cup of tea.

'Niang's will bothers me,' Gregory began. 'It's so unfair. It isn't right that you should get nothing. What do you think we should all do to make Niang's will more fair and to make you feel better? I suggest that each of us give you 10 per cent of our share so that you would end up with 10 per cent of the estate.'

His words brought tears to my eyes. I swallowed hard and waited until my voice came back to me. 'I thank you from the bottom of my heart. I think your offer is more than generous . . .'

'Since I have the largest share,' James interrupted, 'my 10 per cent is equivalent to 5 per cent of the total estate. This will include Niang's flat.' He glanced at Louise, who remained silent with her eyes downcast. No one said anything. 'As I've said before, I'm too old for any legal battles. I want to enjoy my money. So, the answer is yes.'

'That settles it then,' Gregory added, 'I'll speak to Edgar and Lydia.'

Looking at her watch, Louise exclaimed, 'We told Ah Fong that we would be there at ten o'clock. It's almost nine thirty. We still have to pick up Lydia and Edgar. We should be going.'

'I think I'll just go to the hairdresser's. I'm not interested in Niang's jewels or her furniture. All I want is to find Father's will.' Turning to James, I asked, 'Will you give Bob and me permission to go to Niang's flat this afternoon to search for it?'

'I think you're wasting your time,' James replied. 'By all means, go there and look for it. Take any document you wish! Mr Lu and I went over Niang's papers very thoroughly and were unable to find it.'

After a shampoo and blow-dry, I returned to my hotel room refreshed. Immediately there was a knock on the door. It was Gregory.

'I talked to Edgar and Lydia. Edgar refused point blank to give you anything. At first Lydia also said no. I reminded her that our parents had disowned her and, were it not for you, she certainly would not have inherited a cent. Finally she agreed to give you 5 per cent, but on condition that you make a full confession.'

'A full confession? What do I have to confess to?' I was incredulous.

'That's what I asked her. She wasn't sure either. She called your unexpected disinheritance a 無頭公案 wu tou gong an (headless and clueless case). She wants you to confess to the real reasons behind it. It's her Communist training. She likes to hear confessions. They make her feel powerful. In China during the Cultural Revolution, people were confessing all over the place.'

'So Lydia wants to hear my true confession. Well, I would like to know the reasons myself. Tell Lydia to keep her money, Gregory,' I said. 'I don't want anything from her.'

CHAPTER 30

開門揖盜

Kai Men Yi Dao
Opened the Door to Salute the Thief

Bob and I awoke with a start at five p.m., having slept the afternoon away. We rushed out and hailed a taxi to Magnolia Mansions. On the marble landing of the tenth floor we were assailed by Niang's familiar odour of perfume, mothballs and stale cigarette smoke. How often I had waited at this threshold with sweaty palms and palpitating heart! Ah Fong opened the teak front door and outer steel gate.

Inside, all looked the same. There were the antique paintings by Castiglione, the eighteenth-century Italian Jesuit priest in the court of Emperor Qian Long. Niang had cut these masterpieces short to accommodate her furniture arrangement. Against one wall stood four elaborately carved redwood chairs, purportedly belonging at one time to the last Emperor of China. Facing the harbour were her imitation Louis XVI couches. On the Qing dynasty coffee-table lay the silver Tiffany box I had sent her as a birthday present sixteen years ago. Next to it perched a gold cigarette lighter Bob had given her for Christmas. Once, years ago, I advised her to stop smoking. 'Leave me alone!' she had snapped. 'I don't need *you* to tell me that smoking is harmful to my health. It's written on every cigarette package.' After a while she added, somewhat pathetically, 'It's the one pleasure I have left since your father became ill.' I made no reply because what she said was true.

Ah Fong hovered around us asking if we would like refreshment. Suddenly we remembered that we had not eaten lunch. Bob asked her, in his halting Cantonese, if she would make us some tea and toast. Then, not wishing to delay further, we entered Niang's bedroom to start the search.

After the onset of Father's illness, Niang had moved out of the master bedroom into a smaller room facing the steep, green mountain slope behind the flat. It was furnished with a single bed, an antique Chinese writing desk and chair, a night stand with a talking clock we had given her some years before, a free-standing wardrobe and a built-in closet.

I rummaged through the wardrobe and saw a row of dresses neatly hanging, dozens of pairs of shoes on racks like parading soldiers and empty handbags lying side by side on a shelf above. No will there. The sight of her personal belongings brought on waves of nausea. The weak overhead ceiling light and small table lamp by her bed cast sinister shadows. I felt a constriction in my chest provoked by the power of her aura; my senses were saturated with her smell.

I next approached her antique Chinese desk. Six years ago, Niang had offered to leave this very desk to Bob. 'Carved by skilled craftsmen from the finest blackwood during the Ming dynasty,' I remembered Niang saying. Was she already lying then? I looked hard at the elaborate design as I carefully tested the smooth glide of the top drawer and pulled it open.

The stacks of letters struck me at once. Piles and piles of airmail envelopes totalling perhaps two hundred letters, neatly sorted into rows. I stared at the familiar, small, spidery handwriting on the envelopes and the brightly coloured stamps of the People's Republic of China. All came from Tianjin and were addressed to Mrs Joseph Yen. All were written by Lydia.

The sight of these letters rooted me to the spot. Why was Lydia writing to Niang almost every other day? In a trance I pulled out the top letter from its envelope. As I started to read, the ache in my chest gripped me like a vice. I felt dizzy, as if I was standing on the top ledge of a skyscraper, looking down and seeing the earth sway beneath me.

Letter after letter was filled with lies and venom, inciting Niang to hate me. Though I was 'cruel, selfish and miserly', Lydia had written, she was advising Niang to tread carefully in front of the despised Adeline, for Niang was no longer in a position of strength. She accused me of disobedience because I had kept in touch with Susan and had even rallied her and all my brothers behind me in a joint effort to help Tai-way for the sole purpose of sabotaging Niang's commands. The year 1997 was fast approaching when Hong Kong would be governed by Beijing. She played on Niang's fears and paranoia by writing that I was urging James to emigrate so that Niang would be abandoned and forced to live out her last years alone. She then swore Niang to secrecy.

Immediately beneath them were other letters, from Samuel and Tai-ling, making similar accusations. With a leaden heart, I realized that by going against Niang's wishes and helping Lydia's family I had 開門揖盜 *kai men yi dao* (opened the door to salute the thief).

As I turned to show Lydia's letters to Bob, he gave a jubilant shout from his side of the room. He had been searching Niang's closet and was clearly a better sleuth than I. Triumphantly he waved a document in front of me. It was my father's will.

Bob and I sat on the edge of Niang's bed and read Father's will over and over. I heard once again my father's voice. It was as if he had raised himself out of his grave to embrace me. His wishes soothed the ache in my heart.

My father's will, signed long before his illness on 2 May 1974, was radically different from the one written by Niang on 2 June 1988, less than three weeks after his death. Father had divided his estate into seven shares. He left one share to me, one share to Gregory, one share to Edgar, two shares to James and two shares to his grandchildren with the last name of Yen. No share was left to Susan. Father also wrote in his will the following sentence: 'I further would like to record that no share of my estate is to go to my daughter, Lydia Yen Sung.'

Clutching Father's will, I hugged my husband. 'In the end, Niang's will doesn't matter. Whatever happens, *this*, my father's will, is what is important to me. He at least did not exclude me. Perhaps he loved me after all. Besides,' I added, 'James will do the right thing. He is the executor and he is an honest man.'

Randomly, we picked up a few of Lydia's letters and placed them with Father's will in my handbag. Sitting in the cab as it crept back to our hotel, Bob held my hand and said, 'Remember, you'll always have me . . .'

CHAPTER 31

掩耳盜鈴

Yan Er Dao Ling
Steal the Bell While Covering Your Ears

Next morning, James and I met for breakfast at a dim sum shop. We sat facing each other on old-fashioned, low red stools around a matching table. The restaurant was tastefully decorated in the 1920s 'Old Shanghai' style with lazily whirring overhead ceiling fans, latticed windows, gleaming parquet floor, period photographs, potted bamboos and bunches of fresh chrysanthemums. We were the only customers.

Outside, the rain poured down in sheets. Tea was served and we each ordered a bowl of soup noodles. Silently I handed over Father's will. James was astounded that we had found it so easily, repeating that he and Mr Lu had searched 'everywhere' without success.

'I would like to keep this will. It's meaningless, of course, but I want to hand it over to the probate lawyer.'

'Besides the will,' I said, 'we also found many letters in Niang's writing desk. Maybe a couple of hundred. Most of them were from Lydia. We took a few of them with us when we left Niang's flat last night.'

I pulled out the small sheaf of letters from my handbag and laid them next to Father's will. James glanced down at them with a frown. He compressed his lips. I had seen this expression many times before, usually towards the end of a hard-fought chess game, just before his final move towards checkmate.

'You had no right to *touch* those letters, let alone remove them from Niang's desk,' he said icily. 'Those letters are private!'

'I think you should read them. See here,' I said emphatically, 'this letter is dated 7 October 1987. While I was trying to help her children, Lydia was plotting against me.'

'I don't want to read these poison letters.'

'But don't you want to know the truth?' I asked pathetically. 'You can't 掩耳盗铃 *yan er dao ling* (steal the bell while covering your ears)!'

'Is there such a thing as absolute truth?' he answered rhetorically. 'It all depends on a person's viewpoint. In any case, it's all water under the bridge. *Suan le* (let it be)! Besides, I *hate* confrontations! Remember, if you challenge the will, you'll be challenging me. And if you and I end up in court over this, then we would be caught in Niang's trap, because that would be precisely what the Old Lady wanted.'

'You were caught in her net a long time ago. She had always had her way with you. You were no match for her. Lydia alone was devious enough to compete with *her*.'

James laughed. 'You are right! They're two of a kind. You learned this too late to your cost. It was *you* who brought about the reconciliation between Lydia and Niang. If they had not met in 1986, matters would have turned out very differently.' He put down his chopsticks and signalled for the bill. 'Your problem, Adeline, is that you're always transferring your own feelings and reasonings into others. You wanted to believe that we all shared your dream of a united family. In fact, no one cared except for you. Look, it's getting late. I have to go now.' His eyes met mine in a steady and obstinate gaze. He got up, clutching Father's will and Lydia's letters tightly in his hands. 'I'll send you a photocopy of Father's will. As for these letters, they're private and they will be burnt.'

We walked out into the pouring rain. It seemed as if the whole world was weeping. Throughout our childhood, youth and middle age, we had stood shoulder to shoulder on every important issue. Over the years, Niang must have resented this special bond between us. In the end, seeking to destroy it, she had baited James into participating in a fraud he detested. Nothing would have pleased her more than to see the two of us at each other's throats, fighting over her legacy.

As I watched him hurry away, hunched against the rain, I called after him, '三哥! *San ge!* (Third Elder Brother)! It was a great misfortune for us to have had Niang for a stepmother. Don't worry, I won't contest her will. I will never allow her to triumph over me.'

CHAPTER 32

落葉歸根

Luo Ye Gui Gen
Falling Leaves Return to Their Roots

On an overcast March day in 1994, I received a letter from my aunt begging me to go to her in Shanghai. The news enveloped me in gloom, mirroring the unseasonably chilly Southern Californian weather. As I went about my daily routine at the surgical centre, there was an ache which jolted me whenever I thought of her dying alone in her big house.

Inside, a quiet, small voice whispered that this visit would be the last. Instinctively, I recoiled from the intolerable thought that Aunt Baba would soon be gone for ever. Throughout the long flight from Los Angeles to Shanghai via Tokyo, I made elaborate plans to take her to America and have her seen by the best specialists.

Shanghai in the 1990s had been transformed into a city bursting with energy and vitality. Cars jammed the streets. Tall brown cranes dotted building sites. The horizon was sheathed in a hazy film of dust as old buildings were toppled and replaced.

Once more, I entered the familiar lane where she had lived for the last fifty years. It was now littered with broken concrete and construction material. I wound my way around shining motor cycles and imported luxury automobiles. From the garden, I pushed open the newly painted French glass doors, stepped into the old living-room which was now her bedroom and embraced my aunt and all my beginnings. She was bedridden following a fall which broke her hip. X-rays showed that she had cancer of the colon which had already spread. To my surprise, I found her cheerful and free from pain, perhaps because of the small doses of morphine she was being given. She was surrounded by neighbours and friends who congregated at her bedside day and night. In this cosy, noisy, gregarious world of the 'all-Chinese' sickbed, so different from the stark, sterile solitude of the American hospital room, her life had assumed the astounding quality of a continuous farewell party.

Bob, who had accompanied me, had been learning Mandarin. He tried his newly acquired skills on my aunt, though, in truth, it resembled no dialect I had ever heard. After a while, Aunt Baba interrupted him in the middle of a long and convoluted sentence, asking what tongue he was speaking. When told it was Mandarin, she commented mischievously, 'Next time, before you start talking to me in Chinese, please give me advance notice, "I am going to speak to you in Mandarin now." Unless forewarned, my old ears might think you're still speaking English.'

I had returned once again to the warm cocoon of Aunt Baba's world, safe in the knowledge that she was the one person to whom I would always matter. Here, clasping each other's hands and listening to her lilting Shanghai speech, I forgot the throb that had been pounding my head ever since I learned of her illness. Instead of fear and discontent, Aunt Baba was floating in tranquil euphoria. She categorically refused to consider surgery or even hospitalization, gently chiding me for my grandiose plans of rescue which she labelled 'macabre' and 'unnatural'.

'I have had a good run of eighty-nine years. It is time to accept the end. Since there is no hope of a cure, why prolong the agony of dying?'

Up to the last, her anxieties were centred on the loved ones she must leave behind. She wanted to give me strength to come to terms with all my hurt. I nestled on the bed next to her thin, frail body . . . the way I used to as a child when sleep would evade me because things were terrible and life seemed devoid of hope. And she comforted me, just as in the past, by stroking my hair and telling me a story. She called it 'The Incurable Wound'.

'A long time ago, there lived a child called Ling-ling who was a good artist. After her mother's death, her father's favourite concubine began to maltreat her by showing preference towards her own children. Ling-ling had no one to play with and spent her time painting. Her pictures became famous and were sold for many taels of silver. Her stepmother now grew jealous. One night, she crept up to Ling-ling's bed and stuck a dirty nail into the child's hand, spreading faeces on the nail to cause an infection.

'In a few days, Ling-ling's hand became red and swollen. Though the nail was removed, pus poured from the wound. However, Ling-ling continued to paint.

'Now a strange thing happened. The wound never healed, but Ling-ling's paintings became better and better. The more the pus exuded, the greater the beauty of her work. In the whole of China, there was nothing like it. The pain in her hand seemed to imbue Ling-ling with an essence of invincibility, enabling her to 戰而必勝、鬥而必克 *zhan er bi sheng, dou er bi ke* (prevail in every battle, overcome each adversity).

'The Emperor himself heard of Ling-ling's masterpieces. She was summoned to the palace to paint the portrait of the crown prince. They fell in love and married. However, despite the administration of innumerable poultices prescribed by the best doctors in China, Ling-ling's wound would not heal. She continued to paint superbly until her death at a ripe old age.'

Her words were like a gentle breeze, blowing away the dark clouds. Her belief in my worth had always sustained me throughout all my difficult passages. And now, her story touched me with the artistry of a magic wand, bringing harmony and solace.

Day after day, as I sat beside her and watched her lapse into a coma from which she never woke, I believed that my nearness would help her along her final journey. Reflecting on her eighty-nine years, which had spanned most of the twentieth century, I realized how wise my mother had been to entrust me to the care of my remarkable aunt. In her modest and unassuming way, she had guided me towards a spirit of independence which she herself had manifested by rebuffing Niang and remaining in Shanghai. Aunt Baba was not one to dwell on the bitter hardships she suffered during the Cultural Revolution. Love, generosity and humour never left her.

Life had come full circle. 落葉歸根 *Luo ye gui gen.* (Falling leaves return to their roots.) I felt a wave of repose, a peaceful serenity.

Index

ch 14 / yì gēn yì hè
p 139 / One lute; one crane. H. H. Tien. 38 yrs.